CW01655229

TEEN AVENUE

Stephen James Thompson is a screenwriter, producer and jazz musician. He was brought up Pontypridd, moving to England in his late teens as a student. He now lives in West Sussex.

When people ask him who Elisud Jones is based upon he has a simple answer: everyone you've never met.

STEPHEN JAMES THOMPSON

TEEN AVENUE

AN ELISUD JONES THRILLER

Gravity Hill Press
2024

For S & J:
Am byth fy nghariad

Published by Gravity Hill Press 2024

ISBN: 978-1-7385054-0-1

www.gravityhillpress.com

Book design and map by Simon Loxley
Printed by Lavenham Press

Focus on the circle rather than the straight line. The circle of life is the only truth, with every point a blessing.

ABZARI AFIN

Curzon Place
1 Elisud Jones' flat
Charles Street
2 RAK Records
3 Bell Records
Chesterfield Hill
4 Harry Baum
Heddon Street
5 'The Ziggy Stardust door'
Berkeley Square
6 The Astor Club
7 Annabel's
South Molton Street
8 Ryemuse Studio
Bruton Street
9 MAM Records
Conduit Street
10 The Westbury Hotel
Savile Row
11 Apple Records
Bruton Place
12 The Guinea Pub
Bryanston Street
13 Billy Coles' flat
North Audley Street
14 The Marlborough Pub
New Bond Street
15 Chappell's
16 CBS
17 The Chalet Café
Clarges Street
18 ChinniChap
Hertford Street
19 Radio Luxembourg
Curzon Street
20 RCA
Park Lane
21 The Hilton
Lovers' Walk
22 The Joy of Life Fountain

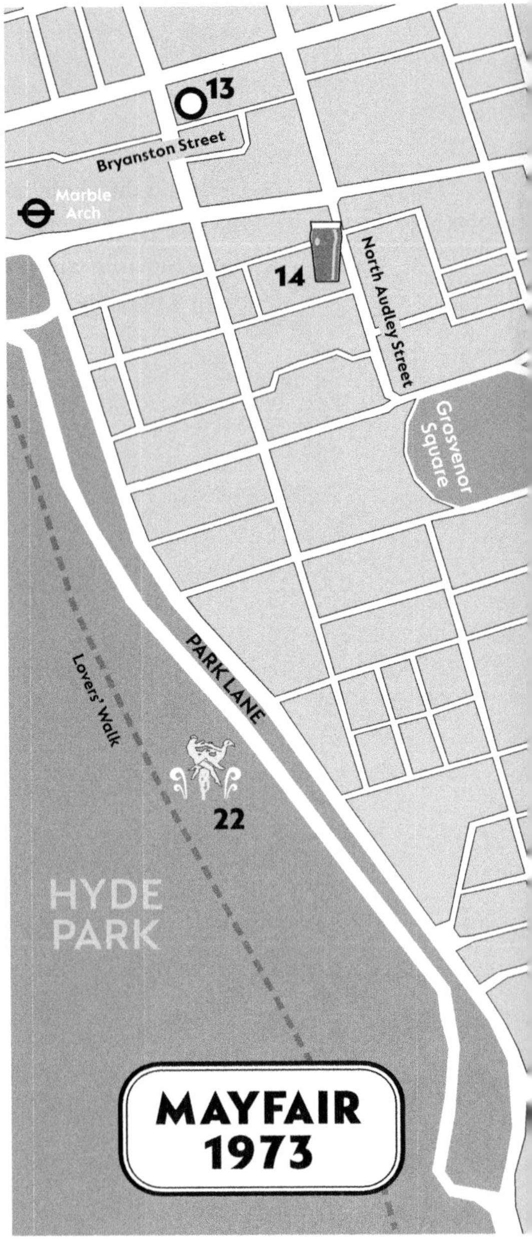

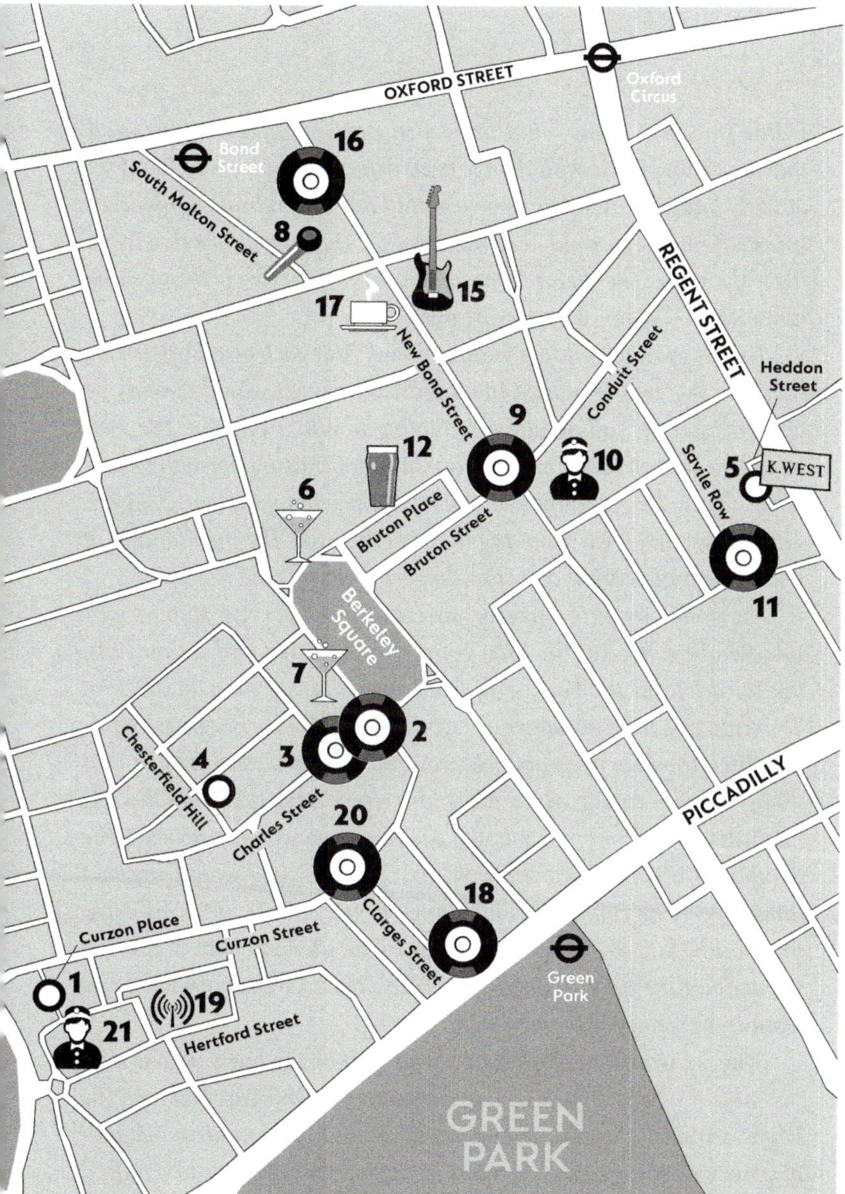
OXFORD STREET
Oxford Circus
Bond Street
16
South Molton Street
8
15
17
New Bond Street
REGENT STREET
Heddon Street
Conduit Street
9
12
10
5
K.WEST
Savile Row
6
Bruton Place
Bruton Street
11
Berkeley Square
7
2
3
4
Chesterfield Hill
Charles Street
20
PICCADILLY
18
Clarges Street
Curzon Place
Curzon Street
1
19
21
Hertford Street
Green Park
GREEN PARK

I didn't need to know what happened next; I could imagine, and that was enough. He would have been driven away, back to London, already badly beaten. His fingers would have been broken; his teeth smashed in. They would keep him awake. There would be no escape from the pain. The torture would be continuous, low level; pushing him right to the point of passing out.

The windows would be wound down. The back seat buffeted by cold air. This was to benefit his captors. The smell would already be terrible after his soiling himself. Talking to him, over him, the men would be keen to maintain a conversation. Chatting normally, matter-of-factly. This is going to happen. This is what you should expect. This is how much we are going to relish the task. The inevitability of it all. The anticipation of a slow, lingering death. The dread.

He would try and imagine an escape. The service station outside Reading: Two of the men going inside for tea and bacon rolls, the third left on the back seat, head turned away from the victim. Thinking this to be compassion, words would form. Begging. Pleading. Then the idea of escape. He would reach for a door handle that wasn't there – cars used for these jobs never have door handles. He might try and shout to a passing car, someone walking nearby. The glimpse of a safe world through the open window would mislead him, suggest he could cross over back to his old life. If he did open his mouth, scream, or shout, he would be silenced with a cosh on the ear, not the back of the head, always the ear. The pain would be instant and sharp, but not incapacitating.

The car would smell of bacon and tannin tea bags, mixed with piss and shit for the stretch into London. The city was waking. The traffic would be heavy. The windows would be wound, no chance anyone was going to see the man in the backseat beaten to a pulp.

A side street basement, a set of steep stairs. End of the line. Get him inside, quick. No one wants to get his blood on their clothes. Someone suggests dragging him by the feet instead. Down he goes, his bloodied head hitting each step like a slow bouncing ball.

Inside there is a chair. A table holds all the instruments and implements. Prisoner delivered, the first set of men leave, the next team take over. The process of torture begins almost immediately. Six hours in, someone important will visit; the person deciding the fate of the man strapped in the chair. He is a villain, one of the worst. There is no pity, no regret. The vengeance is remorseless. Pure.

I could imagine all this because that's how it was when I worked for Terry Sporne in the sixties.

That's how it was when I ended up working for him again in October 1973.

One

October 1973

Danny Marks was vintage Tin Pan Alley muscle, preying on a London that stopped at Regent Street to the left and Charing Cross Road to the right, both thoroughfares acting as buffers, both bouncing him right back into the narrow streets of Soho like a cue ball off a snooker cushion. Anywhere further afield was beyond his imagination; a blank nothing, as vague as an ancient map charting what might be found at the edge of the known world. So, for Danny to have made the effort and travel to Mayfair meant that something serious was on his mind. It took until the third pint for him to prove me right.

'Need you to fix a problem for me,' he said. 'For a man of your talents it shouldn't take you long.'

His sallow skin was sweating alarm and I could smell the anxiety. I should have suggested he head back to Soho and find someone else. Instead, I bought us another round of drinks and a packet of salt and vinegar crisps. The crisps gave me something to do with my hands – I was trying to quit smoking.

Pints safely in front of us, I encouraged him to tell me what it was he wanted. Danny took a rapid slurp and wiped his mouth with the back of his hand. He cast a look around the Grapes Tavern, disappointed not to see any familiar faces.

'I don't know how you stick it all the way out here.'

'Don't you like this pub?' I asked him, suddenly amused by his discomfort.

'Not enough buzz for my taste,' he replied.

It was true. The place was dead. The lunchtime rush had been and gone. Closing time beckoned. We were twenty minutes away from the dead time, those three hours to either sober up or find a drinking club before the pubs opened again. I didn't fancy hearing whatever his problem was while we made that decision. Neater to do the talking now, drinks in front of us. Danny sensed the same thing. He fixed me with narrowed eyes.

'I need you for a thing. I know what you're going to say but it's not how it sounds. It really isn't.'

'How does it sound?' I asked.

'I need you to find a missing loved one for a pal of mine.'

'Who's the loved one and who's your pal?' It was a reasonable question in the circumstances.

'We'll get to that in a minute. But, in the meantime, I should tell you, you stand to earn a monkey from this, Taffy.'

Taffy.

To the old crowd I was always Taffy. The Mayfair crowd tended to call me 'Jonesy', occasionally Elis. But my real name, my birth name, my *Welsh* name was Elisud Jones. For anyone interested, try saying 'illicit' and that will be close enough to the correct pronunciation. Most people weren't interested enough to ever try, especially not Danny.

The landlady was rubbing the small of her back with both hands and staring out of the window. She was tired and fed up. I knew how she felt. I looked at Danny and tried to gauge what I could see before me. He still had that gaunt look; his cheeks sunken on a face defined by a mouth full of rotten teeth. Danny was the old music business. He was Soho, Archer Street, and Denmark Street. He was sheet music and song publishers, band fixers and session bookers. Everyone knew Danny. Danny Marks: Lean and hungry, used to run with Rik and Johnny Gunnell, schlepped for Jeffrey Kruger on occasions, shot a man in '62 and got off scot-free. Soho was now a tale of two industries, film – failing, and sex – booming. Mayfair was the music business these days. Four years had passed since I last saw him, around the time I moved west and began working for music people who every now and then dabbled in villainy. He still worked for villains who dabbled in music. A sudden call out of the blue had prompted this get together and here he was behaving like I was still on the payroll. Something else was off. Lost persons were never even my line of work back in the old days. In Soho, I tended to hurt people, not find them, sorting things that could be sorted with a shove in the ribs or a slap in the chops. Danny knew all that. So why on earth did he think I could help in this situation? I decided to let him in on a little of my thinking.

'Danny, I might not be your best bet on a job like this. Tell whoever sent you I don't do missing persons.'

Danny looked at the floor and bared his ugly teeth in a grimace, like my answer pained him.

'I never said she was missing,' he hissed. 'I know where she is.'

'Then what's the problem? If she's not lost, why is someone paying £500 to find her?'

'It's Angie Bright-Silver,' he announced, checking to see my reaction. We both knew what my next question would be, but I asked it anyway.

'And Terry Sporne is the one looking for her?'

Danny nodded. It was as if an ice cube was slowly moving down my back. The kind of chill you get in graveyards on a cold November night.

'I've never been a fan of dripping taps, Danny. Just give me the lowdown all at once please and put me out of my misery.'

'Seems Angie has terminated her management contract with Terry. Another party has paid for her to record material ready to hawk around for a new record deal. Terry's none too keen on that idea, as you might imagine. Rumour is she's been using one of the Mayfair studios on the quiet. Living here too. Since you're now familiar with this dump of a place it seemed like an idea to call on you and see what you can find out. Why are you smiling?'

There were two reasons why I was suddenly smiling. Firstly, Danny's description of Mayfair: it was a lot of things, but you would have to be pretty insane to ever describe it as a dump of a place. Secondly, and more importantly, I was enjoying the idea of Terry Sporne's current predicament and imagining his discomfort.

'It's not just her contract she wants out of either,' I suggested. 'Angie wants out of their relationship, right?'

Danny shifted in his seat and took a big gulp of his pint. The landlady called time with a ring of the bell. The pub would soon be closed.

'I don't bother myself with the whys and wherefores,' he said, 'but I can see it makes you happy. Me, I'd rather think of it like this: There was a quarrel between a loving couple. The girlfriend stropped off in a huff and is sulking somewhere in Mayfair. We've – you've – been asked to find her and discover what she has been up to. Once you do, the other party can go see her. Cupid arrives with a fresh arrow; you walk away sorted. It's a stroll in the park for £500.'

'Except it won't be an arrow Cupid arrives with, knowing Sporne.'

'Taffy! I'm shocked. You used to be such a romantic. Anyway, what happens after you find her is between them, isn't it?'

I drained the last of my pint and thought it through. If I'd been the one advising Angie, I would have told her to leave the country before trying a stunt like this. You don't walk away from a villain like Terry Sporne unless you had a fortress ready to move into and a small army on call. Clearly, she wasn't thinking straight. She was just like Danny. She had spent too long in Soho. She thought Mayfair was a different country, a different time zone. Deep down, to villains like Sporne, everywhere was just a different shade of the same colour.

'Do we know who the new wannabe manager is?' I asked.

'No idea, Taffy. Anything else?'

I could tell he was keen to get back to the familiar streets of Soho but there was one last question nagging me.

'You coming to me. What are you getting out of this, Danny?'

'I'm helping out a friend and repaying a favour owed.'

It was left unclear as to whether I was the friend or the one owed a favour.

Outside, in pewter daylight, we shook hands; our deal struck as the landlady bolted the double doors behind us with all the finality of a prison gate closing. Danny Marks took off towards Regent Street, his stride short and urgent – almost a run. Soho couldn't wait any longer. I headed through Mayfair at a more leisurely pace. Dozy after four pints, a stretch out on the sofa back at my flat in Curzon Place beckoned. I was also desperate for a fag; a nap might make me forget about those cravings. Reaching the end of Burton Lane, I turned into Teen Avenue.

Teen Avenue: Mickie Most was the one who gave Charles Street that title. Amongst those of us in the business, the name quickly stuck, and rightly so. The majority of what you heard in the singles charts began life there, specifically from two buildings next door to each other on Charles Street – RAK, run by Mickie Most, and Bell Records, run by Dick Leahy. Leahy had David Cassidy, Barry Blue, and Gary Glitter on his label. Mickie had Kenny, Mud, and Suzi Quatro. They were making millions by serving up the sound and look teenagers wanted. They were not the only ones. Teen Avenue was becoming a catchword for Mayfair and the other labels operating nearby. MAM Records in New Bond Street had Lynsey de Paul and Gilbert O'Sullivan. Down on Curzon Street, RCA were doing nicely with the Sweet and David Bowie. A&M Records on Conduit Street had the Strawbs and Stealers Wheel. Chrysalis had hits with Leo Sayer and Steeleye Span. They were based on South Molton Street, right opposite the management offices for Slade. ChinniChap, the song-writing team of Nikki Chinn and Mike Chapman, were writing Teen Avenue hits from a flat in Clarges Street, then recording them using one of the Mayfair studios like Nova Sound or Ryemuse. It was all here. Everything you needed within walking distance. Teen Avenue: Pop music's vertically integrated village. A factory. A pipeline that spewed banknotes. Glam was making people fortunes and I was getting my slice of pie as a freelance fixer. Teen Avenue's Taff. The borough's bagman. Mr Mayfair. I didn't have to work for the Soho faces anymore. Things had changed. Except now they hadn't. And all it took was £500 and the name of a singer I once knew.

Threading my way through to the western edge of Mayfair, I entered the corner townhouse at 9 Curzon Place, climbed the two flights of stairs, and let myself into my flat. Throwing the keys on the coffee table, I kicked off my boots and lay down on the sofa, running the name of the girl Danny had given me several more times before sleep hit me. It was such a pretty name to have rattling around in my brain. There was a sort of poetry to it. Some girls' names are catchy. Some girls' names promise so much. Angie Bright-Silver was both of those things.

Angie Bright-Silver: You did a stupid thing and now someone very bad was paying to find out what you were up to. Angie Bright-Silver, you were somewhere in Mayfair and as soon as I woke up, I would start looking for you.

But first let me sleep and forget about wanting a cigarette, Angie Bright-Silver.

Two

Unsettled, disoriented, I awoke to find the evening had arrived. A carroty glow from the streetlights bathed the front room, adding to my sense of apprehension; a feeling that the city was seeping into the flat, into my life, and there was nothing I could do about it.

I lay still on the couch, listening to the noises about the building and the muffled sounds of my neighbours. Lives through ceilings and floorboards. It helped me think. Anyway, silence can be overrated.

Harry Nilsson owned the flat above. Splitting his time between London and Los Angeles meant he was rarely around. As a result, the place was informally sublet to rock legend pals like Keith Moon, Mama Cass, and Ringo Starr. I had never been up there, but I would hear the goings-on. Tonight, it sounded like a troop of elephants were clog dancing on the ceiling to the Rolling Stones. Simultaneously, my floorboards carried the musical stylings of Michael Herlighey, a high-end Mayfair art dealer and nocturnal amateur pianist, from the flat below. Michael enjoyed nothing more than struggling through a familiar classical piece, familiar enough for me, or anyone else, to notice the mistakes. Right now, he was having a stab at Debussy, perhaps Ravel, I always muddled the two composers. It was a shame Michael wasn't more adept; the tune was a pretty one – when he managed to hit the right notes.

The building's one mystery flat, beyond the reach of my ears, was on the ground floor. I sometimes wondered what those sounds might be like, given the rumour that the place was owned by a Conservative MP's reclusive mistress. Since neither of them were ever to be seen, and, in my case, certainly never to be heard, imagination ran riot, creating scenarios played out in a bordello of drawn curtains, purple wallpaper, black satin sheets and gold framed ceiling mirrors.

I didn't really belong here. I knew that. All this listening and speculating was a constant reminder of why. I grew up in a council house south of the mining valleys, a grey and dismal market town once described as the Damascus of Glamorgan, but better, and more accurately, known as Pontypridd or Ponty. The nightly symphonies through those shared walls would be screaming matches or drunken singalongs, never rock stars and Ravel. I didn't belong here, and yet here I now found myself, listening to elephants tap dancing and piano players wearing boxing gloves. Accommodation wise, I had come up in the world, and it was all thanks to Phil Fratton.

My large, high ceilinged one-bedroom flat was owned by Phil – real name Viscount Philip Royston Fratton of Thakeham – former lead guitarist with the Grass. I was tour manager for his band when they supported King Crimson in 1969. By then, Phil was deep into his heroin addiction. I ended up looking after him and got him clean. He found God, moved to California, took up with a hippy cult called Apricus, and last thing I heard, got himself married. On Christmas Eve, just before he left England, Phil pressed a set of keys into my hand and 'gave' me his flat in Curzon Place, declaring it to be 'a deserved recompense' for saving his life. I moved in that same night. For the first few weeks I had expected the police, bailiffs or worse to turn up. After six months, I started to worry less. Three years later, I never even thought about it. By now, I'm sure, Apricus would have already fleeced their willing convert. That's how it usually works with cults. A pound on the collection plate was never going to be enough. Apricus would have helped themselves to his trust fund, shares portfolio, and even taken a lien on the Fratton stately home in West Sussex. Given the scale of that pay out, they were not going to be too bothered about his flat, even if it was in Mayfair.

With a plan forming in my mind, I rose from the couch, kicked off my jeans and changed into a plum velveteen suit I had bought over the summer. I needed to smarten up for where I was going later. The suit was the best I could do in that department. Grooming wise, I brushed my teeth and splashed cold water over my face. No comb of the hair. No beard trim. *Let It Be* era McCartney, Jim Morrison in his final years – that's the look I was going for. My dark beard was nicely frowsy, the same with my thick long black hair. I had the look, but I could see it aged me badly. Pushing close to thirty, you better hope for good genes if you want to stay looking young. No such luck in my case. I could see my father in the reflected face. It was a face already worn down by life. *Tad* had the excuse of working down a mine and there was probably something noble in that. My face looked the way it did because I had pissed it up and pissed it all away. Worn down by too much booze, too much drug-taking and too much shagging is not noble. But, then again, what else was there to do in life? The music business was booming as never before. There was more than enough of everything to go around, and I was going to get my share while I could, pissing it up and pissing it away. That's what I told the face staring back at me in the mirror. He seemed pleased by the news.

Pulling on my cowboy boots and a leather coat that brushed the pavement, I headed out along Curzon Street and into Teen Avenue. At this time of the early evening, the streets were still peppered with record industry people heading home, or more likely heading off for a bit of pleasure mixed with business. I knew the crowd and they certainly knew me. At six foot three

I was hard to miss at the best of times. Plenty of nods and hellos came in my direction from the record pluggers, publicists, producers, promoters, secretaries, accountants, A&R men, and label executives. Normally, I'm not shy about taking advantage of any friendly greeting. From office to pavement, pavement to pub, pub to nightclub, to home, this was the Teen Avenue routine, a routine I was always happy to fall in step with for some or all of the various stages. I'm pretty obliging in that regard. It would have been easy to collar one of them and make enquiries about Angie, but I needed to be discreet. I didn't want word getting to her too early that there was a search on. Besides, I already had a plan.

Recording studios never sleep. The Beatles had set a precedent and proven a point. Inspiration was just as likely to come at two in the morning as two in the afternoon. Now studios had to be open all hours. Nevertheless, most still tried operating on the old three-hour session system – morning, afternoon, mid-evening, late night. I would be calling in before the evening sessions started, the time when the engineers were getting everything set up and ready. The quiet before the storm.

Doing the round of the Mayfair studios over the next couple of hours, I was fully aware that the chances of striking it lucky and finding Angie were slim. If you're going into hiding, it's not a clever idea to hang about for weeks on end in a studio making an album. My guess was that the backing tracks would have already been done without Angie, possibly recorded months ago. With that in the can, Angie would be able to lay down her vocals somewhere more private. Hidden out of sight. Safe. One of those new portable four tracks would do the job just fine. McCartney did his first album on a small Studer and it came out great. If the room was soundproofed, overlaying vocals would be easy. Mixing down the tracks was where things always got tricky. Whoever was behind Angie's album would need a studio mixing desk for that final stage. If Danny reckoned Angie was still in Mayfair, it was fair to assume the mixing down was also taking place here. With that in mind, I called in at Chappells and CBS in New Bond Street, the Apple studio in Savile Row, as well as Mickie Most's favourite studio at Radio Luxembourg in Hertford Street. I even hopped a cab up to Advision in Gosford Street, which was more Fitzrovia than Mayfair, but I was working a hunch. Musicians still thought of Advision as a Mayfair studio on account of its sixties location in New Bond Street. It was certainly worth a look. If I were making an album with Angie, that was the studio I would use.

In the end, I drew blanks everywhere. There was nothing doing. Advision was full of keyboards, Moog synthesisers and drums – hundreds of drums. Prog rockers ELP had block booked the place since the summer. None of the exhausted studio engineers had heard a whisper about Angie, let alone any album she might be making. After further wasted visits taking in George Martin's AIR, and the in-house studio for Polydor, I was left with one remaining place on my list – Ryemuse. I almost didn't bother. The idea that a well-known star – even one on a downturn like Angie Bright-Silver – would have anything to do with Ryemuse was comical. It was the scruffiest of the lot, well past its best. The equipment was old-fashioned, and the smell of stale hash, body odour and dry rot stayed with you for weeks after any visit. Though this was no place for pop royalty, I liked Ryemuse. Always had. I wasn't the only one. Dick Leahy sent his new Bell artists to record there. Last year, Gary Glitter did 'Rock and Roll' at Ryemuse and had a top ten hit around the world. Heavy bands also liked the stripped-down, gritty sound the place seemed to generate. *Propitious Flavour*, the one and only album by Phil Fratton and the Grass, was recorded there in 1969. That's when I hit it off with the argumentative house engineer, Billy Coles. Though our friendship was initially formed by a shared love of the bottle, the real sealer for Billy was my not being English. A Scotsman and a Welshman taking on the world, it was a nice thought back then. Still was.

'A couple of proud Celts telling the English to mind their own business, and if they don't, they can well and truly fuck off, once told. That's our credo, Jonesy.'

So went Billy's thinking.

Changing my mind about missing out Ryemuse, I headed over to South Molton Street. Billy Coles suddenly felt like the perfect man to ask about what was happening on the Mayfair recording scene. After all, he called it spot on, the last time I'd been there; the time I was trying to help Tony Carter.

Three

Tony Carter started life as a jazz drummer, modelling himself on a combination of Phil Seaman and Philly Joe Jones. Gigs were difficult for him, reading music even more so, on account of his blindness, a condition he had suffered from birth. Nevertheless, he managed to make a name for himself on the declining mid-sixties' jazz scene. Tony held down a long-term residency at the Tally-Ho Pub in Camden on Sunday afternoons for many years, his wife, Sheila, helping him set-up and take down his kit, leading him back and forth from their council flat around the corner. Despite his not inconsiderable disability, he was known to be cheerful and good-natured, as well as an exceptional drummer.

Then he got into drugs.

Not the Charlie Parker, Chet Baker jazz drugs. Not heroin, the drug of choice for his hero, Phil Seaman. Instead, Tony discovered LSD, and it changed his life completely. He took against jazz, and then the ever-loyal Sheila, claiming both were holding him back. Aged forty-three, he grew his thinning hair long, declared himself a hippy, met an exhibitionist flower child named Gracie, and moved into her bedsit in South London. There the two of them began a steady regime of acid trips until Tony decided that he was no longer blind. He still was, of course. It was more a case of the LSD sparking strange, wondrous visions. Gracie was privy to this awakening, quickly becoming an integral part of the next stage, the formation of a new rock-oriented group, Tony's Timepiece.

A two-year spell based in Majorca honed the band into a formidable unit. Boots, a Hammond organ player from Trinidad, and Joao, a guitarist from Portugal, completed the now internationally flavoured band. With Tony's drumming (remodelled in the style of John Bonham and Micky Waller) driving the musicians, they effortlessly navigated complex grooves and time signatures. Gracie's soft, almost spoken word delivery added to this intriguing mix, and the band soon proved to be an unexpected hit touring the discotheques of Portugal and Spain.

Judging the timing to be right, Tony decided to return to England and try and make it big. They needed a manager and they needed a record deal. For a while I was the man who tried to make that happen. So began my first attempts at being an A&R man.

A&R – artist and repertoire – is the fancy name record companies use for talent scouting, offering a commission on signing any act you bring to their attention. Find the right band and it was serious money. With Tony's Timepiece I could see there were going to be issues, issues that had already made other music business folk wary of taking them on. Jazz-rock was not everyone's cup of tea, a fact that would seem to have been confirmed by the low audience attendance at the gig where I first caught them, a festival of similarly minded bands at the Roundhouse. That night, Soft Machine were headlining. And though they did draw a crowd, those lower down on the bill, including Tony's Timepiece, were playing to the proverbial one man and his dog in the cavernous former engine shed. Presentation wise, they were terrible. The sixties were over everywhere except in Tony's mind. His interminable, 'peace and love', 'let's build a wigwam' ramblings in between their songs, combined with his age, were obvious issues, only ever partially offset by the attractions of the robust Gracie wafting around the stage, more often than not, naked. Subsequent discussions about reining in the 'I love Marrakesh and patchouli oil' vibe were met with stony silence. Whenever I pushed the point, Gracie would act as spokesman.

'If love is an energy, you're nothing but a power cut, man!'

Tony soon fell under the spell of some of the Hawkwind crowd, a band he judged to be very much fellow travellers in his mind expansion sensory quest. He decided, like Hawkwind, the band should also have a poet/writer as their lyricist. Sci-fi novelist, Hugh Padley, drifted into his orbit and songs were immediately reworked to accommodate lines such as, 'through the power of a demiurge, we cleanse the path to luminosity, our votive offerings a gift to the Augean master governing us all'.

When I asked Padley what it meant, he offered me an enigmatic smile.

'It's just another way of saying "she loves you, yeah, yeah, yeah"'.

Still, for all that, Timepiece could rock out better than Deep Purple or Sabbath, with more complex musical arrangements than Yes or Genesis. I was sure I could land them a deal, sure enough to stake them the cost of recording a demo, a demo we recorded at Ryemuse. With Billy Coles as engineer, we laid down three tracks: 'Glitter Slave', 'Moons of Varachi', and 'Augean Master'. Each tune consisted of three or four movements, or 'concepts', as Tony liked to call them. The Hammond organ provided the thunderous bass lines, Boots left hand dancing around trying to keep up with Tony's polyrhythmic drumming, whilst Joao's guitar solos were better than anything Jeff Beck could muster these days. Gracie was then called upon to intone during the quieter sections, offering a welcome contrast to the sonic complexity. They sounded amazing. Or so I thought.

Billy had a differing view, as we began work on the demo tracks.

'This lot make Yes sound like a pub singalong band.'

'That's good. Right?'

‘Wrong. Art for art’s sake – but give me something people will buy for fuck’s sake!’

‘They’re an albums band, Billy. Top ten hits don’t matter.’

‘And I was talking about albums! Jonesy, a band has got to look like a band. The reason rock bands look the way they do? They’re in tune with the audience. It starts with a pair of blue jeans and carries on with the long hair. You’ve got a balding Catweazle on drums, Idi Amin on organ, an unmemorable nobody on guitar, and the stripper lassie singing about utter shite.’

It was true. The unsmiling Boots was a little on the portly side, whilst Joao, maybe worried about his immigration/work status, tended to hide behind his amp. When not dancing, Gracie liked to sit down when she sang, which worked for a folky like Penny Sands or Jacqui Mcshee, but not for the front woman of a rocking band.

‘They’ve got their own look, their own vibe,’ I conceded.

Billy shook his head and wished me luck, in a fashion.

‘Tony’s Timepiece is a waste of your time and money. I hope I’m wrong. But I know I’m fucking well not. Still, good luck.’

His pessimistic reading of the band’s chances proved to be accurate. Loyalty took me first to RAK. Mickie Most was excited by the sound – ‘I hear nuggets of gold, Jonesy’. Then he saw the band photograph.

Dick Leahy at Bell hated the band’s sound, but suggested I build a group around Gracie instead.

‘Put Whispering Wendy on a pop record and you might have something. She’s like an acid Astrid Gilberto – Acid Gilberto, there you go.’

His laughter told me he wasn’t really serious about the idea.

The same story was repeated at Polydor and RCA: Liked the sound, hated the look. The only label who showed any interest were Chrysalis, but they wanted the band to put in some time touring the university circuit in England before any money was put down. I took this as very good news, but Tony was getting despondent.

'Record companies! No one wants real music anymore. Jazz is dead. Classical music is dead. Rock is just pop. It's up to jazz-rock to fly the flag for musical inventiveness. Why can't these bastards see that? I'm blind, but I can see! What does that tell you?'

'It tells me we need to show them, Tony. Let me set up a tour. Six universities. I'll invite the label heads. This is how we'll get a record deal, Tony.'

The refectory at Surrey University was to be the first date on the tour. I don't know if it was nerves or just that Tony wanted to be at his 'best' but, in the lead up, I later found out, he was tripping acid non-stop, every day. No longer a way of being able to 'see', the acid was making him paranoid and fearful, reminding him of the dark sightless prison he had existed in ever since he could remember. He was, to all intents and purposes, having a nervous breakdown. Folk singer Penny Sands once told me this acid burn-out was called 'the loss of the psychic-self'. It sounded terrifying. Tony's ravings became so serious even Gracie could see something was amiss. The group never made it to Guildford. She drove the band bus to St Thomas' Hospital in Streatham, where Tony was immediately admitted, sedated and, two days later, sectioned in a mental hospital in Banstead called Downview. This was a real Hammer Horror looking building with a high tower and all the gothic details you'd expect from a loony bin. I went there to visit him a couple of times. The first six months, they pumped him so full of insulin he slept constantly. Later, he was put on a regime of shock treatments. It was hard to discern the Tony I knew. Head shaved, blank, damaged eyes rolling, his speech was unintelligible. More recently though, running into Joao on Teen Avenue, I heard he was in better shape.

'The brain is made up of ingredients, yes? Like a cake. Too much sugar and the cake is bad. Too little and there is no taste. Tony's ingredients were all messed up by drugs, Jonesy. Now they redo the mixture, make sure there is just the right amount of sugar. He will have a good cake again.'

'That's brilliant news, Joao. Do they know when he might get out?'

'What! He's never getting out, man! He's crazy for good.'

Joao stared at me, shook his head and wandered away. He had his own problems. The Home Office were threatening deportation. He'd be kicked out of the country in less than a month. I never asked him about Gracie because I already knew. She was right about love being an energy. A behind someone's back sort of energy. After having a secret affair with Hugh Padley, the two had moved in together, the moment Tony was sectioned.

Tony had packed a lot in from his first trip in 1968 to being imprisoned at Downview in 1972. In just under five years, his life had changed utterly, and now he was crazy for good.

He wasn't the only one.

Crazy for good.

That's me: Traipsing over to a shitty studio to ask questions about a lost singer who would be long gone by now, if she had any sense.

INTERLUDE NO.1

November 6th, 1964: Soho

The first time I saw her. I had just beaten a man close to death in Terry Sporne's Soho office. His blood was there on my cuffs, my shoes. The skin was broken on my knuckles. Sweat, dirt and shame marked my face. I was still breathing heavily from the exertion when the door opened and she walked in wearing a red plastic mac and knee-high leather boots, her big Kohl eyes curious and guileless.

Sporne's irritation was mild, like a parent with a child. 'Now, sweetheart. I thought I told you to wait in the car.'

'But Terry! We're going to be late!'

'Why don't you go back to the car, and I'll be there in just a moment?' he calmly suggested.

She showed no sign of having noticed me and Danny, nor the body of the man stretched out on the easy chair, his face beaten to liver meat by my own fists, his trousers wet with urine after pissing himself.

Bashful as a schoolboy, I glanced at her face.

She had exotic features, like she might have been Mediterranean, perhaps Spanish, despite her strawberry blonde hair. I knew who she was, of course. I had seen her on Ready Steady Go, *singing 'Make Me Yours' with her hands turned out at her sides, her bobbed hair bouncing in time, as she innocently skipped from side to side to the beat. She was gorgeous in black and white, even more so in real life, in colour.*

'Taffy, show Ms Bright-Silver back to the car,' Sporne barked.

I gave a nod and approached her.

'I think I can manage, darling,' she told Terry, even though she was looking at me.

I stepped back and watched her leave. We waited until her foot-

steps receded before turning our attentions back to the man spread out on the chair. Sporne leant over and addressed his comments to the man's bloodied ear.

'I do hope you can hear me, Michael. I want you to view this as no more than a warning. There is no reason why we can't be friends, why we can't trust each other, why we can't do business. Understood? The simple thing I require is that when I ask for one of my bands to be booked into your club you just have to say, 'yes', and not, 'no', and certainly not, 'go to hell frogspawn'. Okay?'

The man gave a whimper of agreement which pleased Sporne. He stood up and looked over at Danny.

'Find him a change of clothes and drive him home. Take Taffy with you.'

Terry hesitated and eyed me inquiringly.

'How are you enjoying the music business so far?'

'Beats wrestling,' I smiled.

'I bet it does. I bet it does.'

Terry left and went downstairs to join Angie. I had wanted to ask him something. I wanted to know the name of the band he was so keen to get booked into the club. They must be good, I thought to myself.

Four

It always tickled me that a total wreck like Ryemuse was located above such a respectable, well-to-do chemist. Whilst the shop front nestled neatly within the tall Queen Anne building, a side door to the right gave the first indication of another world upstairs. Scuffed and stripped of paint, the mullions were warped, the architrave riddled with flaking woodworm. Scribbled messages covered the door and frame. In amongst felt-tip declarations of love from pop fans and groupies were musician to musician communications. Simple instructions for the most part, such as 'Gary, we're down the pub', more inscrutable offerings also caught the eye. My favourite was, 'Paul, Fiona's hamster is moving in with me. Sorry, mate.'

Entry was by way of an intercom system – a dull brass plate with a wire mesh speaker set in the wall. There was only one button to choose from and so I jabbed away until a wary Scottish voice finally crackled out of the wall.

'Who is it?'

'Billy? It's me.'

The door bolt was released with an angry thud, and I went in.

Though the hallway was in darkness, the bulb gone, I could remember the lay out well enough to feel my way upstairs. Unusually, at Ryemuse the control room was across the first-floor landing from the room housing the studio. Closed-circuit TVs allowed the producer and engineer to see the band and vice versa.

It was a weird old set-up, but it seemed to work.

For a time, Billy lived above the studio in a tiny attic room. I'm not sure the owners even knew about the arrangement. Eventually, sick of the leaking roof and scurrying mice, he moved out, sleeping on my couch for a while until he found a new place. I had seen much less of Billy since then, but when I did, we always got on well, though, for anyone listening, our shouted greeting might have suggested otherwise.

'What in the fuck are you doing here? Welsh bastard!'

'Arseholes to you! Scottish git!' I replied cheerfully, joining him in the small room that housed the recording desk and tape deck.

'Seriously. What are you up to?' he asked guardedly.

'Up to no good, as usual, Billy *bach*.'

He spotted my velveteen suit beneath the leather coat and gave a whistle.

'Cinders! You shall go to the ball! You must be off somewhere nice.'

'I could say the same of you,' I replied, noticing his ochre-coloured linen trousers and shirt.

Style wise, everyone was trying to be a peacock these days. Billy Coles had always been a style turkey. Seedy, horse jockey small, he had wiry brown hair and Buddy Holly spectacles perched on a huge nose. His usual look consisted of jeans and a month-old white t-shirt with dried ringlets of dark sweat gathered under the arms like yellowing circles on a tree stump. Billy's reputation for being a smelly, untidy bugger was well known, making this revamp so surprising.

'Don't tell me, you've joined Ravi Shankar's band,' I joked.

'Time for a change around, Jonesy. That's all. You might want a rethink in that department yourself. That fucking velvet makes you look like Little Lord Fauntleroy's evil older brother.'

As we chatted, Billy continued to prepare the desk for the

session. The tape was already loaded on the 16-track. He was now carefully labelling each channel with a black marker pen on the strip of white gaffer tape that ran the length of the desk. Taking a break, he pulled out his smokes and offered me one. Disque Bleu, my brand.

I declined through gritted teeth: 'Trying to cut down on at least one of my vices.'

'Not the booze though, I'm guessing,' he said, reaching under the desk to fetch a bottle of Jack Daniels and two mugs.

'No, never the booze,' I admitted.

'From the cellar of Mr Ronnie Lane, no less. Offered in gratitude for a session I engineered in the summer at his mobile studio.'

We both knew Ronnie. In the sixties, working for Don Arden, I was a sometime roadie, driver, or backup heavy for Ronnie's old band, the Small Faces.

'How's Ronnie faring these days?' I asked.

'Still drinking like a fish. Talking of which…'

He poured out a generous slug for me, then little more than a dribble for himself.

'I've got a long night ahead, Jonesy,' he explained.

We clinked mugs. I could tell Billy was waiting for me to explain why I was sniffing around. I decided to let that hang a while longer. The bourbon was slipping down easy. I was in no rush. Besides, I liked Billy too much to make him think I was only there to grub information, even though that was pretty much exactly what I was there for.

'You still seeing that posh lassie over at MAM?' he asked me.

The 'posh lassie' was Claire Gronwaulde, a publicist for the MAM record label. I started seeing Claire around the same time Billy was sleeping on my couch. His grumpy, smelly sock presence had made things awkward, no doubt prompting Billy to move out.

'Just because Claire went to university doesn't mean she's

posh,' I pointed out. 'Anyway, we're off and on, currently more off, than on.'

I looked around the control room, enjoying my evening being back in studios again. That sense of anticipation for what was about to be. Something out of nothing. Studios were exciting places.

The black and white closed-circuit television was turned off, but from the labelled channels I could see the desk was set up for a classic rock four piece consisting of guitar, bass, drums, and vocals.

'Are you recording, or mixing tonight?' I asked.

'Just a rough mix tonight. A few guitar and vocal overdubs if we get lucky. Bunch of bloody jokers, this lot, let me tell you.'

'Who are they?'

Billy hesitated, as if the memory was an ordeal. 'Blank Verse,' he finally said. 'You wouldn't have heard of them. They're an unsigned band.'

'Who have they got in producing?' I asked.

Billy gave an exasperated sigh.

'Don't tell me they're self-producing!' I laughed.

Billy's annoyance now made total sense.

'Aye,' he confirmed, 'unsigned, inexperienced, and with fickle musician's ears. This is a fucking nightmare!'

'Can I have a listen?' I asked him, reaching for the play button on the desk.

Billy swatted my hand away.

'Get your wee stinking mitts off! Can't you see? I'm still setting up!'

Aware that he was sounding beyond his usual tetchy self, Billy tried to soften his tone.

'I really wouldn't worry yourself about these gobshites, Jonesy. They're just another one of those wannabe, New York, junky bands, hung up on the whole Lou Reed, Iggy Pop kick… wait a minute.'

Billy suddenly wagged his finger at me. 'Now I get why you're sniffing around. You're on the hunt, trying to find another bloody band you can throw Mickie Most or Dick Leahy's way!'

'Why not? They sound good from the way you've described them, Billy.'

He gave a bitter chuckle.

'You're way off, pal. One day, when you hear the finished tracks, you'll see what I mean, believe me. Utter, utter shite. Trust your Celtic brother on this. I was right before. Those other jokers you fancied? You haven't got the ears for A&R. You're too easily swayed.'

'I'm not easily swayed,' I responded. 'I just act on my passions.'

'Tell me something I don't know.'

I shrugged, happy to let the matter drop.

Billy reached for the Jack Daniels and topped up my mug. It was time to ask him about what was really on my mind.

'I heard Angie Bright-Silver is recording again.'

Billy didn't seem interested. I could see I was going to have to push a little harder.

'She's been using one of the Mayfair studios,' I said. 'Not sure which one, mind.'

Billy laughed.

'She hasn't been in here, that I do know. Can you imagine? You've seen the state of the toilets, right? Anyway, Angie's more Royal Variety Show, guest spot on *The Two Ronnies* nowadays, isn't she? She's not even a recording artist anymore. Hasn't been since the late sixties. 'Little Girl's Dream.' Do you remember that one?'

He sang the cheerful melody, fluttering his eyes at me coquettishly. '"Love is a theme, love is a scheme, love is every little girl's dream".'

'But if she was recording again, Billy… would you get to hear about it from other engineers?'

'What do you mean, "hear about it"?'

'Well, I don't imagine you lot all get together for bi-monthly banquets at Grosvenor House, but you probably do talk to each other now and then down the pub.'

'I'd hear about it if I asked people.' He looked at me sharply. 'You want me to ask people? Is that it?'

'It would help me,' I replied.

'What's this all about, Jonesy?' Billy asked.

'Angie's gone missing. Terry Sporne has asked me to find her.'

He took the empty mug from my hand and placed it back under the desk, along with the bottle. I could see he was angry and disappointed, as if I had broken some unspecified oath.

I tried to explain:

'Billy! You know how it is in my line of work: some days you drift, some days you have a mission.'

'Some mission,' he sneered. 'Tracking down a villain's girlfriend! That's bloody murky, even for you.'

'You're right, Billy,' I offered. 'Murky and messed up.'

'And not just any villain. I mean, Terry Sporne! Has it not crossed your mind that Angie has plenty of reasons for going missing?'

'Of course.'

'I thought you'd learned your lesson. I thought…' His voice trailed off as he stared at the black and white monitor for a moment.

'I need to finish getting the desk ready,' he said finally.

That was his way of telling me to leave. I didn't want to disappoint Billy any further, so I did just that.

'Good luck quitting smoking…'

I was half-way out of the door before he finished the sentence.

'...and I will ask around, Jonesy.'

I thanked him and made my way down the dark, precarious staircase, suddenly not feeling so great about myself.

Five

Billy thought too highly of me. The murky was where I worked. It had been that way since the mid-sixties, not long after my move from Wales all set to be a professional wrestler. That initial plan quickly went awry. Back in the Rhondda Valley, as a six-foot three, eighteen stone regional heavyweight champion, I stood out. Not so in London. There were plenty of freaks bigger and heavier than me. Bookings were scarce. Fortune came my way when I met Peter Grant, an ex-wrestler. He had connections with both the underworld and the music business – really the same thing back then. He saw potential in me, introducing me to people who needed help with "forceful negotiations". It was like the Wild West, and I was a gun for hire. Sometimes I felt like Shane taking on the bad guys. More often than not, I was the one dressed in black; Soho's very own Liberty Valance. But making good people bend to the will of a villain takes something out of you sooner or later. It was Peter Grant who rescued me once more. He had started working with an ex-singer from the rock and roll, 2I's coffee bar days called Mickie Most. Though not exactly in business together, the two of them shared an office at the Tottenham Court Road end of Oxford Street. I was put on a retainer to help either one of them, as and when required, which was all day, every day. Peter struck gold and moved on when he started managing first the Yardbirds then Led Zeppelin. Mickie, meanwhile, was doing more than all right with Lulu, Donovan, Herman's Hermits and Jeff Beck, eventually making the move to Mayfair to start his own record label, RAK. I followed him. Phil's flat made the move permanent. I became Mayfair and music, not Soho and Sporne. Except Soho wasn't ready to give up on me quite yet and Liberty Valance was making a comeback as gun for a hire. *Cachu Hwch!*

Down Davies Street towards Berkeley Square and the Astor Club. The search of the studios had been about putting out feelers and roping Billy in to doing my dirty work. The Astor Club was going to be different. That old-time showbiz, black-tie relic of a nightclub had always been Angie's scene, even when she was a successful pop star in the sixties. Of course, times change, people too. These days Angie might be more into snorting coke and dancing the night away in the new clubs like Annabel's or Tramp, along with the rest of Teen Avenue. And if that was the case, all the better. Enough people I knew would see her and I could quickly narrow my search. But my hunch was that Angie would drift back to the Astor out of habit. Could be tonight even. At the very least, I should be able to pick up her trail by asking around. I was just hoping my velveteen suit would be enough to get me past the dress code.

Halfway down Davies Street a gaggle of teenage girls were striding towards me, their wedge heels clomping on the pavement. They all shared the new blue eye shadow and startled Jean Harlow pencil brow look. When I was a kid, girls wore make up to look older. This new get-up seemed designed to make girls look younger, more virginal somehow. One of these startled virgins asked me for a cigarette.

'I don't smoke, and you shouldn't either, it's bad for you,' I said.

Clearly, it hadn't taken me long to become an anti-smoking puritan.

'Piss off!' she replied, her daring making the others giggle.

Encouraged by the sense I was fair game, another of them

piped up. 'Are you in a band?'

'He's far too old!' the first replied for me.

'I think he looks like he's in a band,' her friend persisted.

'No, I'm not in a band,' I stated. 'She's right, I'm too old. Now get home before your parents worry.'

I was treated to a volley of 'piss offs' and wedge heels clomping, as they hurried away.

My guess was they were heading up to Bond Street tube station and from there back to the suburbs after an afternoon hanging around Teen Avenue hoping to meet their idols. Girls like this were a common sight outside the record companies and studios. RAK and Bell were normally good to the fans. The secretaries would hand out the latest singles and promotional freebies, then send them on their way. RCA, on the other hand, would threaten to call the police. 'Looks like he's in a band', the girl had said. What on earth would that band be like, I thought to myself.

Berkeley Square came into view. It was still too early for the Astor, leaving me enough time to have something to eat and relax with a few drinks. I had a sense this was going to be a long night and I knew just what was going to get me through it – a fat juicy steak from the Guinea Grill and a bottle of house red.

The Guinea was situated on Bruton Place at the top right-hand side of Berkeley Square. With its Victorian oak panelling, roaring coal fire and enormous chandelier in the lounge, the pub was straight out of Dickens. The early evening Teen Avenue crowd liked to gather at the bar, sometimes three deep, but where the room narrowed, down towards the back, the eating area began. Sitting there, often the only diner, with that fire kicking in, it always felt very cosy – cosy enough to forget you were in central London. *Cwtch* is the perfect Welsh word to describe being in the Guinea. There's no real direct translation, but imagine being hugged by your mam when you were a child. That's *cwtch*.

Menu wise, the Grill liked to keep things simple: You could have anything you wanted, as long as it was a steak. Luckily, the Guinea Grill served the best steak in London, prepared by the landlord, a small ferret of a man called Gerald. His wife, Paulette, looked after the bar. She was much younger and came from Holland. Some sort of war time incident meant she had a glass eye. When Paulette was in her cups, which was often, she would take out the eye and put it in a glass of gin on the bar. 'I am keeping my eye on the bar,' she would laugh. It made Gerald cross, but he let her do it anyway.

I liked Gerald, and he liked me. Our friendship went beyond mere patron-landlord. At the beginning of the decade, I'd stepped in when some middle-aged Leeds United supporters tried to bust up the place. They'd been doing the visiting Northerners' well-trodden Soho itinerary of dirty mag shops, strip clubs, and a sauna room wank off, before moving further West for a slap-up meal, with a Mayfair discotheque to finish. This lot were at the slap-up meal stage, with The Guinea the location of choice. Gerald asked them to leave and one of them took a swing at him, missed and knocked down Paulette instead. This made the others laugh, and I decided to intervene. Men like that needed teaching a lesson, especially when they were disturbing my evening meal, my feeling of *cwtch*. Besides, a lot of my friends were Chelsea supporters.

Gerald appreciated the gesture and I soon found him to be a good source for gossip and tips on jobs that might be in the offing in Teen Avenue. Tonight though, he couldn't give me anything when I asked him about Angie, though he promised to keep an ear out.

'I mean "keep an ear out" and all, Jonesy. I just have to listen. I stand at the bar, Jonesy, and I hear things. I'm just the man serving drinks to all those record and pop people chattering away.

Invisible. They forget I have a set of lugs and very good hearing. I could make a fortune selling stories to the News Of The World. A fortune! But that's not me. Discretion is important in my line of work, save when it comes to friends, and for a friend like you, the lugs are ready and waiting. The first word of anything on Angie, I'll let you know.'

I had settled into my seat at a far table, trying to forget about my working for Terry Sporne for a while. The steak was on its way, my knife and fork at the ready, when a voice trilled softly, 'not all on your own, are you, Elis?'

English folk music's pin-up, Penny Sands, was standing before me looking beautiful in a diaphanous dress of yellows and golds. Her auburn hair was a little shorter than when we last saw each other, but that glowing skin and radiant smile were still very much in evidence.

'You're welcome to join me,' I suggested, gesturing towards the empty chair opposite me.

'No, I can't. I mean, I'm with Geoff. We're having a quick drink in the bar. I saw you and thought I'd pop over and say hello.'

'I'm glad you did. How's tricks?'

Penny shrugged and comically raised the corners of her mouth from side to side in quick succession to suggest mixed fortunes. I laughed, just like I always did. She had a repertoire of quirky, trademark Penny gestures that made people fall in love with her. That side-to-side mouth business had always been one of my own favourites.

'What about your new album? Any news?' I asked.

'Released next week. I wanted to name it The Sun, the Sky and the Moon. The label prefers Penny Sands Two – such is the poetic grasp of the music industry.'

'Stick with your title. Much, much better.'

'Thank you, Elis.'

I felt a set of eyes boring into the back of my neck. A thin, rangy man was skulking at the bar, staring in my direction with that constipated look jealous partners seem to effortlessly master. I recognised him of course. He was Geoff Birch, once of the Grass, now Penny's mediocre bass player and lousy husband. During one of their many separations, at the beginning of the year, I was road manager for Penny's UK tour. The tour was a success, she was happy, and, with Geoff Birch out of the way, we developed strong feelings for each other, least that's what we told ourselves. After the tour, Penny drifted back to Geoff, and I let her.

Penny's finger traced a pattern on the wooden table, an idea formulating.

'Elis? We're heading off for a handful of dates in Scandinavia this week before the record launch. Last minute I know… but we could do with a good tour manager. You free?'

'Not sure Geoff would like that. Anyway, I'm giving touring a break and staying closer to home from now on.'

'Still trying to get into A&R?' she asked.

'I keep trying but…'

'Close but no cigar?'

'Not even close,' I sighed.

'You must be able to twist Mickie Most or Dick Leahy's arm with someone.'

'You're kidding. My suggestions are as welcome as a turd in a punch bowl to those two.'

Penny laughed.

'Poor Elis!'

'Don't worry, I'll find someone,' I told her. 'Maybe the new band I heard about tonight. A bunch of Lou Reed, Iggy Pop groovers, apparently.'

'Could be good,' Penny enthused. 'What are they called?'

'Blank Verse. Do you know them?'

Penny hesitated, looking over towards Geoff before finally shaking her head. It was a strange reaction. My steak arrived before I had a chance to probe her further for the possible reasons. Penny was quickly back to her quirky ways. She pushed the plate nearer to me, giving me a small bow and a proprietorial wave of her hand to suggest she was the one who had prepared my meal.

'Voilà! Enjoy your steak, monsieur!'

'I most definitely will. Good to see you, Penny. Take care of yourself.'

'You too, Elis. Let's catch up over a drink sometime. We can talk properly.'

I watched her head back to the bar, before leaving with Geoff, walking on the balls of her feet with that impish bounce I always loved; as if she were skipping out of an enchanted forest to meet J.R.R. Tolkien, or off to collect the morning dew with the Fairy Queen. Perhaps it was the folky stuff she sang, the way she looked and moved, but at times Penny felt more imagined than real.

I finished the steak and wine, then took my time over a brandy. The urge to smoke was making my head spin. I ordered another brandy and tried to forget about cigarettes. Somewhere halfway into the second snifter I managed to do just that. It wasn't the brandy that was killing my cravings, it was thinking about Penny and Blank Verse. Curiosity is like that with me. It becomes all consuming. Why had she been lying about knowing them? Didn't she want me to get Blank Verse signed? What was it to her? Unless her label, Island Records, were already in negotiations and she was sparing me the let-down out of kindness. If that were so, I could do without her pity. Blank Verse might be the one to change my bad run. I decided it wouldn't hurt to pop back to Ryemuse after I had visited the Astor club.

Angie first, Blank Verse second.

INTERLUDE NO.2

December 1st, 1965: Columbia Cinema, Soho

She was trapped in the oblong rear view mirror; existing in a letter-box aspect ratio of the car's own creation. Sitting in the driver's seat, I couldn't stop myself looking at her, ever greedy for another view. In front of me, through the windscreen, was Shaftsbury Avenue and Soho beyond. Behind me, visible in the mirror, the aftermath of a film premiere and Angie Bright-Silver.

I made my choice.

She looked beautiful in mink, her hair up, the nape of her neck entwined by a string of pearls. Poking out beneath an eggshell blue evening dress, a pair of fairy tale silver slippers were visible, their glitter matching her sparkling eyes taking in the scene.

Behind her, a large brightly lit cinema sign announced King Rat. To the front, the enquiring flashes of the many press photographers cast a constant, unforgiving glare. Somehow, Angie found herself in a soft wash of shadows, as she waited for Terry Sporne. Only occasionally, as the crowd of guests spilled out from the entrance like a gentle tide, would her face be brilliantly lit. These rare moments of luminescence made her appear even more magical, as if her true, deserved realm was not of this world.

To shouts of encouragement, the waiting press encouraged Angie to stand next to Nanette Newman and Honor Blackman. Self-conscious, but self-aware, the three women giggled and smiled as the photographers circled. 'A trio of lovelies' the headline in the Daily Mirror *would read the next day. Of the three 'lovelies', Angie was easily the loveliest.*

My hands tightened on the steering wheel. I could feel myself getting nervous. Soon I would be driving Terry and Angie the short distance home. My fear was that I wouldn't be able to stop myself staring at her beautiful face, intoxicated to the point of dangerous incaution by her pretty laugh peppering the journey home. I imagined her perfume filling the car, even as I wondered what that scent would be. She would sit feet from me, close enough for me to sense her body warmth, her beating heart, her essence. And no matter how hard I tried to look away, she would be waiting, reflected in the rear-view mirror, each glance fuelling my desire, marking me like a blemish, sealing my fate. I would be the chauffeur who couldn't keep his eyes to himself, who ogled and stared and lusted after a forbidden prize – I deserved every punishment Terry Sporne would rain down upon me.

She was moving towards the parked car, led by an impatient Terry. I could see his face, set to a scowl, he wanted to go home. Film premieres were a means to an end. It was one of the ways he legitimised his brand. He had Angie on his arm for the same reason. He was a gangster who wanted the world to think he was something else.

Only feet away now, I pulled myself together, convincing my breathing to return to something more normal. My resolve was set. I would drive them. I would look forward, never back. Nothing unusual would happen. For her, I would just be another one of Terry Sporne's drivers. Forgettable. Unremarkable. Disposable. For me... it didn't matter – couldn't matter – what I thought.

Angie and Terry moved towards the black Daimler. I climbed out and opened the passenger door. Seeing me, Angie paused. I was worried she somehow knew what had been going through my mind.

'I want to walk home, Terry,' she whispered, more to the night air than anyone in particular.

'Walk home in those shoes?' Terry asked.

'I don't mind. Soho looks so nice at Christmas. Walk with me.'

The matter was settled.

'We're walking,' Terry shouted over at me.

They set off back to the penthouse apartment in Soho Square. I followed on foot, ten feet behind them at all times, my hands in my coat pocket, one holding a cosh, another a knuckle duster. I was there in case of trouble, but I already knew. I was the trouble. I was the thing Terry should have been looking out for.

Six

Back in the early days, when Peter Grant threw me work minding people, I would be in the Astor at least once a month. My job was to make sure no harm came to a visiting Hollywood star like Tony Curtis or George Peppard as they had a night on the town. Sitting two tables away, doing nothing but keeping guard all night, it was tedious, depressing work. The drunker everyone became, the more depressing it was, like being the only sober person on New Year's Eve. Terry Sporne was a big one for the Astor back then, along with all the other gangsters keen to bask in the presence of these visiting celebrities. Angie Bright-Silver would always be on Terry's arm, smiling politely as he and his cronies drank champagne, joked, and slapped each other's backs. Acting on my hunch about Angie being a nostalgic soul had brought me back to this dump. I wouldn't have been seen dead there otherwise.

After an hour of grubbing around the club asking questions, I had hit a dead end. The doorman had not seen Angie, same with the bar staff. Short of her appearing suddenly, the only thing left for me to do was knock on the club owner's door and put out some final feelers. There were good reasons why that might be a mistake, self-preservation being one of them.

The Astor was run by a charmless thug called Bertie Green. Like the club itself, Bertie was a relic from a different age, a different era; a time when the Astor was overrun by car dealers and villains of all shades, the prostitutes swarming about them like flies around a dung heap. From the days when Jack Spot took a razor to Tommy Falco's face on the dance floor for cheeking him; back when the Krays, Richardsons and Terry Sporne were members and regular guests. These days, after endless police crackdowns, and with the Krays and the Richardsons sent to prison, Bertie was trying to make things a little less underworld and a little more respectable. The car dealers had moved on and, despite still having a controlling interest in the club, Terry Sporne stayed away. The place had been given a half-hearted revamp and there was even a relaxation of the strict black tie only dress policy. All this made my asking too many questions about Angie in the Astor tricky. I was summoning up a name from the old days, from a time everyone at the club, particularly Bertie, very much wanted to pretend never existed. I wasn't sure how he might react. It was not like I had a written permission slip from Sporne I could show Bertie. His general paranoia and loyalty to Sporne was going to cast me as a problem and the Astor club had an interesting way of dealing with problems. It began with darkened alleyways and ended with six sets of fists slapping you about. I didn't fancy any of that. Not tonight. I could take care of myself and do serious damage of my own of course, but the odds were never going to be in my favour against Bertie's small army. The safe move would be to get Sporne to ring Bertie and ask him what he knew. Safe, but not smart. You never found out the truth with a phone call. That's why I had been hired.

Settling myself into a booth with a nice Macallan, planning my next move, I worked on trying to block out the tootling big band on stage. The club took a foolish pride in showcasing what they considered to be the top live acts. Even back in the sixties they had been staler than week old bread. It was always Kathy Kirby or Vince Hill or, if not them, a terrible old boiler in a tiara sitting at the piano, warbling her way through 'My Foolish Heart'. Now the

Astor had installed a resident big band. That's how with the times they were at the Astor – a bloody big band squawking their way through a never-ending Glen Miller medley!

I downed my drink and decided I had to speak to Bertie, if for no other reason than to escape the musical torture. Making my way to the entrance, I collared a maître d', telling him I was an old friend wanting to give my regards to Bertie. He made an internal phone call and Bertie soon appeared, as if by magic, from a hidden door. The new relaxed dress policy clearly didn't apply to him. With his immaculate tuxedo and blue-black Brylcreemed hair shining in the foyer lights, Bertie looked like he had just come fresh from playing a game of backgammon with the Shah of Iran.

'Taffy! Barely recognised you with the beard and the barnet. A long time since we've seen you in my humble establishment! What brings you back?'

'Just wanted to say hi, Mr Green. I fancied a night out. Heard good things about the changes you've made here, thought I'd rekindle some memories of my favourite club. I'm glad I did.'

I was pissing in his pocket, but it seemed to be working. Bertie was lapping up the praise.

'What do you think about my big band? Super aren't they?' Bertie's false teeth whistled as he said the word super.

'Unbelievable, Mr Green,' I replied honestly.

'So what are you doing with yourself these days, Taffy? Last I remember, you were schlepping for that rascal Peter Grant. Not still minding Yanks, are you?'

I had my story prepared and launched straight into it.

'No, not anymore. Actually, I'm looking to get into management myself these days.'

'Pop stars?' he asked dismissively.

'No, more the old styles. I was thinking crooners and torch singers.'

His interest was piqued.

'Possibly we can do business if you sign anyone tasty,' he told me. 'The club is always looking for fresh talent.'

'That would be great.'

After an initial wariness, I could tell Bertie was growing more comfortable in our exchanges. In his eyes, I was nothing more than a tradesman doffing his cap. He was used to people trying to sell him something and he enjoyed the power of being able to say yes or no. Since he was expecting a sales pitch, I did my best to oblige.

'This pop stuff is wearing thin, Mr Green. People are desperate for seasoned artistes who can carry a tune. That's why I'm looking for the next Engelbert, the next Matt Monro. Girl singers who can do Bassey…'

I drew breath, watching his face for any sort of response. He smiled agreeably and held out his arms, ready to embrace me.

'Taffy! You find an act like that; we can talk all day long.'

I went for broke, hoping he would still buy my line of bullshit.

'...an artiste with the voice of an Angie Bright-Silver. Do you know what I mean?'

Bertie gave a nod. He was beginning to look less certain. I carried on, wanting to see if he'd bite.

'Talking about Angie, a little bird told me she was now living in Mayfair.'

I stopped. Bertie's expression had darkened. He looked ready to throw me to his dogs.

'The world doesn't need another Angie Bright-Silver, believe me. Stick to what you know, Taff. That would be my advice.'

He offered me his denture assisted smile before turning on his patent leather heels and disappearing behind the same hidden door he had entered from. I braced myself for a not so gentle tap on the shoulder from one of his six trained gorillas, but it never came. All the same, I hurried out of the front entrance as quick as I could, just to make sure it never did.

Walking through Berkeley Square, debating my final move of the night, I was tempted to head over to Annabel's, find the last of the Teen Avenue crowd and enjoy a nightcap in a proper club with proper music. The alternative was to trudge back up to South Molton Street and check out Blank Verse at the studio. I was feeling tired. Annabel's was much nearer. Feet away, in fact. I slowed down and came to a stop, halfway across the square. Annabel's would have to wait. I was going to head back to the studio. That's what a proper A&R man would do, I reasoned. If the band really were terrible, then I had wasted a trip. If, on the other hand, they were any good, then I could talk to them about approaching labels. I would even cut Billy in on the deal.

I reached the side door to the chemist's shop, lifted my finger to the Ryemuse studio entry buzzer, then stopped midmotion. There was no point ringing. The door was already open. Recording studios don't leave their front doors open. Ever. With a sense of foreboding, I went inside and cautiously made my way up the dark stairs. There was no indication of any recording or mixing going on. Even with all that soundproofing there is usually a small amount of leakage in a studio; a low rumbling bass line, a disembodied snare drum or the thin scraping sound of guitars. Standing on the stairs, I could hear nothing. My sixth sense was telling me something was wrong.

I called out.

'Billy? Are you there?'

Nothing.

Continuing up the stairs, a shaft of light from the open door of the control room was visible, breaking the darkness in the corridor. I stuck my head around the door. An Anglepoise provided the only light, but it was enough to show me two things: Billy wasn't around and there was no tape in the machine. The two-way TV monitor, now turned on, showed a black and white picture flickering, as if there was a fault with the signal. I pressed a button and spoke into the small talkback microphone.

'Billy? Are you in there?'

The criss-crossing spectral lines on the monitor revealed a drum kit, various microphone stands and the shadowy outline of an instrument case leaning against one of the amps. The image flickered some more before I realised it was not an instrument case.

My mouth was dry as I walked across the corridor and opened the studio door. The room was lit by a bare red-light bulb. The amps were humming. They'd been on all night. I could smell and feel the valves overheating. A guitar was resting against one amp. What I had mistaken for an instrument case was resting against the other. She was in a sitting position, dressed in the latest glam meets ashram style, arms by her side, legs outstretched and apart, eyes and mouth open. Her neck was snapped, the spinal cord broken, angry red marks showing where she had been strangled. Her twisted head was resting on her shoulder. A small circular pendant of carved bone with a black dot at its centre hung awkwardly from a necklace in her nape. I took a breath, the first since I had entered the room and stared at the face.

My search was over.

I had found Angie Bright-Silver.

Seven

Of the two phone calls I made, the police were always going to be the second on my list. My main concern was to get hold of Harry Baum. I would be dealing with the Metropolitan Police and needed some good legal protection. Harry was a wily old solicitor and easily the best in Mayfair. He lived in Streatham, but his law firm was in Chesterfield Hill, off Charles Street. Over the phone, I told Harry the events exactly as they happened. He listened without comment. We then worked on an edited version for the police, beginning with my omitting any mention of Terry Sporne and my being hired to find Angie Bright-Silver. For my alibi to go unquestioned, any mention of my first visit to the studio would also be omitted along with any reference to Billy Coles. Harry provided me with a blunt warning.

'The boys in blue are in an especially jittery mood, what with the IRA letting off five bombs around London in the previous month. The niceties of policing have been completely suspended. Any quick stitch-up might prove tempting, especially in a murder case involving a famous pop star.'

I knew he was right. The murder of Angie Bright-Silver was going to be splashed across the front pages of every newspaper. With those kinds of lurid headlines, the Met would be looking for a quick collar. A six-foot three Welshman in a leather overcoat and velveteen suit could well be the dream suspect for any lazy Detective Sergeant.

'Have you a handkerchief?' Harry asked politely. 'It might be an idea to do a little light polishing of any surfaces you might have touched earlier; other than door handles and the phone you're ringing me on. Anything that keeps you a bit more removed from the scene of the crime will be helpful.'

Details agreed, I engaged Harry to come and join me at the nick where I was to be interviewed. We both knew the likely location – West London Police Station on Savile Row, only a few hundred feet away from the studio. I finally dialled 9-9-9 to report the crime, then, before the police arrived, went into the control room, and searched out the bottle of Jack Daniels and two mugs. The mugs were there, under the desk, but the bottle had been placed in the wastepaper bin, still half full. I wondered about rescuing it and having a slug. In the end, I just wiped down the two mugs before returning them. Looking up at the monitor, I began processing Angie's death for the first time. The violence would have been extreme. She would have been scared. Then to be left there, alone, snapped and broken under that red light… I stopped myself. For the time being, I had to try and keep it together.

The police held me over for questioning until mid-morning the following day. I sat in an unlocked cell for an hour before anyone spoke to me. They then attempted to begin the "interview", despite my request for a solicitor to be present. When they asked why I would need a solicitor if I was innocent, I explained to them that it was my legal right. Annoyed, they took me back to the cell. Three hours later, I finally returned to the interview room, this time my brief was present. After all that hanging around, the interview, when it began, only lasted another hour. Still, it could have been worse. At least they let me go.

In my witness statement, I told the investigating officers that I left the Astor around one in the morning and decided to call in and see if anyone I knew was recording at Ryemuse on a whim.

I explained that I worked in the music business and had many friends who were musicians. I found the side door open and curious as to why, went inside to investigate. I discovered Angie Bright-Silver strangled and immediately phoned the police and then my solicitor. Twenty minutes later a constable arrived. Two CID officers arrived a little while after that.

My account was given in a small interview room, the four of us bunched around a tiny Formica table. Everyone was smoking except me. I might as well have been, for all the smoke I was breathing in. The two CID officers were DS Seabrook and DI Simkins. Perhaps they allotted officers in alphabetical order. I had their S's today. The younger one, Seabrook, was moon faced with a thin moustache and bulging eyes like Marty Feldman. His superior, Simkins, had the same solid build and baleful stare of a villain. Both policemen were drinking mugs of coffee. Other than sullen looks, they were yet to offer me anything. Harry Baum was sitting alongside in his usual crumpled suit and soup-stained tie. Bald, rheumy eyed, and distracted in manner, Harry might have looked like someone's old granddad, but he was a true legal assassin. All the Teen Avenue crowd used him, particularly to sort out pop stars who were in a legal jam. The two policemen opposite me would have dealt with Harry many times, of that, I was sure.

'Why did you phone a solicitor from the scene of the crime, Mr Jones?' DS Seabrook asked, staring at me before shifting his gaze to Harry. 'Seems strange. Like you had something to hide. And no offence to Harry, but he represents a rogue's gallery of London's more unsavoury characters. It sort of colours how we see you.'

'I knew I was going to be interviewed as a witness at the scene of a crime,' I answered. 'Experience with the Metropolitan police told me it might be wise to have someone by my side.'

The policemen exchanged a glance before DI Simkins cleared

his throat and began.

'Did you know Ms Bright-Silver?'

'Of course. She's a famous entertainer. Pretty much everyone knows her.'

'Did you know her personally?'

'I'm from the world of music. It's a small world. Our paths had crossed.'

'Did you ever do more than just cross her path, if you get my meaning,' Seabrook leered.

'He means did you used to poke her,' Simkins clarified helpfully.

'I'd already got his meaning, thank you. We were good friends a long time ago.'

Harry placed a hand on my arm and leant forward across the table to DS Seabrook and DI Simkins.

'Do I need to remind you officers that my client is here to give a witness statement? If you decide to charge him, you can begin an investigation of my client, but not till then.'

Simkins drew on his cigarette then blew the exhaled smoke my way. He was doing me a favour. I had just decided to give up on this quitting business anyway. I took one of Harry's cigarettes, lit up and blew smoke right back in the copper's face. Judging by his reaction, Simkins was warming to me, I could tell.

'You must have been very upset seeing her like that, neck broken... dead.' He seemed to relish saying the last word and watched my reaction carefully.

'Of course,' I replied.

'Really? The constable said you seemed very calm.'

'Did he?'

Seabrook took over. They were tag teaming me. It was like being back in the wrestling ring again.

'Did you visit that studio a lot?' Seabrook asked.

'I visit all the studios in the area from time to time.'

'Is it always at one in the morning?'

'Sometimes. If there are sessions going on.'

'What made you think there was as session going on at the studio in South Molton Street?'

'There usually is.'

'But not tonight?' Simkins shot back.

'Seems not.'

'And there was no sign of any other people having been present,' Seabrook probed. 'Isn't there usually a producer around or something?'

'Usually. But none that I saw.'

Seabrook kept digging. 'Studio owner said the place was booked in the name Blank Verse. Heard of them?'

'Name means nothing to me,' I replied.

Seabrook continued. 'A house engineer was part of the booking. Fellow by the name of Billy Coles? Heard of him?'

'Yes, but he definitely wasn't there when I discovered the body,' I answered carefully and precisely.

'Not a creature was stirring, not even a mouse,' Simkins sneered.

Harry piped up:

'My client is giving a truthful statement. Derision or scorn simply because you don't like the answer is unacceptable.'

Harry's presence was hindering the two policeman's preferred approach which was to play it rough and go in hard. Simkins finally let out an exasperated sigh.

'Okay, Taffy. What do you think happened?' he asked.

'I don't know.'

'Try,' Simkins pressed. 'Speculate.'

Harry shook his head to discourage me, but I could see the police needed some help.

‘Whoever murdered Angie Bright-Silver would either have had a key or was let into the building since the front door showed no sign of having been forced. The fact that all the amps were on, not to mention the two-way tv monitor means a session of some sort had taken place or was about to take place. However, there was no tape in the recording equipment. Her belongings were also missing.’

‘Belongings?’ Seabrook asked.

‘Her coat, her handbag – her things.’

‘It was a robbery that went wrong then,’ Seabrook suggested.

‘Maybe. Let’s return to the front door business. Normally, the door has an entry system. To get in, you have to be let in. That might put off most robbers. When I found the body, the door was left open. Either the attacker was in a highly emotional state and left in a hurry, too careless to close the door properly, or they left it open deliberately to assist in the early discovery of the body.’

‘You have thought this through, haven’t you, boyo,’ Simkins mocked.

‘More than you have, it seems. Perhaps you were thinking a dead Angie let me in and I murdered her again before calling 9-9-9.’

The policemen’s faces showed me they hadn’t entirely dismissed that as an idea. I drew on my cigarette and let the smoke hang in my mouth before continuing.

‘When you get the time of death, you’ll see how impossible my murdering her would have been. I was in the Guinea grill from nine to eleven. The Astor club from eleven to one. Angie had been dead hours before I arrived. You haven’t got any motive; you haven’t got any evidence of any sort to charge me. Harry will correct me if I’m wrong, but I believe, as a mere witness, I’m free to leave at any time, which I think I’ll do right now.’

Harry and I pushed our chairs away from the table and stood up.

'How's Terry Sporne these days?' Simkins asked.

Harry adopted a bored sing-song voice to restate my rights. 'May I remind you officers that my client is here to give a witness statement? If you decide to charge him, you can begin an investigation of my client, but not till then.'

'A simple enough question,' Seabrook said, 'easy to answer.'

Simkins jabbed a finger downwards to indicate we should sit back in our chairs again.

Reluctantly, we took up our position at the table. With the mention of Terry Sporne, Harry now took charge.

'Unless Mr Sporne is a suspect, I fail to see his relevance as it pertains to my client. Is Mr Sporne a suspect?'

'No. Terry *Frog* Sporne has an alibi,' Simkins began. 'He was at the Empire Pool for the boxing last night. He is not a suspect. However, his relevance to this matter is that your client's name is on file as one of his known associates.'

'All of which still has nothing to do with his witness statement!' Harry shouted.

'The partner of Terry Sporne is murdered, and the body discovered by an ex-employee. It all smells fishier than a summer's day in Billingsgate,' Simkins concluded.

'If you are going to continue with these insinuations, you need to charge my client or I will make a formal complaint,' Harry responded, his voice urgent, commanding.

We stood up again, pushed back the chairs and waited for the policemen to do the same. It took a few seconds, but they followed our lead. The witness statement interview was over.

Hitting the streets, I took Harry for a cup of tea and a salt beef sandwich at the Chalet café on New Bond Street. I bummed another cigarette from him and lit up. A pair of beautiful teenage girls were sitting at a nearby table. They were from the Lucie Clayton Grooming School across the road, I could tell. They looked right through

Harry and me. The school was obviously training them well. Where they were heading, people like us didn't even exist.

'How old do you think she was?' Harry asked.

At first, I thought he meant one of the Lucie Clayton girls, but Harry was staring off in the distance. He was thinking about Angie Bright-Silver.

'She was a year younger than me,' I answered.

'Which means?'

'She was twenty-seven,' I clarified.

'No age at all, is it, Elisud?'

I was so busy thinking about Angie that I almost failed to notice Harry had used my first name, my Welsh name. His pronunciation was perfect.

Eight

I headed back to my flat, armed with the midmorning editions of the newspapers. The moment I got through my front door, I went to the phone and tried to get hold of Billy.

'Yes?'

The voice was female, American.

'I was wanting to speak to Billy Coles. Is he around? I'm a friend, Elisud Jones.'

There was a pause.

'Billy hasn't been here since yesterday.'

'Did he say if he was going away?'

Another pause. 'I'm just his flatmate, Shannon. He doesn't tell me anything.'

Her accent was white South African not American, I realised. She sounded tired or maybe bored.

'Can you ask him to ring me when he gets back?'

I gave her my telephone number.

'It's important he talks to me. Tell Billy to ring.'

'Will do,' she said curtly, ending the phone call.

The flatmate answering was a real surprise, her very existence a shock. I had never been to Billy's new place, other than calling for him on the way to the pub or dropping him off in a taxi coming back from a party. Strange he had never mentioned her. Then again there was a lot about Billy that was strange. It was part of his charm. Was he strange enough to kill someone?

Not a chance. That certainty was what had stopped me mentioning his name to the police. In the cold light of day, I ran the suggestion through my tired brain again, just to be sure. Was Billy Coles capable of being a killer? Same answer. Not a chance. That would have to do for now. But if it wasn't Billy, who the hell was responsible?

I brewed up a pot of tea, boiled an egg, and put on some toast, surprised by my appetite. Hoping for further information, I opened the newspapers to read about a woman I had found dead just a few hours earlier. The words felt calming rather than ghoulish or morbid; the familiar, reassuring newsprint making sense of the inexplicable. They all gave Angie a nice send off, almost treating it as a good news story. Compared to strikes, IRA bombs and the growing Middle East crisis, any story that justified a glamorous accompanying photograph was bound to be seized upon by the editors. Every paper went with a publicity shot Angie used back in the mid-sixties, around the time of her first hit, 'Make Me Yours'. It was taken by David Bailey, when enough misguided people believed London was swinging 'like a pendulum do'. Winking at the camera, long strawberry blonde hair parted in the middle, naked above the waist, nothing but a bowler hat held over each breast to protect Angie's modesty, the photograph was a sixties classic. For two years, between the Beatles' films *Help* and *Magical Mystery Tour*, Angie's face and voice captured that time. The mod, pop art fashions suited her boyish frame. She was sexy but never sexual. Her working-class roots in Stepney were a badge of honour, granting her a Terence Stamp, Michael Caine authenticity that seemed so important back then. Angie never did manage the move to flower power, kaftans, and daisy-chains. She gave it her best shot, but songs like 'Silk Purse Polka' and 'Sitar Sam' never caught on with the public, not like her earlier hits. Then edgier singers like Julie Driscoll stepped in and made Angie

– the "queen of the mods" – appear old-fashioned. This was about the time we became friendly. Sporne kept her on a short leash, but we would see each other at parties, the odd concert. I felt sorry for her. She did enjoy a minor hit recorded just before the decade's end with a Mickie Most produced number, 'Little Girl's Dream', but after that she was singing Burt Bacharach medleys on the Royal Variety Show and appearing in pantos with Lionel Blair. Despite all this, despite not having had a hit for three years, the papers' headlines all went with variations of 'Pop Star Murdered'. Better than popular entertainer murdered. 'Star' sells. The greater the height, the greater the fall, and that's the meat of newspapers. None of the Fleet Street papers speculated on who might have murdered Angie. Terry Sporne was named as Angie's manager, described as 'colourful', but their relationship and his criminal connections were not touched upon. My name didn't appear anywhere. No journalist offered any explanation as to why Angie might have been in Mayfair or alone in a cheap studio. And no one, not even the police, knew of the engineer who had been there earlier. No one was worrying about what happened to Billy. No one except me, that is.

My head began to ache. Both hands were shaking. My eyes were stinging. It was time to tap out as they say in wrestling, but I was straight enough in my head to make sure I got hold of Danny Marks on the phone before quitting the ring. I didn't want Sporne thinking I was a neck breaker, not when the neck belonged to the woman he had hired me to find. There was a number written on a beer mat from the day before if I needed to contact Danny. I tried imagining where in Soho I was ringing. A bookies? A pub? A strip joint? It didn't matter, just that he answered. The phone rang twice before he picked up. A matter-of-fact Danny asked me what happened. I told him exactly what I told the police – that it was just luck or bad luck for me to turn up when I did at Ryemuse. Danny seemed happy enough with my version of events. Why wouldn't he? Sporne had no doubt already heard the same thing from his informer inside the police. The Met were so corrupt they were as leaky as a sieve crossing the English Channel. With the stories corresponding, Terry Sporne would be contained. For now.

I climbed into bed planning to catch a few hours but ended up staying there a whole lot longer. I wasn't just exhausted; I was numb. Discovering a murdered woman can do that to you, I suppose. Must be the grief or shock or something.

The phone rang in the early hours, well past midnight. It took some will power to drag myself out of bed and lift the receiver. Penny Sands was on the other end of the line. She sounded distressed, her voice cracked from crying or drink. Probably both.

'Elis, it's Penny. Have you heard the news? Have you heard what happened in the studio?'

'Penny? Where are you? We need to talk. Talk properly. Not on the phone.'

'She was murdered, Elis.'

'I know. Listen, Penny…'

'She was… she was… "a simple child that lightly draws its breath and feels its…". I can't remember the rest.'

'The rest of what?'

'The poem by Wordsworth…"and feels its life in every limb, what should it know of death?". Elis, I can't believe she's…'

'Are you at home? I'll come to you.'

'He will be here soon. I can't see you. I just wanted to hear your voice, Elis.'

'Did you know Angie was recording in the studio, Penny?'

'I knew I would see you in the pub. I always have a sense with you. There's a powerful bond between us. It sets off a vibration in my core whenever you are near.'

A male voice was agitating in the background. Penny's nervousness increased.

'I have to go, Elis. Bye. I'll ring you again, soon.'

The line went dead. I searched around in my phone book, found her number, and rang straight back. There was no answer. I tried again. No answer. Throwing on some clothes, I hurried through to Park Lane and managed to hail a cab. Penny lived in a cobbled mews near Holland Park. This time of night, the cab would be there in ten minutes. I didn't care if Geoff Birch was around or not. I didn't care if he tried to stop me. I was going to talk to Penny.

The journey took me exactly ten minutes, just as I'd reckoned. When the taxi driver let me out at the bottom of the mews. I couldn't remember the number, just the shape of the house, those uneven steps leading up from the pavement, the broken glass in the top panel of the double workshop doors. Looking for those details, or something else that would jog my memory, I hurried through the mews. My one and only previous visit had been when we met up to talk about her tour. We drank tea, smoked a joint, played mah-jong and ate chocolate cake. Penny was aware I knew Geoff from the days of Grass and Phil Fratton. She was worried I might hold that against her, even though her and Geoff were currently separated. I explained to her how my dislike of Geoff stemmed from the way he conveniently turned a blind eye to Phil's slide into addiction, then used his bandmate's troubles as an excuse to sack him on the eve of a lucrative American tour. But I was sincere that afternoon when I told her I loved her music. With Geoff off the scene, I made a few immediate musical suggestions, recommending Herbie Flowers as his replacement, a session bass player who would massively improve her backing band. I also encouraged her to play a few solo numbers on the tour. Penny at the piano, unaccompanied, singing a traditional song like 'She

Moved Through The Fair' was too good a moment not to include in the set. Leaving her place that day, the business side of things sorted, there was a mutual feeling that we would end up in bed together sooner or later. Might be she was right about that powerful bond between us. Things came to pass on the tour. Passions fulfilled. But touring romances are always funny things. You are separated from reality. Everything is contained, airtight, like a bottle of champagne; all that lovely fizz preserved, as long as the cork stays in the bottle. The moment a tour finishes, the cork is removed, and the champagne quickly goes flat. That's what happened with us, anyway.

I found the mews house with the steps and the broken pane of glass in the door. The bell was also familiar. In a childish handwriting, she had written 'Penny' onto the brick work in felt-tip. I pressed the button and didn't lift my finger. When the front door failed to open, I went back onto the cobbled street and looked up at the first-floor window. No lights. No sign of life. No one was home. It was obvious: Penny hadn't even been there when she rang me less than half an hour ago. So where was she?

The following morning, I rang her label, Island Records, and spoke to Chas Parker, a cheerful Aussie who did Penny's publicity and was someone I knew vaguely. When he seemed wary of offering me up any information, I threw him a line about wanting to know when Penny's new record was coming out, before casually asking again of her whereabouts.

'Penny Sands is doing some dates in Denmark this week, Elis. Left late last night. She'll be back for the record launch next week.'

'"The Sun, the Stars…', whatever it was?'

'*Penny Sands Two*,' Chas corrected me.

'Any chance you could send me an invitation for the launch party, Chas?' I asked.

'You are such a ligger, Jonesy! Sure thing! Just don't forget your life jacket!'

He laughed, ringing off before I had a chance to ask him what he meant.

A sense of helpless frustration was really starting to take hold of me. Chain-smoking a pack of Disque Bleu, three names were spinning inside my brain like kites in a storm: Angie Bright-Silver, Penny Coles, and Billy Coles. There were questions involving all three, but no answers. And all the time, the strings were slipping through my fingers as a hurricane dragged each kite higher and higher, into the clouds, out of sight.

I came to a decision. I needed a pint.

My watch informed me the pubs wouldn't be open for another hour or so. With time to kill, I took a walk north on Park Street, through Marble Arch and onto the Edgware Road. Billy's flat was in a modern block along Bryanston Street. I rang the bell on the entry system and waited five minutes, then rang the bell again before finally giving up, feeling dismal. As I told Danny, 'I don't do missing persons'. The truth of these words was becoming apparent. My record so far: One dead, two disappeared. To add to my depression, I realised I had left my wallet back at the flat. I just couldn't catch a break. Even when the pubs opened, I would have to go back home first.

For no particular reason, and quite by chance, my journey home skirted the eastern edge of Hyde Park as far as the Joy of Life fountain, where I sat on a park bench. The fountain had two bronze figures in the centre holding hands as they danced intimately above the water. People tended to call it 'The Joy of Sex' fountain nowadays after the book of the same name that had recently come out. I watched the water rise and fall, the light playing on the surface. Suddenly nostalgic for Pontypridd, I thought about the people I went to school with and wondered how they would be spending their morning. Would they be sitting in a park waiting for the pubs to open? Possibly. Would they be traipsing about looking for a man who didn't want to be found after a woman had been murdered? Less likely. A wave of sadness washed over me. *Hiraeth* is a word we Welsh have for how I felt. There is no real English equivalent. It means longing, regret and desire all rolled into one. *Hiraeth*: It means wanting to return to a home that never was. So where did that leave me? Where did that leave Pontypridd?

Nine

'Pontypridd is Wales. Forget Snowden – Wales is about valleys, not mountains. Forget Carmarthen – Wales is about coal, not cattle. Cardiff, Caerphilly, Harlech, Pembroke and all those towns with castles? That's not Wales. Wales has a certain working-class grit that makes hatred of inequality a given, not an option. That's why the miners supported the Spanish Republicans fighting Franco, even sent over soldiers to fight the fascists. That's why they took to Paul Robeson, and him to them, and by doing so, took up the cause of civil rights. Class struggle flows through the Rhondda Valley like the River Taff. *"Mae hen wlad fy nhaddau yn annwyl I mi"!* Who wrote the words and music to our national anthem? A father and son from Pontypridd. Need I really say any more?'

My last trip home.

Like every other trip home, we'd been drinking all day. His eyes were swimming, their focus all gone. I knew I was going to have the familiar struggle of getting him back to the house. From the time I first started drinking with him aged thirteen, even then matching *tad* drink for drink, I'd served as his captive audience, someone to lecture, cajole, and browbeat. More importantly, by the end of those sessions, staggering home, I'd become his walking stick to rest upon; charged with taking the key from his grubby pocket and opening up the front door, before carrying him up the stairs to his bed where he would pass out immediately. The last visit home had been no different. Eight years since we'd last laid eyes on each other, I'd wanted him to see how well I'd done for myself since giving up the wrestling. Mayfair, the music business, Mickie Most, all the changes. But my father wasn't remotely interested. Instead, sitting in the front room, the coal fire flickering, he looked me up and down.

'Still in London then, is you?'

'Still in London. Just not doing the wrestling now. These days I work for record companies.'

'Oh! Right.'

He cast an eye at the clock on the mantlepiece before rising to his feet.

'I reckon the bar'll be open down the club. We should go and wet our whistles.'

The clubhouse, belonging to Pontypridd RFC, was a small shack with a bar on the edge of Ynsangharad Park. Charmless, utterly soulless, the main room was large enough to hold a dozen oval tables and plastic chairs. On the walls were photographs of past legends such as Glynn Davies, Russell Robins, Danny Harris and Gareth Payne, all of whom played for the local team and Wales when I was growing up. Rising star, Tommy David, was featured amongst the new crop of players. One photograph caught "Tom the Bomb" in a typical diving pose as he scored a try. I watched him train with the team under the floodlights on that last visit. For a very large man, Tommy somehow managed to move at speed, making him a relentless force of nature, especially when he played in what I could tell was his best position in the back row, blindside flanker. Later, at the bar, his enormous hands engulfing the pint pot, Tommy revealed a modest, affable charm as he assessed Ponty's most recent game. By all accounts, there had been an unpleasant altercation over in Llanelli, the details of which he divulged.

'They were like bloody animals. I don't know what had got into them boys. So, I'd gone up to their captain and says, "any more of this bollocks and we're going to smash you lot's teeth in". Didn't change a thing! They carry on with their punching in the scrum and all that, so now I'm thinking to myself, "I've bloody well had enough of this". First chance I get, I go in hard on their loose prop, head butt him as I make for the ruck, then put my knee right into his privates...'

By now my father was howling with laughter. After all these years of regarding me coldly, the answer to our building a better relationship was clearly my regaling him with tales of violence. And if that was the case, I certainly could offer up some real beauties. There was the time I nearly blinded a man with my fist, then watched his eyeball hang from a thread. Or the occasion I broke the arm – deliberately – of some villain who'd crossed Don Arden. In my Soho days, I'd used knives and baseball bats, knuckle-dusters, broken bottles, hammers and coshes. I'd hit, stabbed, maimed and broken my way across the West End. Violence – real violence, not scrapping on the field of play rough stuff – was my life. Or it had been. I could have told him, but it wouldn't have made any difference. The violence alone wasn't delighting my father. I could see it in his eyes. Tommy David was the son my father had wished for: The rugby player, the boyo, the man. Instead, in me, he got a wrestler first, then a 'hairy hippy', to use his phrase. Of the two, my being a wrestler upset him the most. It took me away from the Rhondda, not just physically but mentally. If I was to do any kind of sport, he wanted it to be rugby, and nothing else. A large man himself, Robert Jones was a fair player in his time. He worked the seams up at the Albion pits and played for the colliery team, Cilfynydd RFC. Like most Welshmen, he had designs on his son playing for Wales the second I was born.

'Imagine that,' he would say to my mother, 'one day we'll have him playing at the Arms Park.'

This refrain would commence after some Sunday game for the school that had taken us up and down and all over the Rhondda, or across into Church Village, Beddau or Llantrisant. Eating our Sunday lunch, he'd go over the game, assessing my performance. In the back row, the number eight, my inclusion in the team was down to size alone – I was already over six foot before I started Secondary School – not any particular aptitude or feel for the game. The multitude of faults in my on-pitch displays were something my father always believed needed urgent addressing.

'It's no bloody good just lumbering about. You got to be the focus for the defence. Hold up the other team's advance. Read the game. Spot their plays.'

My mother would try and change the subject, but he wouldn't budge. Right through to pudding, he'd carry on. It got so I hated rugby, then him.

There was soon just the two of us, after my mother died of cancer. Rugby still dominated Sundays, but now there was no lovely roast afterwards. None of that cwtch feeling you'd have when she was alive, her face smiling as I came through the door covered in mud. Instead, we went to the club, where I'd watch him drink himself insensible, trying to make sense of the pain he felt. Pretty soon I was joining in with the drinking. So that became our thing. Down the club. Father and son. Drinking.

One day, after a suggestion by a schoolteacher, I discovered wrestling. There was to be a training session at a hall in Tonteg. The teacher thought it might be a way to channel some of my already evident aggression. Taking the bus out of the valley and up into Church Village, I found the community hall on the edge of the council estate in Tonteg. The room held the smell of sweat and straw from the mats laid out on the floor. Men of all sizes were rolling around kicking the shit out of each other. Merv "Mountain" Mardy was taking the session. It turned out he wasn't giving lessons, he was recruiting. This was to be an audition for all the big boys in the Rhondda Valley. Merv, an unscrupulous former wrestler turned promoter, liked what he saw in me, signing me to the South Wales circuit. I was fifteen.

I told my father I didn't want to play rugby, told him I thought it was a stupid sport.

'Of all the ways you could have betrayed your mother… you've chosen the cruellest.'

That's what he said. A ridiculous thing to say. Nevertheless, it stayed with me for a long time.

We never saw eye to eye after that. From moving to London, my visits back to Pontypridd were few. When I did return, we renewed our habit of going to the club, glumly drinking pint after pint as a way of avoiding having to really talk to each other. Eventually, his whole 'Pontypridd is Wales' speech would start up, and I'd know the evening was coming to a close.

So it transpired the last time I went back to see him, around the time I was managing Tony's Timepiece.

The night was bitterly cold as we staggered our way over the bridge from the park, crossing the river and making our way up the High Street. From the railway line onwards the gradual hill tested his legs and he leant into me, wanting to be supported, making no effort, a dead weight for me to carry. The house was on the corner of Craig Street. I'd already taken the keys from his pocket ready to open up, though it struck me that he might as well have left the door unlocked. No one was ever going to break into his house. He had far less possessions than most thieves, and certainly nothing they would want. Inside the door, I dragged him up the stairs, lay some newspapers on the mattress, certain that he was going to piss himself, and threw him down on the bed. Then I went downstairs. Out of some misplaced proprietorial sense, I drew the curtains. Fir trees and stars on cream linen: The pattern on the tatty fabric took me back to my childhood. Only now the trees and stars were fighting against thirty years of cigarette smoke in a front room never once aired. Impregnated by a nicotine yellow, the stars looked like they were drowning in butterscotch.

The Albion pit closed in 1966, which was just as well. Miners knew it to be one of the most dangerous around. My father got out unscathed, and never once missed the life. His pension was generous and, other than beer, his outgoings were minimal. As far as I could gather, he didn't eat anything other than nuts and pork scratchings bought down the club. He'd been a widow for twenty years. His life and house showed it. Tumbleweed size dust balls and looming cobwebs collected in the corners of the living room. The perimeter of carpet around his armchair held a collection of stains, cigarette burns and dried sick. It was almost a modern work of art. Cut a section of that out and hang it in a gallery, someone would probably pay a fortune.

Since it had been a day of drinking, I saw no reason to stop that night. Finding his bottle of scotch, I sat in the kitchen and drank the whole lot under a harsh fluorescent light. By the dawn, I had talked to myself, to the imagined ghost of my mother, even thought about ringing Mickie Most back in Mayfair so I could chat to someone from Teen Avenue. If my father had a phone line, I might well have done just that. Instead, I went up to my old bedroom, lay on the bed, and watched the ceiling spin around.

Hiraeth – a home that never was. I had thought going back to see my father might cure me of that painful feeling of loss and longing. Clearly, it hadn't. There and then, I decided I didn't want to ever return to Pontypridd. And so far, I haven't. I haven't even been back to Wales, since that last visit. The only reason I could ever imagine for returning would be for my father's funeral, and, most of the time, that didn't even feel like enough of a reason.

Besides. I had my path.

Mayfair. Music. And murder.

Ten

I sat watching the fountain flow in Hyde Park a little while longer before crossing Park Lane. Mayfair, music, and murder: I could attend to at least two of those things – maybe all three – over a steadying pint. My watch told me it was only another twenty minutes before the pubs opened. Things were looking up.

Back at the flat, wallet collected, there was a soft knock at my flat door. I opened the door cautiously, imagining the worst. The prospect of a pint might have lifted my spirits, but I'd been hired by Terry Sporne the day before, discovered his partner murdered, and lied to the police. My mother was fond of an old expression: *Yr hen a ŵyr a'r ieuanc a dybia* – the old know, the young suspect. I had my way of putting it: If you run with the wolves, sooner or later you better learn how to fucking howl. A little care and caution was advisable. That quickly melted away when I found a striking blonde woman, around my age, standing in the doorway.

'Are you Jonesy?' she asked.

'I am. Who are you?'

'Right now, a bloody messenger.'

Without any invitation, she walked past me into the flat, her fragrant, dreamy honeysuckle perfume taking on the stale cigarette smoke and winning the challenge hands down.

'Sorry to be curious.'

She went to the window and peered outside.

'Wondered what the view was like higher up,' she said.

'Take as long as you want,' I offered.

'Name's Petters,' she said, turning around. 'Gail Petters. We're neighbours. Don't think we've met.'

'You live on the ground floor?'

'Correct.'

She was wearing an old-fashioned screen siren get-up, consisting of a full-length gold satin dress split to the thigh, with six-inch high heels. Not that I'm an expert on these things, but her outfit looked designer and expensive. The very hip Ms Petters was doing that Roxy Music/Bowie trick of making the past seem ultra-new. I should have invited my music journalist friend Rick Kempe over. He liked to write pages and pages about that sort of thing.

'Have you been away?' she asked. 'Only a funny little man came to see you. Apparently knew you and tried ringing you several times. Said man rang my bell asking me to give you a message. Made me come to the front door.'

'What was the message?'

'Tell Jonesy to get in touch with Billy straight away.'

'Did the "funny little man" leave a number?'

'I did ask. He said you'd know where to ring.'

'Would you mind describing the person who delivered this?' I asked her.

'Small, grumpy, Scottish. Had the look of a man who stands outside sex shops in Soho trying to get up the courage to go in.'

I laughed. She had just provided the perfect description of Billy Coles.

'How do you know the kind of men who stand outside sex shops in Soho?' I asked.

'I have an active imagination. You're Welsh?'

'I'm Welsh – *Rydw i'n Cymreig*.'

'Funny enough, I was evacuated to Montgomeryshire during the war. Know it?'

'I'm more the Valleys. Would you like a drink? I was just about to fix myself one.'

'How very sweet of you. I think I will. Scotch straight up if you have it.'

I poured us both a generous slug. She gave the front room a thorough inspection.

'What happened to Phil?' she asked. 'The man who lived here before?'

'He moved to America. Did you two know each other?'

'Not really. I lent him some money. Don't suppose I'll see that again.'

'Was it a lot?'

'Not enough to keep me up at night.'

Gail Petters sat down on the couch. I sat opposite her on the easy chair. She crossed her legs demurely at the ankles and still managed to reveal most of her stockinged thigh. The last woman I'd seen do that trick was Lauren Bacall, and that was in a film.

'How long have you lived here?' I asked her.

'A while. Wish I had your view. Bit dark and dreary on the ground floor. Still, beggars can't be choosers and all that guff. Aren't you going to ring your friend?'

'In a while.'

Since the only number I had for Billy was his flat, it could wait. Gail Petters sensed my inaction.

'He seemed to be in a state. In some sort of trouble.'

'Could be.'

'All the more reason to ring him.'

I made no move.

'Well?' she persisted. 'Are you or aren't you?'

Gail Petters was fragrant, she was elegant, but I wasn't going to let her boss me around in my own flat. I ignored her question and offered her a cigarette instead, taking one for myself.

'Disque Bleu, how very chic,' she said, nodding her approval as I lit both cigarettes with my Zippo lighter.

'It's a taste I acquired growing up in the vibrant café society of Pontypridd,' I explained.

Laughing, her face momentarily lost its brittleness. A nice laugh like that, she really should try and do it more often, I thought to myself.

'I asked the man who delivered the message about you. I wanted to make sure I had the right flat.'

I smiled. 'I'd be interested to know how he described me.'

'He just said you looked like someone who could take care of himself in a fight.'

She looked me up and down.

'I'd say he got it about right. Reassuring to know the building possesses someone who can "take care of himself". The art dealer above me – below you – certainly couldn't.'

'Probably not,' I agreed.

'Makes a girl feel safer. I'm looking for someone who can take care of himself in a fight, point of fact.'

'Going into boxing promotion?'

'Quite the wag, aren't you?'

I shrugged apologetically.

'Point of fact,' she continued, 'I need some assistance with a personal matter.'

I fetched the whiskey, topped up her glass then mine.

'How personal are we talking?'

'Not as personal as you might be thinking, right now. More a case of personal as in private, as in delicate, as in confidential. I'd make it worth your while.'

'Why do you think I might be able to help?'

'Because you're drinking whiskey before midday. Because you have messages delivered to you by seedy little men and because you like looking at women's legs.'

I put down my drink.

'Okay. You caught me looking at your legs. But who delivers my messages is my business and not something I'd appreciate you reading too much into if you wouldn't mind. As for my drinking whiskey before midday, I'd say that's an average teeing-off time for me and, judging by the way you're knocking it back, the same goes for you. Unless I knew any better, I'd just say you were a nosy neighbour who likes to get flirty as she gets sozzled.'

She stood up; her cheeks red with rage.

'You don't know the first thing about me.'

'Then why don't you sit back down, have another drink and tell me. I promise not to look at your legs.'

She slowly sat down.

'Just make sure you don't call me nosy again.'

By the time we adjourned to the bedroom, we had polished off the rest of the bottle. Our breath sour, eyes swimming, we kissed and pawed at each other with pent-up lust. We were sloppy drunk and horny as hell, a comical combination.

Lord knows I needed a little cheering up.

Kenneth Bryce, Member of Parliament for the constituency of Spelthorne was the personal matter Gail hired me to resolve. It was first discussed as we sat knocking back whiskey in my front room. Later, we fleshed out the details in pillow talk following our love-making. Her proposal was simple enough. The Right Honourable Kenneth Bryce had worn out his welcome with Ms Petters. Would I do something to help? She admitted to being his mistress, but contrary to the rumours I had heard, she was not a kept woman. The flat was all hers, and I soon found out how she could afford it. Daddy was a well-connected, multi-millionaire oil trader. He had the ear of Prime Ministers and Sheiks, Presidents and Shahs. A townhouse flat in Mayfair was as fancy as a garden shed to a man like that. Bought it without breaking sweat, I bet. Gail had been introduced to Bryce at one of her father's Christmas parties. By the sounds of it they were the sort of festive gatherings where the Christmas tree was so tall it had to be kept in the hallway, next to the sweeping marble staircase, hanging chandeliers and attending footmen with buckled shoes and powdered wigs. It wasn't too hard to imagine Gail in such a place. The business of her being drawn to some pinstripe politician was harder to square. Sensing my bafflement, she went out of her way to try and explain to me how different Bryce was from the typical Members of Parliament.

'He is one of the youngest Conservative MPs in the House. Ted Heath thinks very highly of him; calls him a rising star. He's everything most Tories are not. He went to Cambridge for a start. He's anti-apartheid, pro-unions, loves modern jazz, smokes marijuana and is really very sweet.'

'And really very married?' I suggested.

'I finally gave him the ultimatum every mistress gives: Divorce the wife or we're over. He hasn't divorced his wife, and he hasn't accepted it's over with me. He has become a pest. An irritant. I need to make it clear to him somehow that we are unequivocally no longer joined at the hip.'

My role was straightforward. I was to be paid fifty pounds to talk to him man to man. He always held a mid-week constituency surgery. It would be easy to meet him there, easy to make a case as to why he should move on and forget all about Ms Petters. I was to tell Kenneth Bryce, or 'Ken', as she called him, that if ever he contacted her again, I would phone his wife and expose the affair. As jobs go, it seemed undemanding. Any lingering doubts I had about taking it on were quickly dealt with by another bout of lovemaking. This was not my normal way of dealing with new clients, but then again, Gail Petters was not a normal client. She had an enigmatic, femme fatale quality that was intriguing, not to mention arousing. If she was Lauren Bacall, then that made me Humphrey Bogart. Who doesn't want to play film stars for a few hours? The little talking we did provided me with the barest scraps of biographical details. She liked drinking scotch and 'reading the work of Victorian occultists, in particular a woman called Anna Kingsford'. Don't we all? Her friends were few and she rarely socialised. Independently wealthy, she had no need to work but chose to help out now and then in a small theatrical costumier owned by her aunt on the corner of Vigo Street and Savile Row, right at the eastern edge of Mayfair.

'What else do you need to know?' she asked. 'As you can see, I'm pretty much an open book.'

That was not true. Not even close. But it felt like nit-picking to point this out as she wrapped a leg around my waist and moved in closer, conversation once more suspended. This was no time to play the pedant.

Eleven

Wednesday. I remembered it was Wednesday – the day the music papers came out. Before catching the train from Charing Cross, I found a good newsagent that carried all the titles. Then, over my eggs, chips, sausage, and beans at the station's greasy spoon, I worked my way through the rock journos take on things.

Record Mirror and *Sounds* had single paragraph mentions on Angie. Sketchy on detail, they did little more than acknowledge her passing. *Disc* had a nice colour photograph of Angie on the cover and the headline 'Bright no More', with nothing else inside. The big two music papers were split in their coverage. *Melody Maker* devoted a half page beneath the "bowler hat" photograph. Their headline tried a little too hard – 'Hits girl now in bits girl'. A sneering obituary then went on to savage Angie for being lightweight and for, of all things, not taking a stand on Vietnam. No wonder no one was buying *Melody Maker* anymore. The recently revamped *NME* had put their new star journalist, and friend of mine, Rick Kempe on the story. He did a generous two-page spread along with a striking photograph of Angie I had never seen before. Apparently taken in Paris 1971, around the time she had a small part in a film that sank without a trace, Angie looked tired and unhappy, as if life were taking its toll. It was an image that fitted nicely with how Kempe chose to write about Angie, playing up the tragedy in her life. As he saw it, Angie's 'slaughter' represented the end of innocence, the end of pop, the end of the sixties dream. That's a lot to put on anyone, dead or alive. Kempe also gave her recording career thoughtful consideration, declaring 'Sitar Sam' the best record of the decade:

> *'Better than 'Whiter Shade of Pale', better than 'Waterloo Sunset', 'Sitar Sam' is Angie Bright-Silver's plaintive offering to Eastern mysticism; a numinous exploration of a soundscape that only Bowie is capable of now fulfilling.'*

All that would have been news to Angie. Probably Bowie as well.

It had been a long time since I had sat on a real train. If you live and work in London long enough you begin to think of all trains as stale prisons that last for two or three viewless underground stops. It was not as if I had now booked a seat on the Orient Express but finding myself travelling overground between Charing Cross and Staines was an unexpected pleasure. I enjoyed the gentle coming and going of passengers as we stopped at each station, the slamming of carriage doors and shrill whistles of the guard. Once under way, I found myself looking outside the window, lost in thought like every other train passenger. Not that the view was especially scenic – it really wasn't – but that was beside the point. Something about the here and gone procession of gas works, housing estates and scruffy dog shit parks of Twickenham, Hounslow and Feltham were helping me organise my thoughts. Or maybe it was simply being outside London. Either way, I came to a few decisions on the hour-long journey. The first of these was that I had to find a way to get in touch with Billy. After Gail Petters left, I did ring his flat several times. There was still no answer. I rang twice on the way to the station and twice from the platform. Zip. It's not that I seriously believed for a second that he killed Angie, but I was getting to be more than a little keen to discover what he knew and what he had seen. Secondly, there were the unanswered questions to chase up surrounding Blank Verse and Penny Sands. My sense was that if I pulled at the right thread the whole ball of wool would untangle.

Arriving at Staines, I clambered off the train and on to a spotless railway platform so neat and tidy it was as if I had travelled back in time; back to a Thomas Tank Engine world of large ladies in fox fur stoles holding dachshunds on leads, teenage boys playing marbles in shorts, and skipping girls with ribbons in their hair. The toy town feel continued as I made my way along the high street, heading towards Bryce's constituency office, apparently based in a Victorian townhouse near the river. I walked past plain shopfronts that seemed untouched since the 1940's, past gents outfitters, ironmongers, grocers, barbers, butchers, bakers, and undertakers. It cast me back to a half-forgotten world, the world of my childhood, the world of dog-eared ration books, long queues for bread, gossiping Welsh aunts and prams the size of rowboats. Dreary, provincial Staines was lost in time. But not for much longer. Apparently, big changes were coming. The word was that they were building a circular road all around the outer reaches of London. Passing a few miles from Staines, this new motorway network was finally going to put the town on the map. Their local MP, Kenneth Bryce was now full of talk about Staines being a town fit for the 20th century. Where once the town's original settlement was justified by a river, now it was to be justified by a road, 'a superhighway to prosperity'. This insight on Bryce's thinking wasn't simple guess work on my part. It was all in the local paper I was reading as I waited in his musty constituency office.

Francis O'Shea, his agent, and a man older than time, had taken my name and problem on my arrival. I gave the name of my old school headmaster, Gwyn Hawkins, and said I had a problem with broken drains. O'Shea was sympathetic.

'A drain is like a bed and breakfast to a rodent,' the old codger noted. 'A *broken* drain is like the Dorchester. Perfect ingress egress you see. Filthy blighters!'

He then offered me a cup of tea which tasted like he had forgotten to put in milk – and the tea bag. Sitting in the waiting room, I could hear a bus driver ranting about immigrants through a closed door.

'It's me that has to carry them back and forth from the town centre on my bus. Gibbering and jabbering they are, and none speaking the Queen's English, needless to say. They don't belong here – and don't tell me, I'm not right.'

After another half an hour, Staines' answer to Enoch Powell emerged red in the face, fully exhausted by the burden of his self-righteous fanaticism. I was really growing to dislike Staines.

Finally, and with great fanfare, I was shown in to meet the MP for the Spelthorne constituency. Two things immediately struck me. The first was the size of the portrait of the Queen in his office. It nearly covered one entire wall, like an advertising hoarding. The other thing that struck me was the man sitting at his desk, beneath the portrait. Contrary to what Gail had told me, the Right Honourable Kenneth Bryce was not younger than me. He was not even the same age. He was, in fact, older than me by about fifty years. I was staring at an ancient fossil.

'Mr Hawkins. Take a seat. I understand you have a problem with the drains.'

His voice was tired and reedy. I remained at the door, resisting the urge to laugh.

'You are Kenneth Bryce?' I asked him. 'The MP?'

'I am indeed. Please sit down and tell me about your problem.'

'I was expecting someone a little younger. I'm sorry for disturbing you.'

'Don't let my age put you off. I still have the fight, commitment, and passion of a man half my age.'

'I am sure you do. Trouble is I was looking for a man sixty years younger who likes jazz, smokes marijuana, and who has been having a passionate affair with a sexy blonde called Gail Petters. Unless I'm doing you a grave injustice you don't seem to fit that description. Not that it's not your fault. Someone's made a sucker out of me. I wish you and your constituency the best, Ken, *butty bach*.'

For some reason, Bryce felt the need to try and get to his feet. He might have been wanting to demonstrate his 'fight' and the other things he had boasted about earlier, but his body clearly had other ideas. He sank back down, thought about trying to get up again, but finally surrendered, his breath ragged. He stared at me with watery and confused eyes. I felt sorry for him. Staines was going places, but Bryce wasn't ever going to live to see it.

I left the office and headed straight back to the station, taking the fast train into London. There was no daydreaming or looking out of the window on the return journey, I was thinking about one thing – why I was set up. I already had my suspicions, but it would take me getting back to Mayfair to know for sure. Billy Coles, Penny Sands, now Gail Petters – the list of people I needed to talk to was growing. I was at the centre of something, but I didn't know what. Meanwhile, those unanswered questions were stacking up like coins in a fairground penny pusher.

INTERLUDE NO.3

June 1st, 1966: 304 Holloway Road, Islington

Cliff was spilling what he knew.

'He's not one for the ladies, Mr Sporne. You haven't got any worries on that score. Straight-up. He got hauled before a magistrate for being an arse-bandit, two or three years back, word is. It was in the papers. He was in some gents up around here when an undercover copper caught him importuning. That's what they tend to call whatever it is them types get up to. Importuning.'

Leaning forward from the plush back seat of the car, Terry Sporne turned his fixed gaze from Cliff, on the passenger side, to me, behind the wheel.

'Alright. Then tell me this: If it's not for him – then why is she there?'

This was the line of enquiry I had been tasked with a few days earlier, the assignment itself proof of my rising in the Sporne ranks. I tilted my head towards the back seat, even as I faced forward, navigating the Daimler through Highbury Corner and onto the Holloway Road.

'My information has it down as been two things: A connection to this group through her label, Pye Records, and the fact that she knows the lead singer from where she grew up. I asked around, Mr Sporne. Everyone is saying the same thing. Her and the band are old friends.'

With the car parked, Cliff jumped out and opened the car door for Terry, who, I could see, was ready for blood.

'When we get in there, bring that toerag outside and sort him. I want him hurt, I want him warned, but I want him to be able to walk away afterwards. Just tell him he's out of the group and he's not to see Angie ever again. Do it out of sight of her. I don't want her upset.'

We marched through a door to the side of the Leather Goods Shop on Holloway Road and made our way up a staircase that smelt of stale cabbage. Reaching the first floor, Sporne threw open the door leading into the small flat.

It was my first sight of a recording studio. Even so, I could see it was home spun and highly unconventional. The drum kit was in the fireplace, bicycle clips were being used to hold the microphones in place on broom handle stands. Everywhere I looked there were wires and cables leading to metal boxes with flashing lights. The room was hot, almost glowing from all the electricity.

The musicians – three men and a woman – and what I imagined to be the producer, were in a small cubby hole that housed the recording equipment. Angie appeared from the kitchen, holding a tray full of mugs of tea. It was all as innocent as a Sunday School outing.

'What the bloody hell are you doing here?' a peevish Angie asked Terry.

The question hung in the air like a Pop Art speech bubble until, head bowed, dumbfounded, the producer approached Terry Sporne.

'I deal directly with Ron and Reggie. Always have. I pay them regular.'

'None of my concern,' Sporne muttered, looking over the band.

'Which one of you is the singer?' he demanded.

'I am,' a tall, thin man responded pleasantly.

'You're from the East End, are you?'

The singer nodded his head. 'Whitechapel.'

Sporne showed no sign of having heard the reply. He turned to the female group member.

'What do you do, sweetheart?' he asked.

'I play the drums.'

Terry Sporne took a deep breath as he stared intently at the drummer and the singer, trying to estimate if they were an item. He was like a man at a poker game, trying to spot the tell. Meanwhile, the producer suddenly thought out loud, relief in his voice.

'You're Angie's manager. You're Terry Sporne!'

'Why don't you have a listen to what we've done, darling?' Angie suggested.

We all stood silently in the studio as the producer pressed some buttons and a large spool of recording tape turned.

'...you walked right by, head held so high, feel like I could die, it's so hard to love you...'

It was a bit old-fashioned, almost pre-Beatles sounding, but catchy. I noticed Terry's foot tapping until his brow suddenly furrowed.

'I don't hear Angie.'

The producer immediately spun a dial and suddenly, as if by magic, all we could hear was a female voice singing harmony. Angie sounded beautiful.

'What do you think?' asked Angie.

'Bloody lovely, darling,' Sporne said.

'What do you think?' she suddenly asked me.

But Sporne, now satisfied there was nothing to worry about, turned to leave, dragging me and Cliff away in his wake.

We followed him back down the staircase smelling of cabbage, out onto the street, and back to the car.

'What do you think?' she had asked me.

Driving away from Joe Meek's place, I silently answered: I think I'm changed forever, Angie Bright-Silver. Seeing the magic of a recording studio and hearing you sing means things can never be the same.

Twelve

Written in a faded gold cursive, the name plate above the ground floor flat doorbell read 'G. Petters'. The anger had been building in me all the way back to London. Real heart pumping anger. I wasn't going to bother with the bell. I hammered on her door, waited, then hammered again. To the sound of turning bolts, released chains and locks, the door opened to reveal Gail Petters. Except it wasn't Gail Petters, the Gail Petters I met and slept with. It was someone I had never seen before.

'Making such a dreadful racket! Who the bloody hell do you think you are? Is there a fire in the building or something?'

Rake thin and ruddy faced, she had an ugly Mayfair Cockney drawl, her vowels elongated and choked at the same time. Making became 'miking', fire became 'far-ya', something 'surmin'. It was a verbal throwback to the 1930's, and the time when Gail Petters, the real Gail Petters, would have been a young woman, already set up as some MP's mistress (if the rumours were true) and learning to hide from sight. A sudden, very powerful smell of cats reached my nostrils. Ms Petters coquettish days, if they had ever existed, were now most definitely long gone.

'I'm sorry to disturb you,' I said, my fury slowly subsiding. 'I made a mistake, another mistake.'

'You're Jones, aren't you? Chap living on the second floor?'

'Yeah, Elisud Jones.'

'Welsh! Yes, yes, it all makes sense. They always mention you being Welsh. Here's me thinking they were talking about The Welch Regiment. I imagined you were a soldier! Not actually someone from the bloody principality. There's a laugh. You have heard of the Welch? Course not! Too young, aint'ya? Welch were good and brave boys. Had it bad in Burma.'

'You said "they always mention". Who were "they"?'

'The people I let in for you, of course! Which brings me to a sore point. May I be so bold as to tell you something, sweetie? It would be a real fucking kindness to everyone if you just fixed the intercom in your flat. I thought that tart was bad enough but this latest character bothering me. Stroll on!'

'When was this?'

'When was what?'

'I think I know who you mean by "the tart". What about the "latest character" you dealt with?'

'Didn't I say? I let him in a few minutes ago.'

I turned and quickly made my way up to the second floor two steps at a time. I could see the damage from the hallway landing. My door had been forced, the flat ransacked. Bookcases lay emptied on the floor. Albums and singles out of their sleeves were thrown everywhere, my television smashed. The sofa and easy chair had been gutted; the white stuffing cast aside in small heaps like drifted snow. In the centre of the front room, amongst all this wreckage stood Terry Sporne's man, Cliff Moses.

An ex-boxer, Cliff still had the build and bearing of a heavyweight champ. Bent over, chin down, his fists half raised, he seemed to be forever anticipating "seconds out". The brotherhood of the canvas ring meant something to people like Cliff. Given I was an ex-wrestler, he was always chummy with me in the past, when we both were doing Terry Sporne's bidding. All that still didn't explain why he was standing in my front room.

'Cleaner's week off, Taffy?' Cliff asked, pleased with himself.

He'd obviously been looking forward to delivering that little witticism.

'It's the new thing, Cliff. Didn't you know? It's been featured in the colour supplements. They're all doing this in Mayfair nowadays.'

I moved closer to Cliff who immediately tensed. Looking down, I pointed in the direction of his left boot which was gently snapping my copy of Roxy Music's *For Your Pleasure*.

'It's brand new,' I explained. 'Do you mind?'

'I thought you got them all free anyway!'

'Not really the point, is it?'

'Don't get your knickers in a tangle,' Cliff said as he reached down, and handed me the LP. I matched the vinyl with the nearby sleeve. He noticed the cover showing a leather clad blonde model with a snarling jaguar on a lead.

'Nice looking bit of crumpet,' Cliff commented.

'Really? The model's name is Amanda Lear. Rumour is that she's a man.'

'Get away! One of them!' Cliff shook his head sadly, as if this were yet more evidence of how the world had gone to pot. He then looked me in the eye and said:

'This wasn't me, Taffy. It was all like this when I arrived just now.'

'Cliff, I know it wasn't you. Whoever did do this went to a hell of a lot of trouble to make sure I wouldn't be here. A lot of bloody trouble! If your boss wanted to turn my place upside down, he wouldn't worry about my being here or not.'

'You got that about right. Who was it then? And what the fuck were they looking for?'

My mind was whirling. Cliff was asking the same questions I was asking. There was something else that was beginning to really give me the terrors. Whoever that was pretending to be Gail

Petters was well briefed. She knew a lot about Billy Coles, enough to be able to accurately describe him. Her knowledge of the building was spot on. There were only a handful of people I had ever told about my getting the flat from Phil, the rumours about who lived on the ground floor even less. Without those details I wouldn't have been so easily taken in, despite all the whiskey and sex. This must have been done by – or at least instigated by – someone who knew me very well, intimately in fact.

'Mr Sporne wants to see you. He's very keen to settle up.'

I had almost forgotten about Cliff being in the room.

'What the hell for?' I asked.

'You did what he paid you to do. You found Angie Bright-Silver, in a manner of speaking. Weren't your fault she was brown bread. A deal is a deal, as far as Mr Sporne is concerned. He's waiting. Wants a chat. I suggest we go now. There's a car outside.'

Cliff, a car, Sporne wanting a chat; it was all code. I was not going to come out of this well. My suspicions were confirmed when Cliff led me to a big old black Rover parked at the end of Curzon Street on the corner of South Audley Street. Two men were sitting in the front. The one behind the wheel had the neutral expression and disinterested gaze that all muscle end up adopting. I was probably the same back in the day. The sidekick on the passenger side was much younger, barely out of his teens. He looked excited, as if this was his first job. He was yet to find the stillness needed in his line of work.

I climbed into the back seat with Cliff and immediately noticed the passenger doors couldn't be opened internally; the handles and latches had been removed. This was how we did it in the old days. It meant that any attempt I made to escape would have to wait until wherever we finally ended up. Once we stopped and they opened the doors, I would take out Cliff, then the driver. The youngster was the least dangerous. I would save him to last.

'Remember Rizzy from the old days?' Cliff asked me, jabbing a thumb over towards the driver.

'How are you doing, Taff?' Rizzy called out.

It sounded more like a warning than a question. I nodded a greeting over his way, even though I didn't recognise his face. Forget memory lane, I was having a hard-enough time thinking straight about my general situation. It struck me that these three were an odd crew to send out to exact a retribution beating or worse. In the old days everyone in the car would have looked like Rizzy. The one sitting next to the mug in the back would always be holding a cosh, ready to strike, not resting back in the seat empty-handed like Cliff.

'You'll never guess what, Rizzy,' Cliff announced, 'Taff here had a break-in.'

'I hope they didn't get anything decent?'

Rizzy appeared genuinely upset for me.

'I didn't have time to check,' I replied, watching the bored youngster bite on a hangnail.

'If you want some help sorting the toe rags what done it give us a shout,' offered Rizzy.

'Thanks, maybe I'll take you up on that.'

We were now heading down Curzon Street towards Berkeley Square. The car then circled the Square and moved towards Conduit Street. Beyond Conduit Street lay Regent Street and beyond that, Soho. They were taking me back to my old stomping ground. I leaned forward in the seat, checked my breathing, and readied myself. It's a skill I picked up from wrestling. In order to strike quickly you have to prepare. I was mentally tightening myself like a coil, every fibre, every bone and muscle preparing for the explosion that was going to happen the minute the car finally reached its destination.

In the end, and much to my surprise, I didn't have long to wait.

Halfway around Berkeley Square the car suddenly came to a halt. We were outside the Astor Club. Cliff could read my mind.

'What? You didn't think you was on for a slapping, did you?'

'The thought had occurred, Cliff.'

All three of them laughed, even the youngster. Rizzy turned to me.

'You're one of the faces, Taff. Why would we hurt you?'

The youngster then ran around to the door nearest the curb and opened it. I was about to climb out when I felt Cliff grip my arm.

'Straight up. You're not in any trouble, Taff. It's just a chat he wants. But remember, it is still Mister Sporne when you talk to him. You might be in Mayfair, but some things never change.'

Thirteen

The place stank of mildew and stale booze, every type of booze. The stink and the rot were seeping into the walls, the floors, the tables and chairs. The Astor really was an ugly place. Daylight only made it uglier.

A brooding Danny Marks was there to greet me with a solemn nod.

'This way, Taff.'

Like some sort of creepy maître 'd, Danny ushered me through towards the back of the deserted club. Bertie Green and Terry Sporne were sitting at a table near the stage. A couple of Sporne's heavies were standing either side, cracking their knuckles and watching my arrival carefully. Bertie wore a queasy smile, trying to maintain the illusion that he was in charge, Sporne merely an invited guest. The angry red swelling below Bertie's left eye suggested otherwise. Things would have been tense before my arrival. I wondered which one of Sporne's minders had belted him. Perhaps it was both. Perhaps they took turns.

Sporne had put on a few pounds since we last met. His face was fatter, his frame bulkier. Embracing the new decade, he wore his wavy dark hair long, close to shoulder length. His piercing flinty eyes were exaggerated behind large, Michael Caine style glasses, a new feature he had adopted. All in all, he still looked like a villain, a healthy, long-sighted villain, but a villain all the same. I felt that ice cube making its way down my back again. Despite

Cliff's assurances in the car, I was on edge.

'Here we are back at the Astor!' Sporne bellowed. 'Remind you of the old days, Taffy? Roulette and a bite to eat at the Colony next door, then wander over here to dance the night away. The sixties were bloody brilliant, weren't they?'

It was a statement not a question, so I kept quiet. Sporne adjusted his specs, carefully lowering them on his nose till he could look over them and study me.

'Just been having a catch up with dear old Bert here. It appears he wholeheartedly backs up the alibi what you told the police and Danny. Smart move you checking-out the old club. Should have thought of that myself.'

I began to relax just a little bit. He'd had Bertie slapped about to make sure, but my confirmed alibi put me in the clear as far as Angie's death was concerned. The question still making my legs shake was why Sporne wanted to pay me personally. Why drag me to the Astor?

Sporne continued. 'Bertie just had me laughing, as it goes. He mentioned the flannel you gave him about moving into management. I explained to him that was just your way of grubbing information about Angie. I'm right, aren't I?'

'I didn't mean any disrespect to Mr Green, I was just being careful, given who I was asking about and her connection to you, Mr Sporne,' I confirmed.

After four years of being away from their world I was finding it hard to play along with the necessary bowing and scraping deference these bastards demanded. The whole 'Mister Green', 'Mister Sporne' bullshit was really hurting my pride. They might not have changed, but I had.

'Smart boy is our Taffy, Bert,' Sporne said. 'I always wanted him to stay working full time for my crew, but he seemed keener on schlepping for Don Arden or Peter Grant or even that bloody

Mickie Most for some reason. Almost hurt my feelings he did.'

Dented pride or not, I felt this might be a good opportunity to say something in the way of a commiseration.

'I wish this wasn't the way it ended up. I mean with Angie. I'm sorry about that.'

Sporne looked past me. I wasn't even sure he had heard me.

'Nearly ten years me and Angela were together. First off as her manager then as her… well you know. She had some daft bloody ideas, but I always loved her. That says a lot.'

Bertie Green now felt compelled to say something.

'She was a fabulous girl, Terry. A fabulous girl! When she used to come in here, I would say to anyone who would listen, "look at that fabulous girl". She was, and I think the fellows would all agree with me, a fabulous, fabulous girl.'

He looked at me and Danny, then the muscle, as if we were all expected to chorus our approval. No one said anything. His repeated use of 'fabulous' with its sibilant 's' had created a whistling denture symphony. If they were like me, they were trying not to break out in nervous laughter.

'That's kind of you, Bert. Now put a sock in it.'

Sporne rose to his feet, leant over the table, his knuckles almost digging into the wood.

'Taffy, there has to be consequences. You can understand that, can't you? Consequences for what they done to my Angie. Otherwise, we're allowing anarchy to run riot in our city.'

Sporne drew breath and patted his hair at the back, making sure it wasn't caught in his collar. We all watched him and waited. Finally, he sat down again, gesturing for me to join him at the table.

'Do you fancy something to drink, Taffy?'

I nodded. A belt of something would make all this a lot easier.

'Bert, go make us a pot of tea. Bring a few biscuits and all.'

His humiliation now complete, Bert hesitated before finally leaving. I sat down in the vacated chair. We were getting to the heart of the matter, I could tell. Sporne's voice became quieter, almost gentle.

'Danny believes it might have been a rival business associate sending me a message.'

'They can't get at you Mr Sporne, so they get at poor Angie, instead,' Danny piped up.

'What do you reckon, Taffy?' Sporne asked me.

'That doesn't fly, not for a second. There would have been far easier ways of sending you a message. Easier people to target. Danny for instance.'

Danny smirked, amused by my suggestion that he was an 'easy target'.

I continued. 'Besides, unless things have changed, going for wives and girlfriends was never a thing. Especially taking things as far as murder.'

Danny had another shot. 'Then it's like the police are saying, Mr Sporne. It was someone off the streets. A deranged lunatic, a violent thief. He murders Angie after scaring off whoever was in there at the time.'

'Is that what the police are saying?' I asked the room, even though I was addressing only one person.

Sporne began sharing what he had been told by his informant.

'They see it as a robbery that went wrong. What little effort they are putting into this is based on that line of enquiry. Like you, I'm not so sure. I had Cliff and the boys go talk to the studio owner just to be sure the version of events he'd told the police was on the level. The boys were good and thorough, thorough enough to make me believe he was telling the truth. It seems the studio was hired by telephone under a false name and number. There was no producer or engineer booked on the sessions. We're still trying to establish if one of the usual house engineers was around on the night. Know any of them?'

The last thing I wanted was Sporne hunting down Billy, not till I got to him first.

'I don't see any of the engineers being mixed up with this,' I said, praying Sporne couldn't tell I was lying.

He fixed me in his gaze.

'Give me your thoughts, Taffy. If you don't think it was any of my rivals, or some nutter breaking in, who do you think it was?'

'I really don't know who killed Angie,' I told him.

A sound escaped from low down in Sporne's throat. It was both a groan of frustration and a cry of despair. He was hurting inside. He was genuinely grieving. For a second, I felt sorry for him. I quickly continued:

'I don't think a recording session took place the night she was murdered. The amps were on, but the studio wasn't set up for the whole band. There were no mics on the drums for a start. The console was ready for a four-track mix down, with a fifth channel for a few overdubs. If I'm right and they were just mixing the recording, it also means there was hardly anyone in the studio that night.'

'How can you be so sure?' Danny asked. 'The whole band could have been there listening to the mix down. Maybe, they'd finished doing the drums earlier. You can't be sure, Taffy.'

'No, I can't. But think about this: Who would murder someone in the middle of a session? Let's say for sake of argument it was a typical band recording, with musicians, roadies, liggers, girlfriends, producers, engineers. What did they all do while Angie was being strangled? Stand around and watch? Even if they did, that leaves a lot of witnesses, a lot of loose ends. Something would have come out by now, don't you think? There would be whisperings, people with a story to tell or sell. No, I can't make this work in my head any other way than Angie was there on her own with just one or two people.'

'And one of them was the person who killed her?' Sporne asked.

'That's right,' I suggested. 'Someone in the music business certainly works better as a theory than it being someone off the street, and certainly not a robbery gone wrong.'

'You seem so very sure of yourself again,' Danny interrupted. 'Why couldn't it be that a tea leaf murders her then nicks what he could?'

'Then why not steal the guitars?' I asked. 'Instead, the only thing missing from that studio, as far as I could tell, was the recording tape, and most people wouldn't think that to be worth anything. No, whoever took that tape knew that what was on it was important.'

Sporne nodded. I was confirming his own privately held opinion.

'Go on, Taffy. Keep it going. Spit it out.'

'Whoever booked the session was doing this on the quiet. They certainly didn't want anyone to know that it was for Angie Bright-Silver. No producer, no engineer, just a few select people, people familiar with a studio, people who wouldn't blab.'

Sporne digested my comments. I could now see what had been happening. This was a witness interview just like the one I had endured with Seabrook and Simkins, except Danny was playing the role of the bad cop. Like the police, not only did Sporne want to be sure I wasn't the man who strangled Angie, he wanted to know if I had any leads on who did. He had now reached his judgement. He began calmly:

'You think you know someone. All them years together, me and her. Straight up, if she wanted to make another bloody record, I could have got her in somewhere classy. Recording I know about.

Abbey Road or Olympic. Studios what have a bit of something about them. Places with top producers and all. Instead, she goes to Ryemuse? If she wanted to record in Mayfair, why not Advision or Apple? That I could just about understand. But Ryemuse? It's the last place you'd expect to find my Angie. Why go there?'

'Because it was the last place you'd ever expect to find her,' I suggested.

There was a moment of calm as my words sank in. I knew it was going to be short lived. Summation over, "Judge Terry", was ready to deliver sentence.

Sporne tensed his fists, struck the table, snorting air in and out of his nostrils, the words exploding out of his mouth.

'All in all then, we are left with fuck all. No cunt knows who booked the studio, there were no fucking witnesses, and even the filth are drawing a blank. Meanwhile, Angie's killer is wandering around. There's no way I'm living with that.'

The merest of glances from Sporne sprang Danny into action. A thick envelope bulging with banknotes was laid on the table before me.

'A monkey as agreed for work already done, a bag of sand to find her killer,' Sporne declared.

I stared at the envelope.

£1,500. It took most people six months to earn that sort of money. The difference being most people didn't have to work for Terry Sporne to do so.

'If I do find the killer…' I began.

'Let me worry about what happens after that. You just find them, Taffy. Keep them warm until I arrive with my specialist crew.'

Sporne smiled at me. The prospect of the "specialist crew" seemed to please his vengeful thinking. Try as I might want to, I couldn't smile back. It was now clear to me. I was to be the first stage in a process where revenge would eventually be exacted. Or to put it another way, I was to be an accomplice to a murder. The specialist crew he was talking about were infamous. In the old days, Frankie Fraser earned his nickname "Mad" by heading up this firm. They had a house in Bermondsey and a chair with straps. Teeth were pulled, testicles electrocuted or bashed with a hammer or worse. At the end of the punishment, if you were still alive, you were given a clean shirt. The messed-up logic being that it wasn't right your wife had to see all the blood stains when you went home. Punishments soon became known as 'getting a shirt from Frankie'. I never set foot inside that horror house, but I dropped off a few poor souls who were soon introduced to Frank's unique form of dentistry. Thankfully, Fraser was in prison now, but the specialist crew never stopped operating. I heard that Sporne had set them up in a basement somewhere in Soho. I didn't want to know where because I had no plans to ever go visiting.

Sporne waited for me to pick up the envelope of money. The moment I did, he stood up, offering his hand. I blindly followed his lead, and we shook on the deal.

'Brew's up, gentlemen!'

A triumphant Bert reappeared with a teapot and three cups and saucers on a silver tray. It was too late. Sporne was already in motion, leaving the club, Danny and the muscle following in his wake.

'I'm assuming you don't need a lift, Taffy?' Danny inquired pleasantly, as he passed.

I nodded my head. I reckoned I could still make my way around Mayfair, despite being weighed down by that envelope of banknotes. I was certainly looking forward to the fresh air. The Astor made me feel like I had crawled inside an unemptied ashtray.

With the club to ourselves, Bert joined me at the table. Deflated as a punctured beach ball, he began pouring two cups of tea.

‘So, you’re working for Mr Sporne again, Taff?’

It was all I could do not to slap Bertie in the face. I dug my fists in my coat pocket just to make sure. I wasn’t working for *Mister* Sporne. Payment or not, his interests coincided with mine, and that’s all.

‘Sugar?’ Bertie asked.

‘No tea for me. I have to be going.’

‘Drop by again anytime, Taffy.’

I left him drinking his tea, alone in a club he ran but did not own. Maybe, like me, Bertie told himself that he didn’t work for Sporne, told himself that theirs was nothing more than an overlapping of interests. We tell ourselves a lot of things to keep going, I suppose. All I knew was that Sporne and I both wanted to find Angie’s killer. We differed on our reasons. Sporne was driven by a desire for revenge. I was driven by a desire for justice. I knew the police would never find the murderer. And that didn’t seem right. Angie was counting on me. That’s what I was telling myself. That’s what I had to keep telling myself just to carry on down the path I had chosen: Mayfair, music… and everything else.

Fourteen

Leaving the Astor, I couldn't face going back to the heartbreak of my ransacked flat. Besides, there was the little matter of the bundle of cash I was carrying from Terry Sporne. I needed to find a safe home for all that money. With Seabrook and Simkins sniffing about, that wasn't the sort of amount I could just deposit at the Midland Bank. I made my way around the corner instead and called in at the Guinea.

The lunchtime session was ending. I found Gerald busy collecting the empties from the empty bar.

'Jonesy! Officially we're closed. Unofficially, I could slip you a medicinal scotch.'

He poured me a generous triple and with my medicine duly administered, I got to the matter in hand.

'I could do with a favour, Ged. There's something I would like you to look after.'

The contents within the envelope I passed across the bar were obvious, and he assessed the bulging package with a weary, knowing expression.

'Given up keeping your loot under the bed in a biscuit tin?' he laughed.

'My flat was just broken into, so yes, I've given up on the biscuit tin.'

Gerald gestured to me to follow him upstairs, as he shouted over to Paulette to finish closing up the pub. The suggestion didn't go down well. She was sitting to one side resting her legs on a stool and already looked fed up.

She shouted back at her husband. 'Merde! Mais je suis épuisée.'

Gerald provided the translation, as we navigated the narrow staircase leading up from the bar.

'She reckons she's knackered, moody mare. To think back to when I first met her. Full of beans, even with her one eye. And looks? Like a Merle Oberon, she was. Now, look at her. Lazy and gone to seed.'

I passed no comment. I'd had enough of men telling me about their partners for one day.

Going past the small flat, we arrived at a back office where Gerald placed my envelope in an old lead safe.

'That envelope will be there when you need it,' he assured me.

Gerald looked me over, as if deciding whether he wanted to share something on his mind.

'This Angie Bright-Silver business got a bit nasty, didn't it?' he finally said. 'A lot of sad faces at the bar the last few nights. Your crowd are in shock about the whole thing. Are you still sniffing about, or has that enquiry been resolved by what transpired?'

'Sniffing about still,' I said, adding, 'even more so now she's been murdered'.

Gerald nodded.

'Then, I might have something, Jonesy.'

Twenty minutes later, after taking a cab up to Camden, I was in the lobby of the Euston Tower, the tallest office building in London, and home to a new commercial radio station going on air in less than a weeks' time.

With that deadline looming, the atmosphere at Capital Radio's headquarters was understandably far from calm. Carpet was still being laid. An enormous sign bearing the new logo was being erected on the far wall. Both these things required a lot of shouting, drilling and hammering. Elsewhere, teams of men with toolboxes and ladders were marching up and down the MGM-Hollywood scale staircase, off to perform urgent tasks. Pretty secretaries clutching single pieces of paper were making the same journey, running between departments on different floors. The explanation for this labour intense, old-fashioned communication system was suggested by the teams of engineers buried in a mess of exposed telephone cables next to the reception desk. There were only three phones in the building that worked. My enquiry at the front desk had sent a battlefield messenger running off upstairs. Curious to see how effectively the system was working, I took a seat in the lobby, offering nods of recognition to some familiar Teen Avenue faces also milling about. These were mostly song pluggers, press secretaries, and artists' managers already feathering nests by appointment at pop music's newest outlet.

It turns out the female dispatches system obviously worked just fine. My battlefield messenger must have been a real Hermes. I'd only just settled into my chair when a voice called out:

'With suspicious types like yourself, I am delegated to enquire whether you have an appointment and the nature of your business.'

I looked up at the tall, thin man approaching me.

'And what happens when they tell you to fuck off,' I responded.

'I appeal to their better nature.'

'I haven't got one, Dave.'

He laughed, as we shook hands.

'Jonesy. What have you been up to?'

'This. That. And the other.'

'Well, I hope it's all time well spent. Come on. Let me take you upstairs. What do you think of our new staircase? Until a month ago, all we had was a ladder to get between floors. Then they commissioned this ridiculous thing – 'Dickie's folly', we're all calling it.'

'Dickie' was the esteemed actor, Richard Attenborough, who was heading up the new radio franchise along with another old film star, Bryan Forbes, and fifth Beatle, record producer, George Martin. The station owner was a former dentist from Weybridge with the made-up sounding name of Barclay Barclay-White. Given none of them had any experience running a radio station, people thought they'd be out of business within weeks. The one person who did know a great deal about radio, and might just stop that happening, was their production manager, and the man leading me to his office, Dave Cash. Dave was a popular former Radio One DJ, who had developed his broadcasting style on pirate radio stations and a spell in Canada, which explained the curious American accent, something he played up no end, particularly with a catch phrase, 'groovy baby'. He had influenced many younger 'radio jocks' (as they liked to call each other) with his relaxed, zany delivery. Many, if not all DJs, were copying that approach, particularly Tony Blackburn and Kenny Everett. It was Everett who once explained to me that their typical listener was not a teenage girl, but a young housewife who had just seen her husband off to work and was set to do a bit of housework, naked, with the radio on. The purpose of jocks like Tony, Dave and Kenny was to serve as her lover for the day. It was hard to see how that seduction worked, given all the silly voices and puerile jokes. 'We laugh them into bed,' Everett clarified, when I quizzed him further on that matter.

Capital Radio had a lot riding on Dave. As well as overseeing the station, he had been given the plum afternoon slot as DJ, pitting him up against the much-loved David Hamilton on Radio One. Never a Dave, Hamilton relied on his nickname, 'Diddy', given to him by Ken Dodd, to create an informal persona. I was no judge of these things but I couldn't see why, given a choice, bored housewives would contemplate pleasuring themselves to someone called 'Diddy', over Dave's exotic American drawl. Dave was certainly of the same view. Sitting in his grand office, he was a charming mixture of confidence and extreme nervousness. I was certain he had nothing to worry about. If the success of his radio show was set to replicate the view from his window, London would soon be at his feet.

Over our encounters in the past few years, Dave and I were always friendly but never close, only ever tolerating each other due to our mutual dependence. Rick Kempe summed up the position of radio DJs like Dave as being akin to feudal lords.

'They descend into Teen Avenue licking their lips, ready to enjoy their *droit de seigneur* with the young virginal, unplayed, unreleased singles from the various record labels, whisking them off to some castle, where they will be played pitilessly on their radio stations.'

It was a great analogy, though, to be fair, the labels were willing accomplices in this grubby transaction.

Teams of song pluggers were hired by the record companies to get new singles on the top of the pile, often using a range of questionable incentives. Over the last few years, I'd been hired to make a few tacky moves on behalf of the lesser labels, with the hope of getting some lousy single played by DJs like Dave Cash on Radio One. Dutch crooner, Hein Van Clojt, and his single, 'Lovely Love Is Lovely' was a low point in my faltering song plugging career. Even the most elaborate bribes didn't break down Dave and the others' resistance. Finally, in the end, I managed to get Hein's 45 played three times by a particular DJ in exchange for the paid services of a dominatrix in Edmonton.

Given all this, it was only natural Dave assumed I was here to plug him something.

‘Tell me please, please, please you’ve got me something groovy from Mickie? Or Dick? We’re very fond of lovely David Cassidy here at Capital. What about MAM? I was rather hoping to have an exclusive to help launch the first broadcast.’

‘I’m not here selling. Sorry, Dave.’

‘You’re not? I just kinda assumed…’

‘But even if I was here plugging records, I wouldn’t need to twist your arm to play an exclusive, would I?’

Dave grinned at me.

‘Are you saying, Jonesy, you could get me an exclusive early play of something groovy for my afternoon show?’

‘I might have a word with Claire Gronwaulde at MAM. For a favour, I could get you the heads up on a Gilbert O’Sullivan release. I know he has something set up to come out next month.’

‘We like Gilbert here at Capital! The Irish navvy look? Spot on. Jonesy, Jonesy, Jonesy! Go make it happen. An advance copy of Gilbert O’Sullivan’s single! Groovy baby! A gentleman and a scholar as always, Jonesy. I knew you’d come through for me.’

‘Hold on, Dave. I’m saying I could try and see. But, either way, I’d want a trade.’

‘Anything. Just don’t ask me to play another baked turd by Hein Van Clojt. I have my pride…’

‘Angie Bright-Silver. That’s the trade, Dave.’

‘I’m not sure what you mean, Jonesy.’

‘Don’t give me that. You know how I work: Always one step ahead of everyone else on Teen Avenue. You were overheard shooting your mouth off down at the Guinea.’

‘What’s it to you?’

‘I have a professional interest in information. So I’m asking again. Angie Bright-Silver?’

‘If I tell you, you’ll get me an exclusive on Gilbert’s new single?’

‘I will certainly try.’

Dave chewed over his options before clapping his hands like a street trader.

'Deal! But I'll be straight with you, what I've got is pretty thin stuff. It's nothing to wet your pantaloons over.'

'Duly noted. Let's hear it, anyway.'

'Sure. Then, if you're sitting comfortably, Uncle Dave will begin. A few days ago I was rung up anonymously by a man claiming to have an album Angie recorded just before she was murdered.'

'A few days ago? Could you be more precise, 'Uncle Dave'?'

'It was the day after she was found dead.'

'That's two days ago, then,' I clarified. 'Carry on.'

'He was excited, telling me about some acid rock album she'd just done. Did I want an exclusive? And how much was I willing to pay?'

'What did this man sound like?'

'Shifty.'

'Come on Dave. I know you like doing the whole Yank bit, but I also know you've seen Dixon of Dock Green. We're now at the bit when they ask for a description.'

He stared at me blankly.

'Let me put it another way,' I continued. 'Was there anything distinctive about the voice?'

'Sure, sure. He was polite, but like I say, shifty.

'Old? Young?'

'Definitely our age. He used words we use, you know? Like "cool", "hip", "far out", that kind of stuff. He had a Scottish accent. Did I mention that?'

I looked at Dave with a reproachful raised eyebrow.

'No you didn't. Anyway, did this Scottish voice suggest a price?'

'It was more along the lines of "what are you prepared to offer?". So I said, "fifty squiders". He bit my arm off right up to the elbow. I could have offered a lot less, I'm sure. But fifty quid was still one hell of a good deal. I was already planning the show as we spoke. We'd do a big evening special on Angie. Maybe Dickie could do the narration and really lend the thing a bit of class. As part of her tribute we'd play the tracks from her latest recording – a voice from the grave, her last will and testament, creatively speaking. Can you imagine it, Jonesy?'

I could. One last indignity for Angie to suffer – paraded on a commercial radio station to boost ratings. And all for fifty quid.

'When and where did you arrange to meet?'

'Yesterday evening. Six o'clock, Waterloo Station, by the barrier at Platform Two. I was told an intermediary would approach me with the tapes.'

'Only they never showed up.'

'Nope. I stood there like a lemon for over an hour, looking for all the world like I was trying to find a hooker – which is not difficult down there by the way. Have you seen that place, recently? It's a disgrace.'

'And the man never rang you again?'

'No. Never heard from him again. That's all I know. That was the story I was telling the gang later on, down at The Guinea. I'm guessing that's how you found out. Someone overheard me? Who was it by the way? Penny Sands?'

'Why do you say Penny Sands?'

Dave shrugged.

'No reason. I know she's friends with you and she's been down the Guinea a lot recently with that useless bass player husband of hers. What's he called?'

'Geoff Birch. Anyway, it wasn't Penny or Geoff. They're both away on tour. And as to who did tell me, a good detective never reveals his sources.'

'Are you a good detective?' Dave asked. 'Or just a nosey bastard?'

'Comes to the same thing. Ask Dixon of Dock Green.'

INTERLUDE NO.4

July 30th, 1966: The Astor Club

Everyone was celebrating in the Astor Club but me. It was a bad night to be sober. England had won the World Cup. Bloody England. It was a bad night to be Welsh.

She handed me a glass of champagne, leaning in, her face nearly touching mine, the warmth of her sweet breath on my cheek, her perfume enveloping me like a caress. The intimacy was startling, and I froze as I listened to her words, the first she had ever spoken to me without Terry Sporne listening in.

'I always see you standing in the shadows, in the corners of a room, watching what's going on in front you, interested but somehow uninterested at the same time. Visible but trying your best to appear invisible. I see you all the time and all the time I think one thing...'

'Which is?'

'What is it that you do?

'I help people,' I smiled back.

'Like a saint?'

'More like The Saint. I get paid.'

'Didn't Francis of Assisi have a daily rate?'

'I don't think he was big on the idea of money.'

'Probably not. He'd have a hard time fitting in here.'

'You sound like "here" is somewhere you're not too keen on.'

'Do I? Here is where I am right now, so I suppose I must like it a little bit. Then again, here is always with the now. Here and now.'

'As opposed to the there and then?'

'Exactly. I can see you're someone who understands. My name is Angie Bright-Silver.'

'I know.'

'Am I allowed to know your name?'

'You are. My name is Elisud Jones.

'El...?'

'Elisud. It's Welsh.'

'Sounds like you're saying illicit.'

'Then say illicit, if it helps. Or just Elis.'

'I think I'd prefer Elis.'

'Not many people do.'

'I've heard. They call you Taffy. Do you mind being called that?'

'I don't mind. I grew up a few feet from the River Taff.'

'By the same logic you should call me Thamesy.'

I clinked her glass with mine.

'To Thamesy and Taffy, in the here and now,' I said.

'One day to be in the there and then.'

'Good point. How about we drink a toast to here, there and everywhere?'

As we clinked glasses again, I wondered what the hell I was doing flirting with Terry Sporne's bird.

Fifteen

It seemed like an idea to do the two miles from Camden back to Mayfair on foot. Walking would help me think. The mystery Scottish man who had tried to sell the tapes to Dave Cash was obvious. The question was, having made the deal, why didn't Billy Coles go through with it? Could it be he got a better deal elsewhere? Fifty pounds seemed a pittance for a pop stars' last recording. He must have been desperate.

Coming into Mayfair along Conduit Street, off Regent Street, my thoughts turned to Gail Petters. I'd bought into her story about Billy so quickly because it chimed with my view of the relationship between the two of us. Of course, I would be the friend Billy would turn to in an emergency. Or so I liked to believe.

Suddenly smarting over how I'd been set up by the phony Gail Petters, I spent a pointless twenty minutes exploring the nearby Vigo Street, looking for the theatrical costumiers she had mentioned in our pillow talk. There was no such place of course, but it seemed important to at least check. She had played me superbly, offering up just enough detail to make the lie appear real. Back when I was a wrestler that's what we always tried to do. There is a certain way of landing, crying out, or spinning off the ropes that makes the fakery seem real. If you believed in it, the audience would do the same. 'Selling the gag' wrestlers call it. My phony Ms Petters could certainly sell a gag.

Back at the flat, thinking about my days in a ring, I dug out and rescued my wrestling scrapbook from all the mess. It was the first thing I did. I didn't even take my coat off. I just wanted to make sure it was still intact. Thankfully, it was. All the bills, programmes and cards from my bouts were there, from my first professional outing at Maesteg Town Hall, January 29th, 1961, to my last at West Ham baths on June 10th, 1964. It was hardly a glittering career, but I like to think that when I did quit, I showed a bit of character. In that last bout, I was up against Johnny 'Jungle Boy' Zaire, a Black wrestler from Coventry. Johnny was no more from the jungles of Africa than anyone else there that night, yet they dressed him in a leopard skin loincloth and stuck a fake bone on his nose, just to make sure everyone got the idea. The referee even made an announcement that he had seen Johnny in the changing room warming a massive pot over an open fire, ready to cook me alive if I lost. All this put the audience in a bloody mood. There were catcalls, jeers, and terrible racist chants as we made our way into the ring. That level of hatred towards Johnny was something I'll never forget.

We began the bout, and, to great cheers, I immediately had the better of him. That was no surprise, not to the two men wrestling. The routine was already agreed. Johnny was going to lose. In a big finish, I was due to throw Johnny over the ropes then kick him into the crowd, at which point 'Rule Britannia' was going to strike up on the public address system. Leading up to this, out on the canvass, Johnny proved himself to be a good wrestler. He sold all the gags, all the stunts, expertly. I liked his grace and athleticism. Even though I had a good five-inch height advantage, and the longer arm reach, Johnny was much quicker getting in and out of holds. In a fair fight he would have beaten me hands down. But that was never going to happen, not in the East End. They wanted blood. They wanted to see a Black man suffer. So we played out the bout as agreed and I kicked him into the crowd. Out of the ring, still on the floor, some men began using their feet and fists on Johnny. I jumped over the ropes and started laying into the crowd, protecting Johnny as we both made our way back to the changing rooms, with bloody 'Rule Britannia' playing out all the time. A huge crowd gathered, beating on the backstage door. If they had broken through, we would have both been killed, no question. The promoter eventually called the police, and the venue was cleared. It still wasn't safe for us to leave till two in the morning, when a police van took us all the way into central London, dropping us off in the West End. Johnny and I decided to go for a drink and ended up at the Flamingo Club listening to Georgie Fame. I was pretty shaken by the earlier experience, but Johnny seemed to take it all in his stride.

'Human nature isn't it, Jonesy?' he said in his sing-song Midlands accent. 'A Black fellow like me is always going to get hell from an English crowd, especially in the East End.'

'But you're a brilliant wrestler, Johnny. Doesn't it make you angry that the crowd are too stupid to see that? Doesn't it make you angry having to lose all the time?'

'It's how I earn a wage, Jonesy. Better than working in the car factory back home. Unions there make sure us dark fellows are always doing the menial jobs on the lowest wages. White boys hang nooses in the canteen, spit in our food. Compared to that, wrestling is better, believe me.'

In the end, we had a good night. Georgie Fame and the Blue Flames were brilliant. There was lots of drinking, funny stories swapped, and some dancing done – more by Johnny than me. He also met a pretty brunette who invited him back to her flat in Primrose Hill. At dawn's first light, Johnny and I made our drunken farewells beneath the Eros statue in Piccadilly Circus, promising to stay in touch. I decided to give up wrestling that morning, left it for good, and never saw Johnny again. I later heard from Peter

Grant that Johnny had damaged his back and ended up working in Longbridge on the production line making Mini Coopers.

With the bookcase off the floor and upright, I put my scrapbook on the middle shelf, pride of place. It felt important to remind myself of that chapter in my life, especially the way I quit the wrestling business. I'm not sure why, but looking it over again spurred me on to spend the rest of the early evening cleaning up the flat and repairing my front door as best I could. The mortice lock was gone so I dug out an old key for the unused deadbolt and managed to get that working. It was far from perfect but at least the door was secure for now. After a couple of hours tidying, all the bookcases were back upright, the books and records in place. I used heavy gaffer tape to fix the slash marks on the sofa and threw a heavy bedspread over the whole thing as a disguise. The easy chair was too far gone, so I moved it into my bedroom and used it as a dumping ground for my mountain of discarded, unwashed clothes. For the most part I had the flat looking a little less like a crime scene. There wasn't anything I could do about my record collection being scratched and damaged to hell and that's what hurt the most. Cliff was right, of course. Most of my records were freebies acquired from the record companies over the last five years. But it still pained me to find *Houses of the Holy* snapped in two and what looked like cat claw marks down side-one of *Hunky Dory*. My signed copy of *Propitious Flavour* had luckily escaped without too much damage. I put on side two nice and loud, loud enough to hear in the kitchenette whilst I cooked myself an evening meal of tinned spaghetti on toast. With the flat secure, something warm in my stomach, and Phil Fratton's guitar solos still ringing in my ears, I felt a whole lot better. It was time to think through what I knew so far about the crime Sporne had hired me to solve.

Angie's death, my being sent on a wild goose chase and the

break-in were somehow all connected. If my hunch was right, someone who knew me well was behind all three things. I took a pen and notebook and drew up a list of my Teen Avenue friends who had knowledge of the following things: Phil Fratton giving me the flat; the other tenants in 9 Curzon Place; Billy Coles. These elements were all part of the phony Petters hustle. Since I didn't know her, someone must have given her the details. There were loads of my acquaintances who knew one of those criteria, a few who knew two, but only seven people who had knowledge of all three. Following on from that logic, I was left with this list of suspects:

1. Billy Coles
2. Phil Fratton
3. Peter Grant
4. Harry Baum
5. Penny Sands
6. Rick Kempe
7. Claire Gronwaulde

Billy Coles was the most obvious suspect. He was missing, and with the business of selling the tapes to Dave Cash coming to light it made him seem guilty as hell. But the other stuff? Strangling Angie? To begin with, he was so puny I doubted he had the strength to strangle a hamster. Angie would have batted him away like a fly. Then there was the sophisticated job done on me, sending me to Staines and so forth. That just didn't seem like a Billy Coles play. For all that, he was in the studio the night Angie was murdered and had now gone missing with the tapes. He knew as much about me as anyone, visiting my flat on many occasions, even sleeping on my couch for a time. We were good friends, fellow Celts no less. That's the point, we were good friends. Was that blindsiding me?

Moving on, I eliminated the next two names almost straight away. Phil was burning incense in California and dancing naked around a firepit, never to be seen again. Peter Grant was also in America with Led Zeppelin. The ransacking did have Granty flourishes, but he would not have bothered sending a pretend Gail Petters if he had wanted something from me. He would have just asked me. And anyway, Granty was one of the good guys in the business.

Third on the list, Teen Avenue's favourite solicitor, Harry Baum knew all about Phil Fratton giving me the flat. I had asked him for a legal opinion a few months after I first moved in. I'm sure I also told him about the art dealer below me and the MP's mistress (I remember Harry used the term 'inamorata') on the ground floor. Harry would also have certainly crossed paths with Billy Coles. I doubted Harry was the strangler, but his phone book was full of the names of thugs that he could have hired. The rest of it though didn't play. Harry was with me at that police interview. I saw his ashen face in the Chalet. No one can fake that level of sorrow.

Penny Sands, on the other hand, was a big tick on all the criteria. Good friends with Billy Coles, she was in the vicinity around the time of Angie's murder and behaved strangely when I mentioned Blank Verse, the band supposedly recording in the studio. The other details about my neighbours could have come out on the tour. Hours doing nothing but sitting on a bus between gigs means you end up prattling about all kinds of stuff. Throw in our pillow talk and Penny would probably be capable of writing an encyclopaedia on my life. As far as the evidence was concerned, she was in at number one with a bullet. It was ridiculous to even think her capable of murder but her name could not be discounted. She stayed on the list for now.

The next two names were good friends I crossed paths with on my usual day-to-day in Teen Avenue. Rick Kempe was a music journalist whose star had risen since landing a job at *NME*. Claire Gronwaulde was my old girlfriend from MAM records. I drew a line through Rick's name almost immediately. We had become tight in the sixties when he was working on the underground paper *Frendz*. In exchange for top quality grass, I would get Rick access to people in Mickey Most's orbit like Jeff Beck, Jimmy Page and Donovan for interviews. He was a laid-back intellectual, about as threatening as a limp daffodil. I also viewed Claire's name as being too farfetched to seriously leave on the list. Then again, we were intimate. Was there anything in the whole 'woman scorned, hell hath no fury' expression? None that I could see, not in her case. Claire wasn't much given to fury, and as for the scorning, my taking up with Penny Sands wasn't the reason we fizzled out over the summer. We were just one of those doomed couples everyone else considered a perfect match. 'A couple of facetious bastards made for each other,' was how Dick Leahy once described us to Mickie Most. 'Jonesy and Claire': invited to every Teen Avenue press event and junket. Piss-takers, the pair of us. Shame was, none of that sense of fun helped in the sharing of feelings or emotions. Humour was our hiding place; sarcasm the castle walls standing in the way of true love. And that's the trouble about being a 'couple of facetious bastards'.

I drew a line through Claire and looked over my list once more.

Motive! I was forgetting motive. Something would have had to drive any of these people to murder. Who stood to gain from Angie's death? That was the missing piece in the puzzle. I stared at the names for another ten minutes. If it was there, I couldn't see it. So much for motive.

With great reluctance I circled the first name on the list. Billy Coles. He was clearly the most likely suspect. Immediately, as if hoping he could defend himself there and then, I picked up the phone and rang Billy. No answer. Next, I rang Ryemuse to see if they were open again. It took five minutes waiting but eventually the phone was picked up.

'Ryemuse, if you are ringing from a newspaper, kindly drop dead,' a tetchy voice declared.

'You might want to think about your choice of words, given someone was murdered at your studio,' I pointed out.

'Yeah, yeah, shove it up your arse, mate.'

I sensed the phone was about to be put down.

'Wait, who is that? Is that you Paul?'

Paul Richards was a freelance engineer.

'Yeah,' the voice responded. 'Who's that?'

'Paul, it's Jonesy. I'm trying to track down Billy Coles.'

'You and everyone else at Ryemuse. The owner's having kittens. We got bands booked and he's not here, Jonesy. I'm covering for him. Why don't you try his flat?'

I thanked Paul for his useless advice and replaced the phone.

Where in hell was Billy? Since I could safely assume the phony Gail Petters' story about him visiting my flat was false it meant that three days had passed since his last sighting by me in the studio. Three days would normally be long enough to report a missing person. Perhaps I should tell Seabrook and Simkins, use the police to find Billy.

I was so busy concentrating on playing the detective that I jumped when the phone rang.

'Jonesy? I've been trying to get hold of you. I need you tonight – I needed you two days ago – but I especially need you tonight.'

I recognised the voice straight away. It was Dick Leahy, head of Bell records.

'What's happening, Dick?'

'David Cassidy is flying into Heathrow and there's going to be five thousand girls who want to try and molest him.'

'You want me to protect him?'

'No, I want you to protect them. That randy bugger has no shame.'

'Where's he staying?' I asked. 'The Dorchester?'

'He's not staying anywhere! He's flying in and flying straight out again after an hour.'

'Dick, you're not making any sense.'

'I'll tell you all about it. Get yourself over to Teen Avenue, now.'

Sixteen

Last minute arrangements for Cassidy's arrival and departure were still being thrown together when I arrived, putting the Bell office in a high state of panic. An added complication was coordinating the TV crew that was set to film the American star singing his wistful hit, "Daydreamer". Cassidy said he could only spare an hour before boarding his return flight home. The film crew wanted two hours. There was also the question of where to do the filming. Dick was at the centre of this confusion, calmly dealing with the various Bell staff manning the phones, the latest foul-ups and complications coming thick and fast.

'Hilton Hotel says we can't film in any of the rooms!' someone was shouting.

'We're not allowed to film on the plane without written permission from the Aviation Authority,' someone else informed Dick.

'...his people are insistent. Immediately on landing, Cassidy wants champagne, a meal, and a lady companion,' a third person announced.

Given all this chaos, Dick appeared remarkably relaxed.

'Haven't we already rustled up a delightful popsy to satisfy his amative carnalities?' Dick asked.

'We have, Dick,' someone shouted.

'Splendid,' Dick beamed.

Only a few years older than me, Dick Leahy was currently one of the top people in pop music, second only to Mickie Most.

Everything seemed so easy with Dick, success always a given. With fashionably long hair hanging like an Afghan dog's ears about his kind face, Tommy Nutter suits and mink coat, Dick was famous for his style and, just as importantly, for treating people with respect. I liked him and I particularly liked the manner of his rise to the top. It was a route I aspired to. Starting in the Philips record warehouse, he moved into A&R at Fontana records and now managed the most successful label in the country. On the way he had convinced Philips to release Bowie's 'Space Oddity' and fought hard against the label's ban of Serge Gainsbourg's 'Je t'aime', which would have earned them a number one and a small fortune if only they had listened to him.

As soon as Dick noticed me enter, he came bounding over.

'Jonesy, glad you could make it!' He handed me a set of keys. 'Let's go, go, go! Car's waiting.'

I drove us to Heathrow in the brand-new company Jaguar XJ. I had never been behind the wheel of a faster or more silent car. Ninety miles an hour felt like we were doing a sedate thirty, the engine purring like a pussy cat all the way. Dick sat next to me, enjoying my enjoyment of the car.

'Caroline doesn't let me drive this beast,' he remarked. 'She reckons I'd end up driving too fast and crashing. She's probably right.'

Caroline was Dick's new wife. I had gone to the wedding with Claire in the spring. Their abundant happiness seemed like a rebuke; a comment on our own relationship, somehow. Still, I was happy for Dick, happy someone had found love, at least.

'What's the deal with Cassidy?' I asked, wanting the lowdown on my task.

'Tomorrow night is the 500th episode of *Top of The Pops*. They badly, badly want Cassidy to be on. We also badly, badly want

Cassidy to be on. The only way we can do it is by showing a pre-recorded film of him singing, or at least miming to his hit. Naturally, we weren't given much warning, hence why the whole thing is a kick, bollock, and a scramble. I just want you to keep an eye on young David, keep the press away and any fans who show up. It's all been hush-hush, but you never know.'

As we made our way to Heathrow, we caught up with each other's latest news. Wanting to keep things light, both of us were careful to avoid mentioning Angie Bright-Silver's murder. Dick started telling me all about his latest signing, Alvin Stardust, who, by his account, was, all set to be the next Gary Glitter.

'He looks just like that old rock'n'roller, Vince Taylor. Jonesy, girls are going to go wild for him, trust me.'

I reminded him that the last time we had met he was making similar predictions about a bunch of clowns from Edinburgh called the Bay City Rollers. They were a struggling band with a minor hit from a few years ago. I was roped in to mind them during a stay at the Dorchester. To my ears they were useless, but Dick had always seen something in them.

'You rather took against those boys, as I recall,' he laughed.

'I picked up one of them passed out on the floor of the hotel bar, carried him up to his room and got called a "cunty-baws" for my troubles. I don't mind talented shits, but I draw the line with the talentless ones, Dick.'

'Talent is overrated,' Dick declared. 'Ask Gary Glitter!'

He went on:

'The Bay City Rollers get one more single. If that doesn't dent the charts, I'll have to drop them. Strangely enough we are using Ryemuse next week to record their new A-side. All a bit weird after the sad business with dear old… you know who.'

Now that he had touched on Angie's death, I decided to quiz him a little.

‘Who’s going to engineer the session?’ I asked.

‘Engineer? Don’t you mean produce?’

‘Both.’

‘Coulter’s producing. I’ve no idea who the engineer is. Probably that funny little Scottish chap that Ryemuse often use. What’s he called?’

‘Billy Coles.’ I answered.

‘That’s the one. Why are you asking?’

‘Billy was telling me about a great new band called Blank Verse,’ I said. ‘Heard of them.’

Dick shook his head and laughed. ‘Not another one of your discoveries? You give me a hard time about the Rollers – what about that lot you tried to get me interested in after Mickie Most passed on them? What were they called? Willy and the Wombats?’

‘Tony’s Timepiece.’

‘That’s them. They had a deaf drummer, didn’t they?

‘Tony was, or is, blind.’

Dick’s derisive laugh, usually so infectious, left me cold. I let a few seconds pass before I asked him another question.

‘What if someone came to you with the master tapes of a new Angie Bright-Silver album? Would you be interested? Now that she is dead, I mean.’

‘What? Are you suggesting that she was in Ryemuse recording new stuff? I just assumed she was visiting someone. You, maybe?’

‘Me? Why do you say that?’ I said, meeting his amused gaze.

‘I always thought you two were hot for each other.’

‘Only ever friends, Dick.’

‘Okay! Just pulling your plonker, Jonesy.’

I was annoyed with Dick and I had let it show, even though he was only parroting what people suspected back at the end of the sixties. Tongues wagged; I knew that. Perhaps we were hot for each other, the good it did us, since neither of us were insane enough to take on Terry Sporne. I moved the conversation back to the missing master tape.

'Imagine Angie had been doing some recording and someone came to you...'

Dick stroked his chin, the prospect of an Angie Bright-Silver recording intriguing him.

'So, I am to imagine there is a new recording, and work on the assumption it was good stuff...'

I finished his sentence. '...would that be of interest to Dick Leahy?'

'Not to me. Not at Bell. We are all about bubble-gum, top-ten records. Records by dead people is not our bag. That is not to say there wouldn't be other companies who might be tempted. EMI certainly. Philips probably. Who was she with before? Pye? They would jump at the chance. More than if she was alive. Remember Otis and 'Sitting On the Dock of The Bay'? Being dead doesn't half help sales. That song was Redding's biggest hit by a mile. By a mile! This is all hypothetical, Jonesy, isn't it? Or are you telling me you have a recording of Angie Bright-Silver?'

'No, not at all. I'm just curious.'

'Well, you are certainly being that,' he replied, the trace of a smile on his lips.

David Cassidy was ridiculously good looking and alarmingly small. His sensual lips and eyes were almost feminine. I wondered what went through the minds of those prepubescent girls as they gazed up at his face adorning the posters over their beds. In many ways he was the perfect first crush; unthreatening, familiar, sensitive to those needs and desires of a teenage girl because he gave every appearance of being a teenage girl himself. Unlike Alice Cooper, Cassidy's teenyboppers could imagine just *talking* to their idol. Breathless, giddy, dreamy, he'd want to chatter about dresses and ponies, make-up, and boys. Cooper, although only a few years older than Cassidy, looked like someone who would ask a girl to round up a couple of her friends for a threesome, take photographs, then leave them all with an unpleasant STD – attractive and thrilling in its own way to those girls who wanted danger, but not enough of them to sustain the true fan mania Cassidy enjoyed. Until his looks went, David Cassidy was all set to rule the world.

Dick had arranged for the film crew to capture Cassidy singing his hit song in an aircraft hangar on the far, far edges of the airport. A buffet of sorts had been laid out on a trestle table that included a roast chicken, caviar, scotch eggs and about thirty bottles of champagne. Without clearing customs, Cassidy breezed into the hangar on an airport fuel transporter and made a beeline for the food. A separate transporter arrived with his hairdresser and personal stylist. As the two of them went to work on David, David went to work on the buffet, giving the scotch egg a suspicious poke with his finger before turning his full attention to the caviar and champagne. He looked hungry. And thirsty.

'David! Welcome to England!' Dick exclaimed with an outstretched hand.

'Hey man! Wrap that chicken for the trip back to the States, will you?'

'Of course.'

Sensing Cassidy thought him to be no more than the caterer, Dick tried a different approach.

'As managing director of Bell Records UK can I say how delighted we are to have you here filming your segment for *Top of The Pops*.'

'You're Dick Leahy?' Cassidy said, finally offering his hand. 'Dick, I've only got ninety minutes. An hour for filming and half an hour for relaxing.'

For some reason he winked at me, as if I would know more about what he meant by 'relaxing' than Dick.

'Your "relaxation" is being taken care of as we speak,' Dick assured. 'Now David, the director was wanting a technical rehearsal…'

'No rehearsal. I just sing. I just feel it. One take. That's all they get.'

Dick's effusive smile beamed, as if this had been the plan all along.

'Absolutely! I'm sure they'd be happy to do it your way. No rehearsal. One take. Just feeling it.'

So, at twenty past two in the morning, still chewing on the last of the caviar, David Cassidy began wandering through the hangar, miming his hit as three cameras attempted to follow his erratic movements. A tiny cassette player played 'Daydreamer' as a guide, though the sound of aircraft landing and taking off often drowned this out. Cassidy didn't need the playback. He was a pro. He knew the song inside out and really sold it. In the end, no doubt buoyed by the champagne and the prospect of a blowjob, he was generous enough to perform his song twice for the cameras. A total of twelve minutes and he was done. I was impressed. The arrogant shit did have talent.

My workload was less than minimal. Being so far away from the main airport meant we had no security worries from fans or the press. Occasionally, I had to throw a few menacing looks the way of some nearby ground crew who wandered too close, making it clear they must stay away from the star. Mister Cassidy will not be signing autographs tonight.

While David was skipping about on the second run-through, an airport car arrived with his companion for the night, an extremely attractive woman in her 20's. Dick gestured for me to smuggle her through to the small office at the back that had been set up as David's dressing room. A petite blue-eyed brunette, she was far more wholesome than I had ever imagined, given the short notice.

She was holding a garment carrier. 'You're changing?' I asked. I thought her jeans and t-shirt looked fine.

'I want to look my best,' she replied in a plummy, Home Counties voice.

'I'm not sure he's that worried about what you're wearing.'

'You'd be surprised with these pop stars, especially the Yanks.'

In the office, amongst the wall charts and filing cabinets, she kicked off her shoes and began to change in front of me, getting down to her knickers and bra in no time. Unzipping her carry bag, she revealed her outfit: A gold satin dress that was all too familiar. She noticed me staring, not at her, but the dress.

'What do you think?' she asked me.

'Making the old new,' I said, remembering the phony Gail Petters and her identical get up. 'Very Roxy Music. Very Bowie.'

'If you say so. All I know is that it's an Ossie Clark and looks fabulous.'

'Memorable,' I agreed, leaving her to prepare herself for David's relaxation treatment.

In the hangar, the filming over, I found Dick wrapping the chicken in tin foil. David was talking to a Heathrow official, no doubt explaining why he needed to relax before being transported back to the runway and his waiting plane.

'How's the popsy?' Dick asked me.

'More than adequate.'

He passed me the chicken.

'See that David gets this. Would you drive the jag back to London? Just park outside Bell and put the keys through the letterbox. I'm going to go with the film crew and check they've got what we need back at the 'Beeb'.'

'Okay,' I said. 'No problem if I also drive the girl back into town?'

'Jonesy! You romantic devil! Be my guest. Talking of which, come along to the BBC tomorrow for the *Top of The Pops* special. Bring the girl. I'll put you down as a plus one. It's going to be a fab night! Loads of people there you'll know.'

Dick hurried off with the film crew. I gave the chicken to the Heathrow official, grabbed a bottle of champagne, and sat on an abandoned boarding ladder, swigging away, smoking a cigarette and all the time feeling like a real detective. I was thinking about that gold satin dress, my first real lead. In the distance planes were landing and taking off. Even at night the world is in motion, I thought.

Seventeen

Night was fast becoming day by the time a laughing David Cassidy emerged from the 'dressing room', his willowy arm wrapped around the girl as he whispered sweet nothings into her eager ear. To anyone watching – and this was probably the calculation – they looked like long-established lovers, a golden couple destined for years of bliss. He even gave her an affectionate kiss farewell, just as if she were the one true love of his life. In its own way, it was touching. Unnecessary, but touching all the same. Little David was clearly a romantic; 'a daydreamer walking in the rain' as his song described. At the very least he could fake it and that was commendable. As he untangled himself from his partner, we exchanged a few words.

'Dick had to get the film back to London, but he told me to tell you how great it was to meet you,' I said.

'Tell him thanks, man,' David replied sniffing the air. 'Hell, I don't know how you guys can live somewhere so fucking damp and cold.'

'It's character forming. You should try it some time, you might even grow to like it.'

He turned his head to one side and gave me a hesitant look that suggested he wasn't sure if I was taking the mickey or not. When the girl laughed, he eventually did the same.

'You English and your sense of humour,' he said.

'I'm Welsh,' I pointed out.

But David Cassidy had stopped listening. Mentally, he was already on the plane, a flight away from a scorching sun, swimming pools and palm trees. He blew a kiss in the direction of the girl, hopped on his airport transporter, and disappeared into the black void beyond the hangar.

The call girl was pleased to be getting a lift back to London, especially when she saw the car would be a brand-new Jaguar. She hurried back to the dressing room and changed into her jeans and t-shirt, folding away the satin dress – the same satin dress I had seen the fake Gail Petters wearing. When she emerged, we were the last people in the hangar. The handful of curious ground crew had already helped themselves to the buffet leftovers and moved on.

Climbing into the car, I offered her a cigarette as we exchanged names. I went with Jonesy. It was too late at night to go through the whole Elisud routine. She told me she was called Molly. I knew it wasn't her real name, but it helped keep things agreeable. She even chose to sit in the front next to me. That surprised me. For some reason I was fully expecting her to sit on the back seat.

'Did he like the dress?' I asked Molly as we hit the M4.

'Not half,' she laughed. 'He kept on saying how classy I was.'

'There's a lot of teenage girls who would have loved to have been in your shoes tonight.'

Molly rolled her eyes and made a face like someone who had just been offered a plate of raw offal. 'They're welcome to him. I've never been with a man so hairless and smooth. I'm serious! It was like fucking a clammy pebble.'

Molly had a nice way about her, or 'emanation' to borrow a favourite term used by Phil Fratton. A very nice emanation indeed.

'Been doing this long?' I asked.

'This?' she asked.

'The service you provide.'

'A year or so. You won't believe this, but I'm actually trained as an actress. I graduated the same year at RADA as Stephanie Beacham.'

'I don't know who that is.'

'Really? She does films, and she's on TV all the time: *Jason King, Special Branch, The Protectors*. Big shows.'

'Haven't seen them. I only ever watch *The Good Old Days* and *Magic Roundabout*.'

'You are kidding?'

I shrugged.

'First job she got after graduating,' Molly sighed, 'I mean the *very* first job, was a Michael Winner film with Ryan O'Neal. Second film was with Brando. Makes you sick.'

'How'd you do with the acting?' I asked.

'I did alright for a while. Flashed my tits in a foreign film, did a panto. I was understudy in *Godspell* at the Roundhouse before it got transferred to the Wyndham theatre.'

'Did you ever get to go on?'

'One night only,' she explained. 'Poor Julie Covington had terrible flu – she played the tomboy, Robin – so it meant I sang the best number.'

'Day by Day?'

'That's the one. You saw the show?'

'No, but the outfit I sometimes work for, Bell records, had a hit with 'Day by Day' last year. Bell also produced the cast album. They even tried to sign the guy playing Jesus, David Essex, but CBS made him a better offer.'

'Dave's certainly come out of it all very nicely! He was singing adverts for bloody Pledge furniture polish two years ago.'

She had a way of making her bitchy bitterness seem funny. I found myself chuckling.

'Did he invite you to that big party the record company threw at Quaglino's to celebrate his signing?' I asked.

'You're kidding. Actors who have made it can never be around those who have yet to make it. Lack of success is a curse. Why? Did you go?'

'It was a slow Sunday night. Quaglino's is only a few streets away from where I live. It was that or 'the Good Old Days' on telly.'

'A few streets away? Don't tell me you live in Mayfair?'

'I have a nice flat there, though someone tried to burgle me the other day.'

I watched her carefully just to see if there was any reaction. She didn't show anything, other than sympathy.

'Getting burgled is just not cool,' she said, 'though getting invited to parties at Quaglino's is very cool. You must be a big deal in the music industry.'

'I'm just the sump oil that helps the big cogs turn.'

She liked that. I went on to tell her how launch parties were usually boring. The one at Quaglino's had been no different. The only thing I could remember about it was the way CBS's top brass were standing around looking like the cats who'd got the cream. They were right to be so smug. David's first single 'Rock On' was still a massive top ten hit. His debut album was certain to go gold.

The mention of Quaglino's and Essex had made Molly reflective:

'Stephanie Beacham and David are the lucky ones. You need luck in the world of acting. Unfortunately, I just never seemed to have any. One day the work dried up for me, my agent wasn't interested anymore, and I was shoplifting tins of baked beans just to be able to eat. Then a girlfriend told me about this line of work. I know what you're thinking. But believe me there are worse ways to earn a crust.'

'But plenty less degrading.' I wish I hadn't said it, but I did. I couldn't help myself.

She shrugged and gave a sad nod of the head. I didn't like that

I had made her sad, so I said:

'Look, we all do what we have to do. I'm not judging. I've been for hire since I can remember. I've done some pretty bad things, things I'm not proud of.'

She raised a quizzical eyebrow. 'Thereby hangs a tale.'

I smiled. 'A hell of a tale. I'll tell you about it sometime.'

'I hope you do.'

I stole a glance at the woman sitting next to me. She was intelligent, good-looking and with a flair for the dramatic. If they were all like her, it made sense that my phony Gail Petters would come from the same stable. We were getting on well, surprisingly well. It seemed a shame to spoil the party, but I needed to find out what she knew about my Gail Petters.

'My boss said he might need someone for tomorrow night. How do we make the booking with your boss?'

'The usual way,' she replied.

'Meaning?'

'Put an order in for a dress, of course.'

'I don't usually do the booking. Explain.'

'You phone up the office and request a dress. Yellow for a blonde, brown for a brunette, red for a redhead.'

'Apparently they need a blonde. Cut glass English accent. Haughty. You know the sort of thing.'

'They'll find you someone,' Molly said.

'They used someone like that before, about your height, very well spoken. Do you know her?'

'No. Blondes don't mix with the brunettes, or the redheads for that matter. The manageress is keen we operate in isolation. She's paranoid we might form a union, or something.'

'One last thing. What if I wanted to do this face to face? Rather than phoning?'

'They're not keen on people coming into the office.'

'But if I needed to, is it still the same office?' I was pressing hard, sounding like a policeman, but I had no choice.

'Same office: Heddon Street, right opposite the Ziggy door,' she said.

I knew Heddon Street. It was in Mayfair. The fake Gail Petters had almost revealed the whole set-up when she made up her tale about working for an aunt in Vigo Street – Heddon Street was the next street up from Vigo Street. Her describing the business as a theatrical costumier was also dangerously close to the truth. And the whole different colour dress code business? *Duw*, she virtually gave me the whole thing on a plate.

We were still ploughing down the M4, about to pass through Chiswick. Molly was yet to give me any hints as to where she wanted dropping off.

'Where's good for you?' I asked.

'Didn't I say? Off the Caledonian Road. Near King's Cross.'

'Lived there long?' I was back to sounding casual after the earlier questioning.

'A year or so,' she answered.

'Like it there?'

Now I was sounding like we were on a first date, not that Molly seemed to mind.

'Well… it's not Mayfair,' she smiled, 'but it'll do. There's three of us in a shared house. All of us actors or musicians. Great vibes. Very spiritual. Very, very creative. Trouble is that the council want to knock down the whole street. It's just not right. Have you ever read Orwell's *1984*?'

I shook my head.

'But you do know it, right? Big Brother, newspeak, thoughtcrime, obliteration of the self and all that? Orwell based the area where his proles lived on the streets around King's Cross. Maybe even our street. Crazy, right? Now the council – or Big Brother

– wants to destroy people's homes. It really is the very definition of irony. You should read the book sometime. It's all about being free. I reckon you'll enjoy it.'

Dawn was breaking when we finally reached her house. What the Luftwaffe hadn't managed, unscrupulous landlords had achieved through neglect. Like the other dilapidated terrace houses in the road, it was boarded up and surrounded by a jagged fence of rusting corrugated iron. Hidden in the nearby shadows, like yellow sleeping giants, hydraulic breakers and backhoes with wrecking balls stood poised, ready for action, ready for orders to flatten the whole street.

We sat in the car a moment, neither of us saying anything. I was staring at the bleakness of where she lived, and she was watching me.

'You live in a squat,' I said.

'I suppose I do. Are you shocked, Mister Mayfair?'

'Not really. I live rent free in a flat I don't actually own.'

'I see,' she replied, 'a fellow squatter. Like I always say: One man's hovel is another man's garret.'

'And who do you say that to?'

'People who don't live in hovels,' she giggled.

It was crazy but I suddenly felt sorry for Molly, as if she needed rescuing. I still wasn't sure what from, but whatever it was, I would be happy to put myself up for the job. David Cassidy's romantic nature was clearly rubbing off on me.

'Do you fancy going for a drink sometime on one of your days off?' I asked her on impulse.

Without a moment's hesitation, she grabbed a pen and a piece of paper from her handbag.

'I don't have a phone,' she said. 'Write your number down and I'll give you a ring sometime soon.'

I wrote down my name and my number and passed back the

piece of paper along with the pen. She climbed out of the car but leant back in before closing the door.

'I bet you're not smooth as a pebble,' she laughed.

'Hairy as a gorilla,' I answered.

'Thought so.'

With that, she was gone. I watched her squeeze her way through a loose panel on the corrugated iron fence and disappear. It was no surprise she didn't have a phone. Her house didn't even look like it had a roof.

Eighteen

On the third time of walking up and down the length of Heddon Street, the true meaning of the 'Ziggy Door' finally came to me. When Molly first mentioned it the night before, I had taken it to mean a club or a fashion boutique. Finding nothing like that, it felt like I might have been sent on another wild goose chase. Then, it suddenly came to me in a flash – a Ziggy Stardust flash.

The 'Ziggy Door' was a reference to David Bowie's *Ziggy Stardust and the Spiders from Mars.* Shot in Heddon Street, the cover showed Bowie, guitar in hand, standing in a doorway – the Ziggy door – beneath a distinctive sign reading 'K West'. It gave a lot of people in Teen Avenue a proud thrill to know that Bowie had chosen Mayfair as the backdrop for his album cover. Not that many of the music crowd would ever visit this non-descript cul-de-sac. Other than Brian Ward's photography studio and a post office, it was a street more tied up with the garment trade. In fact, I remembered hearing a funny story from Harry Baum after the Bowie album first came out. Konn (the K of K West), a struggling furrier firm in Heddon Street, tried to sue RCA for featuring David Bowie outside their premises without written permission and for denigrating their business with such an "offensive" image. The legal action was quickly seen off by a team of top New York lawyers. As they pointed out, very few teenagers knew what the sign Ziggy Stardust was standing under referred to, and even if they did, far from denigrating Konn's business it probably made it a thousand times cooler.

I found the K West sign and the Ziggy door on the wider section of Heddon Street, the side parallel to Savile Row. Turning about and facing the other side of the road placed me opposite a soot covered four-storey warehouse with a large set of double doors on the ground floor. A smaller door within these doors had several brass plaques detailing the various firms and the room number and floor where they could be found. I crossed over the road and started looking for a likely candidate amongst the names. They were all connected with the rag trade. There were more furriers, a couple of woollen companies, and a milliner called Wunderba Tit Fer, a name coined in a more innocent time, presumably. Nothing suggested the office I sought, but my gut was telling me this was the right place.

Inside the building, the ground floor packed with bales of goods and raw materials stored on pallets. A set of stairs at the far end led to the upper storeys. An old-fashioned lift big enough to park a car was alongside. There was no one around to stop me so I took the stairs.

Dark and narrow, the layout of the corridors on the upper floors was haphazard, chanced upon rather than planned, and all done with much smaller people in mind. Hallway ceilings would occasionally dip and pitch, forcing me to stoop just to keep going. It also felt peculiarly warm, with an unpleasant smell of astringent chemicals assaulting my nostrils. Behind each door, I could hear banging and scraping, sewing machines whirling, and loud voices calling out as people went about their business. All the doors displayed either the names of the proprietor or, at the very least, some indication of the trade they were engaged in – all the doors until I reached the fourth floor. Next to 'Samuels & Son – Bespoke Tailors', I found a plain, unmarked door. Putting my ear to the door to check, there was no sound to indicate people working away inside. Maybe the office was empty. Or maybe, just maybe, this was the very office I was looking for. I knocked, and not waiting for an answer, went straight on in.

A very large lady in a pink velour catsuit was perched on a high stool; a stubby pencil behind her ear. Her close cropped, heavily lacquered black hair formed a wonderful kiss curl at the front much like Bill Haley. Though a phone and a scribble pad rested on the bar counter in front of her, she was currently engaged in carefully painting her nails a shade of scarlet and had no intention of looking up until she had completed her last stroke. It gave me a chance to take in the rest of the windowless office. There wasn't much to the place, so it didn't take me long. No furniture, no filing cabinets, no desks, no typewriters, the only things in the room were the counter, the lady, and behind her, on the walls, faded posters of couture collections from a time well before rock and roll was invented.

'All done,' the nail lady said.

'They look nice,' I commented.

'Rufous passion. That's the colour. It's a range from Boots. I saw it in my lunch hour and decided to give it a whirl. I usually prefer something darker, but you have to switch things around sometimes.'

She had a pleasant voice, like one of those old-fashioned radio announcers I would hear as a kid introducing *Listen With Mother*. This airiness of tone almost made you forget her imposing form. I guessed her height to be about six foot and probably pushing twenty stone in the weight stakes. I wondered if she had ever done any wrestling. Her frame was perfect.

'I was looking to hire a dress,' I said.

She stared at me blankly.

'A yellow dress,' I clarified.

Expressionless, she picked up the phone on her counter and

rang a number, using the pencil to dial. Without saying anything, she immediately replaced the receiver and smiled sweetly at me. Some time passed. Nothing happened.

'Is it always so busy here?' I asked.

The large lady had given up smiling at me and was blowing her nails.

'Still, it makes the day pass quicker – when you're rushed off your feet like this,' I said.

The door finally opened, and a bulky, suited up Black guy came running at me with speed. The first thing they teach in wrestling is to use an opponent's velocity against them in any takedown. He was laying it on a plate for me, making it easy to knock him off balance with a leg trip. As he was falling, I switched to a double collar tie and fell with him, landing on top and winding him with my full body weight. I rammed my elbow into his jaw for good measure. He was now dazed, gasping for breath and out of action. I got to my feet and turned to the large lady.

'Do you need to make another phone call?'

She dialled again. This time there was no sweet smile.

I leant over the man on the floor. 'Breathe in through the nose, take in the air long and slow… there you go…'

As he regained his breathing, he looked up at me.

'Was that a Bruce Lee move you done on me?'

'No. Mike Marino. He's a four-time champion.'

'In what?' he asked, accepting my hand as I helped him to his feet.

'Wrestling,' I told him.

The door opened again, and a teenager appeared. He was long haired, well dressed in a silk and chiffon sort of way, and wearing a lot of jewellery, with rings on his finger. A gold medallion nestled in the gap between his open shirt. I instantly twigged him as a Marc Bolan fan.

He stared at the still gasping Black guy, at me, then the large lady, before turning his attention back to my way. There was something of a pregnant pause, until his asking: 'I understand you wanted to order a dress, sir?'

'Yes, I do. For tonight.'

'Then if you would come this way, please.'

The Bolan fan ushered me past his still incapacitated bouncer, into the corridor, and through the neighbouring door I had noticed earlier. As we entered, I thought for a terrible moment I had got it all wrong. This looked like a proper firm of tailors to me. There were men chalking patterns and cutting fabrics, half stitched suits sat on dummies and a large steam press was busy ironing razor sharp creases into a pair of trousers.

I was led through to a wood and glass partitioned office with a desk and a couple of swivel chairs. The Bolan fan took the seat behind the desk; it suited me fine to take the chair in front, that way I could see London outside and the wash of a grey afternoon sky. It was the first bit of daylight I had seen since entering the building.

He cleared his throat and addressed me:

'We have found, through trial and error, that the best way for our dress business to work, and by that, I mean work mutually, is that clients make their order by phone in the first instance. May I ask why you called in person?'

'How old are you?'

'Nineteen.'

'And this place?'

'Belongs to my father. He has been unwell for a prolonged period of time, sadly. For the foreseeable future, I am the current manager.'

I nodded. The picture was coming into focus. The father asks the son to mind the shop. The son isn't happy just making cheap suits. The son branches out into pimping, hiring his boyfriend to help out.

'To answer your original question, I was passing,' I said.

Since I was planning on going to *Top of the Pops* later, there was no harm incorporating that into my cover story.

'I want to order a dress on behalf of someone at RAK records. It's for a job at the BBC, White City, tonight. Things are a little desperate.'

The Bolan fan looked me over. He was more curious about me than the assignment.

'Is that why you attacked my associate, Brutus? Out of desperation?'

'Firstly, he attacked me, and secondly, anyone who goes down so easy isn't a good person to hire as muscle. Just some friendly advice.'

The Bolan fan nodded, as if taking my advice on board.

'About my desperation,' I went on, 'my boss asked me to sort this last minute.'

'Well, we don't want you desperate, do we?' he reassured sardonically.

Perhaps remembering his father's tailor training about the customer always being right, he quickly took on a more conciliatory tone.

'The world of entertainment, particularly music, is our speciality. We cater for little else. If you tell me precisely what you want, my assistant, Ms Ghisham – the lady you met next door – can make the necessary arrangements.'

I elaborated. 'You helped us out last night for a social event in Heathrow. We were all pleased.'

He nodded graciously.

'The event at the BBC tonight also requires something special,' I continued. 'A friend described to me someone you sent to a private residence in Mayfair a few days ago. Would you know the one I'm talking about? Blonde, bespoke, specific to a client's particular needs. Quite exceptional, I'd imagine. One of a kind, in fact. If you had some pictures, I could pick out the one I'm talking about from my friend's description.'

The Bolan fan shook his head.

'We have no pictures. No files of any sort. Ms Ghisham has everything committed to memory, every detail, every measurement, every number. It helps keep things discreet for our clients. She really is quite invaluable.'

Without saying a word, he got up from the desk, left the office, walked through the workshop and into the corridor. Brutus suddenly appeared and joined me in the office. We exchanged a nod as he took up a stance, leaning against the window.

'Football's more my game,' he said after a while.

'You play for anyone?' I asked.

'No one right now. Had trials for Leyton Orient though when I was younger.'

It was his way of telling me he did possess skills, even if they weren't as a hardman. I nodded to show I understood.

'Brutus your real name?' I asked.

He shook his head. 'That's his idea. My name's John Brutan.'

'I'll keep an eye out for you on Match of the Day, John.'

That cheered him up. We spent the next few minutes in silence until the Bolan fan returned, calmly resuming his position behind the desk, extravagantly ignoring his associate's presence.

'Ms Ghisham knows the dress of which you speak,' he stated.

'Would you like cash in advance?' I said reaching into my pocket.

I left the building and took a last look at the K West sign, thinking about the Ziggy door and Ms Ghisham all alone in an office without filing cabinets. Her gift for recall must have been like Leslie Melcher. A memory man variety act, Melcher was able to recall at random any page of Wisden's, the cricket reference book. It was such an amazing ability people reckoned he might be some sort of an alien, an alien from Mars even. Melcher eventually retired just like that other Martian, Ziggy Stardust. I doubt if people cried when Leslie Melcher left the stage for the last time, but they did for Ziggy. I'd seen it with my own eyes at the Hammersmith Odeon earlier in the summer. I was backstage minding Jeff Beck, there to sit in on three numbers. As Beck came off, he stood alongside me watching from the side of the stage as Bowie unexpectedly announced he was retiring.

'...not only is it the last show of the tour, but it's the last show we'll ever do. Thank you.'

'Blimey, was it something I said?' Beck laughed.

My Jeff Beck duties provided me with an invite to the post show party at the Café Royal, where everyone was talking about Bowie's shock announcement. It was a very starry affair. I sat next to Ringo Starr, passed Barbara Streisand an ashtray, and later found myself having a pee in the next urinal to Lou Reed in the gents. He began talking to me, or at least began talking.

'Know where I can get some horse?'

There was someone a short taxi drive away who could sort out Lou, but after my experience with Phil Fratton I never wanted anything more to do with junkies and heroin.

'No,' I lied.

'Then what purpose do you serve?' he asked before answering his own question. 'None at all, none at all.'

I started to walk back into Mayfair, running through the arrangement I had agreed with the pimp. Before going on to the BBC, I would pick up the 'yellow dress' in the Marlborough Head, a pub in North Audley Street, around the corner from Marble Arch tube station. The Head had two bars – a snug and a lounge – separated by a shoulder high glass partition. The meeting was set for five o'clock. At that time of the day, the saloon would be busy, but not crowded. Half hidden by the partition it would be easy to watch the fake Gail Petters enter the lounge. Hopefully, I could then go round, corner her, and find out who had hired her to send me on that wild goose chase to Staines. That information would then help me find out who killed Angie.

So that was the plan.

And that was my purpose, Lou Reed.

INTERLUDE NO.5

March 16th, 1967: The Speakeasy Club

The room had star power: Robert Stigwood, Kit Lambert, Chas Chandler, Marsha Hunt, Terence Stamp, Jimmy Page, Pete Townsend, Michael Herlighey, Phil Fratton, Mitch Mitchell, Eric Clapton, and Angie Bright-Silver.

Amongst the church pews for seats, ancient mariner beams, and stately home wainscotting we found each other.

'Is Terry Sporne with you?' I asked.

'I'm all alone.'

'No muscle keeping guard?'

'Other than you?'

'I don't work for him anymore.'

'No, that's right. You don't. I think he's a little cross about that.'

'People and situations change, Angie.'

'Not for me. My 'bodyguard' is waiting in the car. Do you know him? Cliff Moses? He knows you.'

'You asked him about me?'

'He asked me if I knew you. I said yes. He likes you, Elis.'

'And I like him. He knits me mittens every Christmas.'

Angie laughed.

Hendrix and his band shambled onto the stage.

'Dig. People. We're all here for a groovy new record label run by some groovy cats, Chris and Kit... Track Records, man. A circle of light in this mind-blowing darkened universe. Track Records. Out-tasight! And like, this is their first single. It's by me and my brothers from the Experience and we hope it blows your mind.'

He began playing a guitar riff that made my stomach knot with excitement. I looked at Angie. I could see she felt the same.

'Purple Haze, all in my brain...' Hendrix sang.

People started dancing. Angie took my hand.

'I don't dance,' I warned her.

'Then stand still and watch me, Elis.'

So I did. I watched her move in time to the music, hips swaying, head nodding, each thrust of her torso describing a circle, every move and gesture directed towards me. She never lost eye contact, holding her smile throughout.

'...is it tomorrow or just the end of time?' Hendrix continued.

The song finished and people cheered. Angie took both my hands, bringing me nearer so our bodies were touching. I wondered if she could feel my heart beating. I swear I could feel hers.

'What do you think?' she asked.

'About your dancing?'

'We can start there...'

Nineteen

By six o'clock, the Marlborough Head was getting busy with office workers, shoppers, and the odd embassy staffer – both American and Italian – from nearby Grosvenor Square. I took up my place at the partition between the two bars and waited. My date was ten minutes late, but when a beautiful blonde woman entered, carrying a copy of the *International Herald Tribune*, heads immediately turned. The newspaper had been the pimp's idea, a way of helping me to identify my 'date'. It was easy enough to play along with his suggestion, even though I knew I would be able to recognise her with or without any newspaper. After all, I was meeting the woman who came to my flat and shared my bed. I was meeting the phony Gail Petters. The decoy. Beautiful though she was, the blonde who had just walked into the pub was most decidedly not her. Ms Ghisham had sent a blonde, but not the blonde.

I made my way over to her and leant in. 'Hello, I'm the one who placed the order,' I said.

Just out of her teens, she was perky and peachy skinned. A sky-blue peasant dress, barely covering her bottom, met thigh high multi-coloured leather boots wrapped around long shapely legs. A huge floppy hat completed the outfit.

'Aren't you going to offer me a drink then?' she asked with a giggle.

'What would you like?'

'Cinzano, thanks ever so.'

I ordered her drink, at the same time fighting my anger and trying to work out if the pimp had deliberately sent me the wrong hooker. I had a lot of things all ready and prepared to say to my Gail Petters and now I was left with no target for my rage.

'Are we really going to see *Top of The Pops*?' she asked.

'We'll get to that,' I said. 'I'm just deciding whether to march you round to Heddon Street.'

'Why?' she asked.

'Because you're not what I ordered. I was expecting the same blonde sent out on a job a few days ago. You're not her. I should know. I was there. Got the hurt pride to show for it.'

'Hold up!' she protested, her Liverpudlian accent becoming clearer in anger. 'If you don't like what you see, be a gentleman and just say, but don't be making up excuses. There's only one blonde – I mean one yellow dress – that young Mr Samuels uses. Only one, and that's me. So, I don't know who the hell you think you're talking about. And, what's more, I'll tell you this: I haven't had any complaints so far.'

People were looking our way. Her raised voice was casting me as the big lump picking on the pretty girl. Before soon, some fool ready to play the hero would step forward wanting to protect the damsel in distress. That was messy aggravation I could do without. Time to take the temperature down.

'Okay, okay. I didn't mean any offence. Come on. Let's grab a seat.'

We took our drinks to a nearby table.

'I'm Jonesy. What's your name?'

'Barbara,' she answered, cheering up. 'Here, I like your accent. All dreamy, like Richard Burton.'

'More like Stanley Baker if it's like anyone. He was born in Ferndale, a few miles from me.'

Barbara shrugged, Baker's name meaning nothing to her.

'Don't you remember *Zulu*?' I asked.

She obviously did not. Swinging her outstretched legs in front of her as she sipped her drink, I was beginning to wonder if Barbara was younger than I first thought. My mind went back to the teenager who had asked me for a fag and told me to piss off when I refused. The teenagers of Teen Avenue were taking over the world.

'Are you being straight with me?' I asked. 'Are you really the only blonde they send out?'

She nodded. 'They only have one of each type. Easier to keep tabs on everything. It's all very bijou there. Exclusive. Pays to be judicious.'

'Judicious?' I laughed.

'What? Can't scousers use fancy words?'

'I didn't mean that,' I said. 'And don't be so touchy! Are you an actress by any chance?'

'How did you know? First year Mountview Academy.'

Another actress. Another pretty face. The pimp's business approach was clear now. He operated at the high end of pimping. A small outfit that could find hookers who didn't even think of themselves as hookers. Bespoke, like the suits he made, these girls were tailored to the client's needs. If Barbara was being truthful, it meant my phony Gail Petters had never worked for them after all. The gold dress certainly linked her to Molly, but it didn't link her to the Heddon Street operation. I was left with the clue but no answers.

'You and the other girls that work for Mr Samuels?' I asked. 'I don't suppose you ever share clothes?'.

'Course not. We're probably all different sizes. You ask weird questions.'

'I guess I do.'

She eyed me warily. 'Are we really going to *Top of The Pops*?'

'Only if you want to. You're no longer on hire, Barbara. As

far as I'm concerned, you've already done everything I required. You're off the clock.'

'What? That's it? I've only sat here drinking bloody Cinzano.'

'And you did it beautifully.'

'I was hoping I might meet Gary Glitter. Wouldn't that be something?'

Barbara was still excited by it all, by life and the limitless opportunities it seemed to offer. She was a few years off where Molly found herself – where I found myself – after the inevitable setbacks and disappointments of life. That is why I probably preferred Molly. She was weathered. Level-headed. Closer to my world view. Barbara was all cherry coke and fairy tales. Still, it seemed mean to not let "Little Miss Naïve" get her chance to meet Gary. I was going to the BBC anyway. What was it to me if she tagged along?

'Drink up then,' I said, 'and we'll get a cab.'

David Cassidy's film, or 'video' as I heard someone call it, went down well with the kids. Any other week it would have been the highlight of the show, but this was a special night. Dick Leahy had been right; I knew lots of the people who were on the Top of the Pops hour long show. From the opening number, featuring RAK's Cozy Powell (on drums with a big band performing the new theme tune, "Whole Lotta Love"), to over half of the twelve acts, the Teen Avenue labels dominated. The line-up included Gary Glitter, Dawn, David Bowie, Cliff Richard, David Cassidy, Lynsey de Paul, Sweet, The Who, and Bryan Ferry. From MAM to RCA, Bell to Track Records, Island to EMI, it was as if Mayfair ruled the pop world.

'Oh! Such a night, such a night,' presenter Jimmy Savile gurned into the camera, as the Who ended both the show and the useful working life of most of their musical equipment with a powerful, destructive climax. Savile was flanked by a pissed Sandie Shaw on one side, and a quietly seething Lynsey De Paul on the other. There had been some earlier unpleasantness when Savile felt Lynsey up introducing her new single, 'Won't Someone Dance With Me?'. Savile had offered to do a lot more than just dance with her, and Lynsey was having none of it. The DJ quickly forgot about Lynsey de Paul once his introduction was concluded, homing in on a couple of teenagers in the audience. Much more his type. Accompanying this revolting seduction, the Who sang their song, '5.15': 'Girls of fifteen, sexually knowing...' Really?

Up in the packed green room, Dick Leahy and Mickie Most – Teen Avenue's very own Svengalis – were celebrating, along with everyone else. This week it had been mostly Bell artists on the pop show but next month it would be RAK's turn. That was why theirs was only ever a friendly rivalry. With money and chart success granted for both, why squabble when you could enjoy the fabulous ride?

At the far end of the bar, the Sweet, Gary Glitter, and the Who were in competition to see who could be the most badly behaved. Keith Moon was winning, but Glitter was giving him a good run for his money. Girls from the television audience had managed to sneak in. Combined with the plentiful alcohol available, their arrival energised the already charged atmosphere. Pretty soon, it was a sexual free for all with kissing and groping openly taking place everywhere. I felt protective towards my date, but luckily Barbara had found herself talking to Cliff Richard, the one pop star in the room who didn't seem set on finding someone to fuck.

I was well into my third triple vodka when I spotted the *NME* journalist Rick Kempe at the bar chatting to Lynsey De Paul. They made a funny couple. Rick: Pale, wild haired, spidery limbed and swivel eyed. Lynsey: Elegant and poised, with the perfect features of a porcelain doll. Already gone in the legs, I went over and joined them.

'Jonesy, welcome to ancient Rome!' Kempe laughed; his voice thick with drink. 'I imagine this is what it would have been like if Caligula had been a pop star.'

'Except some record company boss would have made him change his name to Johnny Tiber,' Lynsey pointed out.

She was a pop star who knew all about changing names. Someone at her label, MAM, had made her switch from Lynsey Rubin, her real name, to Lynsey de Paul. Less Jewish they had told her. Lynsey and I had met a number of times when I was dating Claire Gronwaulde, one of the publicists at MAM who helped promote Lynsey's sinister, bleakly erotic pop song, 'Sugar Me' to the top of the charts last year.

'Who was that girl I saw you come in with?' she asked me in a sharp tone. Lynsey was being loyal to Claire, obviously unaware that we had finished over the summer.

'Just a friend,' I told her.

A scream of laughter intruded. Nearby, self-styled "madcap" DJ Kenny Everett was dancing in front of Barbara with two oranges down his t-shirt and a banana sticking out of his flies. Barbara clearly thought it was hilarious.

'She's still new to this kind of thing,' I explained, the three of us now watching the pathetic spectacle.

'Just keep her away from Savile,' Lynsey said darkly. 'He's positively priapic this evening.'

I didn't know what priapic meant, but that didn't stop me nodding, pretending I did. Mickie Most had once told me Lynsey was always the most intelligent person in the room, always the most beautiful. I could see exactly what he meant.

Kissing Rick on the cheek, Lynsey wafted away majestically.

'Say hello to Claire when you see her next,' I called out after her.

Turning back and smiling she said: 'Do you want me to do it in a Welsh accent?'

'If you don't mind,' I answered.

'Then you can piss off, can't you?' she said breezily.

Rick clinked my glass. 'We should do as the Ancient Romans and drink a toast to the immortals,' he suggested.

'Bugger that!' I said, sinking my vodka. '*Lechyd da* and down the bloody hatch.'

By now, Barbara had joined a conga line started by the Who's roadcrew and Pan's People. At least she was heading in the opposite direction to where Savile and Gary Glitter were standing.

Rick produced a joint and lit it up. After a few tokes, he passed it over to me. Right back to when I first met him, when Rick was working at the underground newspaper, *Frendz*, he always had the best grass. I filled my lungs to capacity.

'Were you interviewing Lynsey just then?' I asked in a raspy gasp, letting the smoke escape slowly.

'Sort of. I was getting her take on it all. Context. Dispatches from the battlefield. Feeding it into a piece I'm writing about tonight's celebratory show. I can't decide which way to go at the moment.'

'What are the alternatives?'

'The usual Spengler pattern work, decline of the West bullshit.'

'Or?'

Rick used his hands to describe an invisible headline. 'Glam's graduation – not just a trend but a teen movement.'

'How about this: More musical mayhem from Mayfair?' I suggested.

'Not bad. I like the alliteration. I'll pay you for that.'

'By the way, Rick. That was a great piece you did on Angie Bright-Silver.'

'Good job I did it, since none of the other papers bloody

bothered,' he moaned, 'though I hear *Melody Maker* are going to have another go next week.'

'I'd like to get your thoughts about Angie's murder, Rick,' I said in another cloud of exhaled smoke.

'Would that be thoughts other than the symbolic and allegorical?'

'It would.'

'In that case let's do it properly. Call in at the *NME* office tomorrow. I'll give you a quid for the Mayfair mayhem headline and we can have a proper chat about Angie. Right now, I need to have a word with Pete Townsend.'

'Tell him there's an important difference between girls being aware of sex and girls being sexually knowing. That song? 5.15? Bloody awful.'

With a pat on my back, Rick headed off.

I considered doing the same. The vodka was kicking in, Rick's grass likewise. Everything was getting out of hand. Time to tap out. If I could make it to the foyer, I could ring a cab for me and Barbara. I looked around for her but couldn't see her anywhere. She had disappeared. But then what was that to do with me? I had enough trouble looking after myself, let alone anyone else. Right now, I had enough trouble standing up. It was time to go back to Mayfair.

Before I had a chance to act on that realisation, Mickie Most, Cozy Powell and Suzi Quatro suddenly joined me, each carrying what I believe are known as jeroboams. Most offered me his cheekiest of smiles.

'Jonesy! Fancy a nice glass of champagne?'

Twenty

I was submerged underwater, trapped inside a piano, as Lynsey de Paul performed the Who's "5.15", each note low and booming, the hammers striking my head, the strings strangling me, restricting my air flow. Looming bloated dead girl's faces joined me in my piano coffin and started screaming with laughter. I tried to escape, thwarted by arms and legs that were no longer working...

It was time for me to wake up.

I began by opening one eye at a time. That went well. Next: Time to find out where I was. I lifted my head. My living room was staring back at me. I had made it home – thank God, I had made it home. In between deciding to leave and actually leaving the BBC last night, I remembered drinking my way through bottles of champagne with Mickie Most. From then on things were pretty hazy. A splintered memory of sharing a cab with Cherry Gillespie from Pans People wormed its way into my waking mind. I think I asked her to marry me. Her husband, who was sitting next to her in the cab, was surprisingly understanding about my proposal, considering I had earlier tried to punch him. I was guessing he carried me up to the flat. Either that or I crawled the two flights on my own.

The music had started again, this time an insistent ringing instead of Lynsey's piano. It took a while to realise it was someone ringing the building entry bell. An earthquake was going on in the room as I staggered to let in whoever it was. I rested my head against my front door waiting for the knock to come, the footsteps on the stairs getting nearer and nearer. The knock was insistent, prolonged. I swung open the door to be presented with DS Seabrook and DI Simkins, each carrying zip briefcases like insurance salesmen.

'Wish I could have a lie in whenever I fancied,' a surly Simkins remarked, handing me my mail.

'I went to a party,' I explained. 'It finished late…'

I glanced at the mail and noticed the Island Records logo on one letter. Chas Parker had come through for me. It was Penny Sands' album launch invitation. I folded it and tucked it in my back pocket, to be opened when I had more physical strength. Right now, keeping my eyes open felt exhausting. The battery was flat. The starter engine fried. I was 'babalass', to use a term Mickie had picked up in South Africa. As if to confirm all this, my legs suddenly buckled. Seabrook and Simkins carried me, one arm each, to the dining table and dropped me on a chair.

'The morning after the night before,' Simkins continued. 'Always have to pay the price the next morning, don't we? Must have been a hell of a party.'

'Like the one we've just come from,' Seabrook added sourly. 'That must have been a hell of a party.'

Simkins nodded. 'King's Cross – go up there much?' he asked.

'Not if I can help it,' I managed. They were tag teaming me again and this time I was in no shape to cope.

'And what about Mary?' Simkins asked. 'See much of her these days?'

'Mary Hopkin?' I asked.

'Mary Shearer,' Seabrook clarified.

'I don't know anyone called Mary whatever you said.' I could feel the acid in my stomach rising. This really was the mother of all hangovers.

Seabrook looked at me, his lip curled in disgust. I knew I must have smelt wretched. 'What is it you do, Mr Jones?' he asked.

'I work in the music business. I told you before.'

'Lot of drugs in the music business,' Simkins remarked. 'Easiest bust there is, finding a musician with drugs.'

'Especially when you lot plant the evidence.' Not a bad comeback given the circumstances. They were beginning to irritate me now.

'Look, get to the point. I'm planning on throwing up any minute now.'

'You might want to rethink your story before you do,' Seabrook said with a smile.

'What story?' I asked.

'Did you know Mary Shearer was a drug addict?' Simkins probed, as he started walking around the flat, checking out the bookshelves, the postcards standing on the mantlepiece – standard police snooping kind of stuff. Hard though it was, I started to piece together what was going on here. They were trying to tie me to something serious. I was in the frame for whatever went down last night, whatever happened with Barbara, whose real name it seems was Mary Shearer.

'Look,' I said, 'last I saw of her she was in a bloody conga line in the BBC bar. I got a cab home; the details are a little on the fuzzy side, but I don't think she was with us. Drug addict? Hard to imagine but then I don't know the first thing about her. I mean, I only met her last night...'

I paused. Simkins and Seabrook were exchanging a quizzical look.

'Last night?' Simkins asked.

'Six o'clock, near Marble Arch,' I confirmed.

Simkins reached into his zip briefcase and fished out a piece of paper. 'We found it next to Ms Shearer's bed, if you can call it that.

Strange thing to have for someone who doesn't know you.'

He handed me the piece of paper I had given Molly two nights earlier with my name and number. I looked at it for an age trying to make sense of why the police would be handing it to me.

'No… I gave this to a different… wait… what colour hair does this Shearer girl have?'

'Why don't you take a look at her yourself,' Seabrook said, reaching into his zip briefcase to fish out a black and white photograph.

Simkins adopted an official, giving evidence to the court tone. 'We believe her to have been dead a day or so. Cause of death: Overdose.'

They didn't have to show me that morgue photograph.

They could have described her and left it at that. I would have told them about Molly. I would have said I dropped her off the night before last. I might even have mentioned what a fun person she was. But they showed me that photograph because that's what cops do. Bastards. A lovely photograph it was too of her lifeless face and marbled torso, her breasts on show, her eyes still open, submissive and hopeless after drawing her last breath…

I ran to the kitchen sink and was violently sick.

It was the photograph, it was the booze, it was Molly; I was just sick of it all, of people dying, of beautiful women gone before their time. I was just sick.

I filled a shot glass with vodka, took it to the bathroom and cleaned my teeth, dipping the brush in the alcohol. It really is the only way to cure a hangover. Don't believe me? Try it some time. I stuck my head under the shower set to cold then splashed some Brut over my face and the back of my neck, cursing my stupidity when Seabrook and Simkins first threw the name Mary Shearer at me. Without the hangover, I might have been a lot quicker on the up take. After all, in Wales, and probably the rest of the country, Molly was a common enough pet name for Mary. It was as common as Stewart to Spike, John to Jack. Mary to Molly – Mary Shearer didn't overcomplicate things coming up with her working name.

Emerging from the bathroom, feeling a little more awake, I found the two policemen quietly discussing the case, their paperwork and photographs laid out on the table.

'What made you think she was an addict?' I asked, interrupting them.

'Why don't you tell us what you know about her first?' Simkins said.

I wanted to keep them focused on the overdose and try and find out as much as I could. 'I saw her arms and legs. I didn't see any track marks.'

'She wasn't shooting up, she snorted the stuff,' Seabrook said.

'Where's your proof?' I asked.

For no reason other than petulance it seemed, Seabrook passed me a close-up photograph showing the scene where her body was discovered. I glanced at it. The flash of the camera had cruelly illuminated the small, upturned fruit box that served as a bedside table. Amongst the clutter was a mirror with the remains of a powdery substance chopped into lines. Alongside, next to a paperback book about some sort of new age nonsense, was a necklace with a small carved circular pendant of bone. I couldn't be sure, but that circle and black dot looked similar in design to the one that had been around Angie's neck. The dress tied phony Gail to Molly. Did the necklace do the same with Angie?

I was busy weighing up the facts and had tuned out from what the policemen were saying for a moment. Focusing in again, it appeared, to Simkins' evident disgust, that Seabrook was showing his inexperience by talking too much.

'…toxicology said it was top grade heroin on the mirror…

autopsy will show it was in her system… anonymous tip off told us she had OD'd and where we could find her.'

'Was it one of the flat mates?' I asked.

Seabrook shrugged. 'Could be. The place was empty when we got there. Any longer, the rats would have done for her.'

Molly's description of her house came back to me: *'Great vibes. Very, very creative space.'* A garret or a hovel – it is all about perception, I guess.

'Male or female?' I asked Seabrook. 'The person who called it in?'

'Female apparently,' he replied.

I had a last look at the photograph before Simkins snatched it from the table and buried it away in his briefcase. Something was bothering me.

'Where's her stuff, her heroin?' I asked.

Simkins shrugged.

'Because if it's gone,' I said, 'it means the person who tipped you off was probably a user as well.'

Simkins rolled his eyes. 'Or they were hiding the evidence before ringing the police. Did you think of that?'

'Then why leave the mirror?' I shot back.

While Seabrook and Simkins pondered that little piece of logic, I came to a decision. The pimp, Ms Ghisham, the whole operation – I was going to shut it down. It's not that I'm particularly moral about pimps and their trade, or how their girls earn a living. But I couldn't get that lifeless face out of my head and I needed someone to blame. Today it was Molly – Mary – we were talking about. How long before it was Barbara?

Over the next hour or so I gave Seabrook and Simkins everything I knew about the whole Heddon Street operation; how they chose struggling actresses for their girls, the colour dress code, Ms Ghisham. I told them about driving Molly home from Heathrow after her assignation with Cassidy, explaining she must have been booked by his American management. That would keep Bell and Dick Leahy off the police report. Seabrook and Simkins didn't seem too worried about that side of things. Unless they were being paid off, the police always liked to go for the pimps. It was noisy and splashy and satisfied the angry of Tunbridge Wells contingent. Given the elaborate secrecy around the pimp's operation, it was doubtful he was bribing anyone in the police. All in all, that meant I had given Seabrook and Simkins a nice collar and the tabloids a nice lurid headline. The pimp would be demonised, Ms Ghisham too, far beyond their actual crime. Did they really deserve that? Maybe not. But he could have stuck to making cheap suits and she could have gone on the stage with a memory act or even taken up wrestling. In my mind it was simple. They used those girls and one of them was dead. Something had to give.

After I had finished serving up Seabrook and Simkins the whole operation, a strange silence descended. They knew they would have to immediately report what I had told them. No doubt a raid would take place in the next few days, they might even be involved. I knew I had to get back to chasing down Angie's killer. It was like the quiet in the dressing room ahead of a fight. A moment of peaceful contemplation before the onslaught. They rose to their feet, gathered the paperwork, and made to leave. I could see the strain on Seabrook's face. Murder, overdose – the detective inspector had also seen more than he could stomach over the last few days.

'How do you think he got all those lovely birds to go on the game?' Seabrook asked quietly, to no one but himself.

'The pimp or Ms Ghisham, more likely, chose well,' I theorised. 'Probably told them it was still a form of acting. A different play every day. A different script. And every night a standing ovation.'

At the front door, just before he left, Simkins gave me the sternest of looks.

'I'm getting fed up with seeing you, Mr Jones. No more non-sense. Keep your nose clean. Stay out of trouble.'

Stay out of trouble? I wasn't even getting started.

Twenty-One

With the policemen gone, I set to work.

Danny, whose judgement I trusted when it came to criminals, had promised over the phone to rustle me up a top housebreaker. With little fuss, the meet was set up outside Marble Arch tube station just after midday. I almost suggested my contact carry a copy of the *International Herald Tribune*, but Danny seemed certain they would be able to spot me without any difficulty. Sure enough, at the agreed time, a slight figure approached me as I stood at the station entrance. His severe prison yard haircut and shiny brown polyester suit several sizes too big made me think he was fresh from a jailbreak.

'I'm guessing we're both friends of yer man Danny,' he muttered sideways out of his mouth, his accent a rich Falls Road Irish.

Given his chosen profession, the small workman's tool bag he was carrying seemed a bit of a giveaway to my eyes, and for any policemen who might be watching. He must have noticed my staring.

'I'm to be missing my lunch, so the wife made me sandwiches.'

He produced a hefty ham and pickle cheese sandwich and took a great big cheerful bite. I noticed an apple, a bag of crisps, and a flask were also in the bag.

'I don't like working on an empty stomach,' he explained. 'I get so I can't concentrate when I'm ravenous.'

Still munching on his sandwich, he reached for his apple, but decided against it, instead casting me an apologetic look.

'You're probably in a hurry and here I am stuffing my face like a proper eejit. Lead on and show me the way.'

Off we went. I was still feeling tenderised by a hangover pressing down on my brain like a ten-ton weight. At a phone box on the corner of Edgware Road and Bryanston Place, I called Billy's number, leaving it to ring for over a minute. When there was no answer, we continued. Reaching the apartment block, my accomplice cast an expert eye over the front door.

'Sure, I'll have you in there in a jiffy,' he declared.

'This bit I can handle myself,' I told him.

On the entry panel to the side of the door, I pressed all the buttons at random, hoping someone was expecting a delivery or a visit. Sure enough, the door buzzed open, and we went inside.

'Handled like a professional,' my housebreaker said admiringly.

Avoiding the lift and walking quickly, but not so quickly as to draw attention, we made our way to the second floor and Billy's flat. Outside Billy's door, the Irishman again studied his adversary.

'Nothing to it,' he suggested. 'I'll open that in the blink of an eye.'

Since his bag only contained a flask and an apple, I was unclear on how he was going to achieve this, but then he reached inside his jacket and fetched out half a dozen small keys on a piece of string. He selected one, licked it, placed it in the front door lock and bumped it back and forward. The key turned gradually, and, with a click, magically opened the door. He smiled at me, enjoying my amazement.

'Bump keys,' he explained. 'Everyone's using these Yale type locks nowadays. Makes my job so much easier.'

We both entered the flat and stood in a long corridor of closed doors, listening for signs of life. There were no sounds in the flat other than our own breathing and the lock picker's rumbling stomach. Satisfied we were alone, I opened the first door to reveal a spacious front room.

'I'll finish my lunch, if you don't mind, while you do whatever you have to do,' my lock picker suggested, immediately settling himself down on a small futon couch.

I set about searching Billy's flat. It was much bigger, tidier, and feminine than I would have imagined, with a hippy/new age feel that I found difficult to square with the Billy I thought I knew. There were candles and incense, bead and bamboo blinds, Indian rag rugs and Eastern deity statuettes. All the paintings on the wall showed primitive representations of the sun. I was no expert, but the artwork looked Aztec, maybe Mayan, maybe Maori. Like I say, I was no expert.

In one corner of the room there was what appeared to be a private shrine in front of some sort of prayer mat. On the shrine stood a saucer sized white circle of carved ivory or bone with a black dot in the centre. Thumb cymbals and sticks of incense stood either side.

'This place looks like the Chinese restaurant round the corner from where I live', the lock picker chuckled.

I toured the room, hoping I might find something that would indicate what had happened to Billy. There was nothing; no paperwork, letters, diary, shopping list or anything to suggest the character of the person who lived here. The lock picker was right. It did look more like a restaurant. This was no normal living room. Then it came to me. What it looked like was a place of worship. A temple. I left my fellow Celt pouring himself a tea from his flask as I went back into the corridor to explore the flat further.

The second door led to the main bedroom which had been thoroughly ransacked, much like my flat. Clothes were thrown everywhere, paperback books splayed on the floor, their spines broken. The mattress had been slashed and gutted. Whoever was here before me was searching for something, just like I was. I picked through the mess. Other than a few Hugh Padley sci-fi novels, most of the books were New Age paperbacks about astral plains, ley lines or studies of UFOs and alien gods. One title caught my eye, *The Paranormal and The Forest of Dean*. I don't know how long Billy had been reading this rubbish, but he had never once mentioned anything about it in our times together at the recording studio or down the pub.

The next door opened onto a smaller bedroom. Here there were more paintings of suns on the walls, and another shrine, again with the white circle and dot, thumb cymbals, sticks of incense, and prayer mat. A wardrobe to the side of the bed was full of women's clothes in the glam meets ashram style. On the bed lay a woman's fur coat and a small leather satchel containing a purse, lipstick, tampons, and a red driving license booklet. There was no mystery as to who the license belonged to, but I opened it all the same. The name read: Angela Bright-Silver. I now knew where Angie had stayed after leaving Sporne, where she had stayed while recording her album in Ryemuse, only a ten-minute walk away.

I sat on the bed and tried to make sense of the discovery. Billy had seemed so disappointed the last time I saw him, when he found out I was back in the pay of Terry Sporne and looking for Angie. Now it was clear: That wasn't disappointment, more like worry that I might uncover their secret. *Their* secret? Billy and Angie? It seemed doubtful that Billy masterminded the relaunch of Angie's career, almost as far-fetched as him murdering Angie. Whoever did commit the murder brought her belongings back to the flat, then trashed and searched Billy's room. Unless Billy trashed his own room, the only way any of this made sense was if there had been someone else in the studio, someone else in on the plan, someone else covering their tracks. At some point, say after the murder, things fell apart and Billy struck out on his own, taking the tape with him. That's what the other person or persons were looking for in his room. That's what they were looking for in my flat. Then when they couldn't find the tape, they looked for clues as to where he may be hiding out.

I ran my hand through the expensive clothes hanging in the wardrobe, all of them designer labels, all of them chic and couture. It was difficult to picture Angie in this room, lighting incense and clicking her cymbals whilst knelt in prayer to whatever the hell that circle religion was supposed to be. I tried to imagine what Terry would make of it all, how deep the wound would go when he found out Angie had rejected the luxury penthouse flat they shared in Soho for this communal spiritual enlightenment.

I moved on to the last but one room in the corridor. There was a mattress on the floor, a cardboard box in the corner filled with identical pamphlets. Still thinking of the old Billy, the Billy I thought I knew, I had half expected the box to contain pornography. At first glance that initial thought seemed correct. The glossy photograph on the cover of the pamphlet featured a blissed out naked couple enjoying the sunrise on a sandy beach. The man and woman were very much from the dated, Woodstock era, Californian branch of hippiedom. Beneath the picture, a caption in bold suggested the reader 'WELCOME THE SUN'. This, it transpired, was no nudist or naturist mag. Inside, it was like a sorcerer's handbook with ancient Eastern texts and mystical diagrams of spheres, circles with dots and ouroboroi. Perhaps to offer a little light relief, the centre pages had a personal statement from someone called Abzari Afin, shown grinning like a mad man from a passport size photograph at the top of the page.

'Nature is incapable of the straight line. The perpendicular is a contrivance. Focus on the circle rather than the straight line. The circle of life is the only truth, with every point

a blessing. Sincerity meets devotion meets renewal meets devotion meets sincerity on and on and on, like an ever-revolving wheel, like the constant waxing and waning of the moon in the night sky, the rise and fall of our nourishing sun. Life and death are meaningless distinctions. The circle is all powerful just as the sun is all powerful. The sun is all powerful just as is the circle. Light comes from the sun, enlightenment comes from the circle, the circle is light, the sun is enlightenment…'

'Kumbaya my Lord, kum-fucking-baya,' I said out loud in exasperation at what I was reading. These thrown together, guru on the make religions were ten a penny in the sixties. It seemed hard to believe people were still falling for this new age nonsense but, by the looks of it, Angie, Molly and Billy had been willing converts. Billy Coles! He was involved in all this deeper than I had ever thought possible. Billy, the house engineer who used to live above a studio had become Billy, the caretaker for a temple or shrine, welcoming in fellow devotees and converts like Angie. Now it made sense why that bottle of Jack Daniels was in the studio bin when I went back. The man who once drank for Scotland, renouncing alcohol in the name of some crazy religion. That was devotion. And all for circles and dots. This outfit were no better than the cult who entrapped Phil Fratton, I thought, before turning the pamphlet over and glancing at the back page. There, in big letters, was the name of the organisation responsible for the pamphlet, Apricus. This wasn't *like* the sinister cult Phil had fallen for – it was the very same cult. Billy was mixed up with Apricus, as was Angie, as was Molly, as was Phil… I was getting closer to finding the answers I needed.

The last door led to the bathroom. There were two toothbrushes in a glass beaker by the sink. Women's toiletries were mixed with men's on the windowsill. It was a comfortable, domesticated arrangement. Billy and Angie as platonic flat mates. It was still taking some getting used to. I remembered the voice that had answered the phone when I rang the morning after the murder. South African, guarded, to the point. A pretend flat mate? Like my pretend neighbour, like my Gail Petters. I'd bet my life the phony South African, Shannon, was busy searching Billy's room when I rang. She'd let herself into the flat using a key, then, intrigued or worried enough by my call, decided to pay me a visit a few days later. This time she didn't bother with a South African accent. When she knocked on my door, she went the full cut glass English and introduced herself as Gail Petters. Someone had primed her with all the details she would need, and so she improvised her character beautifully. To look the part, she even selected a knockout outfit from the wardrobe Angie's clothes were hanging in and set about fully committing to her role. My earlier words to Seabrook came back to me: *'A different play every day. A different script. And every night a standing ovation.'* Job done, she must have then given the dress to Molly. But how did those two know each other? How was she mixed up with Billy and Angie? And who told her all about me?

The answers were not going to be found here. I headed back to the living room. It was time to leave.

'Something I don't get about this place,' the lock picker said as I joined him. 'There's no television. Who doesn't have a television these days?'

'Who indeed?'

I passed him over the twenty pounds we had agreed upon.

'I'm all done here. Let's get going.'

'What?' he asked. 'Is that it? Are you not going to help yourself to anything? Some of those wee statue things would be worth a tidy sum.'

'I was just looking for clues to a puzzle,' I told him.

'Sure you're like one of those detectives. Have you seen the new fella on the telly, Cannon? Big fatty he is. Do you know the man even has a phone in his car!'

He narrowed his eyes and gave me a significant look.

'If being a detective fella is your line of work, you'd be needing a gun. Some of the boys I know back home would be happy to oblige for a small contribution to the cause. Their armoury is a bit on the old side, but those shooters still fire just fine.'

After declining his offer of a gun, we left the flat separately. I looked for him out on the street, to make sure we were heading in different directions, but the lock picker was already gone. I smiled, remembering what he said about the television detective. A phone in your car! That would be something, I thought.

Twenty-Two

The rest of the afternoon was supposed to be set. I was to meet Rick Kempe at the *NME* offices on Long Acre, though knowing Rick, the afternoon would quickly extend to become the evening. On my way through to Covent Garden, I made a last-minute decision to call in at MAM records before I left Mayfair. Seeing Lynsey de Paul the previous evening had got me thinking about my old flame Claire Gronwaulde. Since she had been on my list of seven suspects, it might be beneficial to talk to her and find out if she knew anything. There was also the matter of the deal I had made with Dave Cash about trying to get him an exclusive. None of that really was uppermost in my mind. Truth be told, I just wanted to see a familiar face. Right now, I needed a friend.

MAM – short for Management, Agency and Music – were opposite the Westbury Hotel, on the corner of New Bond Street, occupying the top three floors of a modern grey concrete building. The head man, Gordon Mills, and the accountants were on the very top floor; the artists' agency was on the floor below, and below that, on the floor Claire worked, were the MAM record company offices. All three entities were floated on the stock exchange. By being a public company, it meant that anyone owning shares in MAM technically also owned a piece of their chief assets, which included Tom Jones, Engelbert Humperdinck, Gilbert O'Sullivan and Lynsey De Paul, not to mention the people they represented as agents, such as Welsh warbler, Mary Hopkin, and radio presenters, Jimmy Young and Tony Blackburn. It was a very strange set-up and probably as shady as it gets, what with their famously underhand business practises and various offshore accounts in the Caribbean Islands. When not on tour, the main shareholders, Jones and Humperdinck, would often call in, partying on the top floor with Mills, before adjourning to the nearby Westbury Hotel, accompanied by the latest Miss World or glamour model they had managed to ensnare. They were having a right old time of it there at MAM. A lot of the other Teen Avenue crowd felt they were spoiling it for everyone else by being just a little too flash, a little too vulgar. I wasn't so sure about that. Though I never could warm to the insecure, egotistical Humperdinck, I always rubbed along well enough with Tom Jones, the few times we met. Because of our surnames, people often assumed we were related, or at very least knew each other, especially since we both came from Pontypridd. Neither of these things were true. Besides, I grew up in the Graig area, Tom in Treforest. And, although I saw him about town with the other 'Ponty Teds', I had already moved to London by the time he was singing. As for being related, Tom's real surname was Woodward, so nothing to do with my branch of the Jones clan. I did know Tom's bodyguard, Dai Perry and his manager, Gordon Mills, the other two Rhondda Valley boys at MAM, a lot better. As a boy, Mills sang and played his harmonica in the pubs and working men's clubs around where I grew up. These days, someone playing harmonica conjures up images of Sonny Boy Williamson or Muddy Waters. Gordon was more from the 'Theme tune from Genevieve', 'Under Paris Skies' school of harmonica, but that's what gave him his first start in showbusiness. Dai Perry had been a teen tough nut, always starting trouble in the Pontypridd pubs. Six pints of Fernvale under, he once tried to pick a fight with me in the White Hart until I punched him in the face, breaking his nose. He left it unfixed, apparently liking the way it made him look menacing. It was strange to think we were all now in England, all operating out of a tiny square of London. *Cymru am bith.*

I walked up to the third floor of the building and was waived through into the open plan office by the friendly receptionist. Claire was on the phone, lounging back in her office chair, her heels kicked off, her pretty feet resting on the office desk. No bra, in a flowing floral dress, she looked good, just like I always pictured her in my mind's eye; her dark hair swept back behind either ear, those intelligent green eyes blazing proudly, her face flushed with her latest passionate enthusiasms. I immediately realised how much I had missed her.

'...she's London's pocket rocket Aretha Franklin, I'm telling you... the East End's answer to Etta James and, I kid you not, she's barely eighteen...'

Claire gave me a nod and rolled her eyes to indicate her opinion of the person on the other end of the phone. She passed me an 8" × 10" showing a young doe-eyed girl leaning against a set of railings – the subject of her conversation. I gazed at the photograph, enjoying the challenge of estimating the level of hype Claire was employing in promoting the youthful singer.

'...is she pretty? What a question to ask me! She's beautiful... beauty is as beauty does, as my mother used to say, and what this girl does will knock your socks off... believe me, everyone will know the name Tina Hoskins by the end of the year. Just meet her, get to know her, take some pictures, listen to her story, and help yourself to a great big juicy scoop courtesy of yours truly... okay... okay. Thanks, Bob. Ciao.'

Claire sighed, replacing the phone on the hook.

'All publicity is bullshit, but this girl needs shovel loads. Shouldn't be that way. Amazing voice, lovely smile, huge tits... but glam is a boys' game and doesn't need or want women it seems.'

'What about Suzi Quatro?'

'A butch girl who looks like a pretty boy dressing like the plain girl next door.'

'What about Lynsey?'

'Lynsey de Paul is a brilliant songwriter who can sing a bit. She also happens to be every man's fantasy blonde.'

'Couldn't this girl be every man's fantasy brunette?' I asked, tapping the publicity photograph.

'We had to keep her off the cream buns for a month before that photo was taken. I love Tina to bits but, compared to Lynsey, she's just a dumpy Jewish girl from the East End.'

'And Lynsey's a Jewish girl from Cricklewood.'

'And I'm a nice Jewish girl from Camden. The Jewish thing isn't really the point. The love of cream buns is.'

'What are you going to do then?' I laughed, glad to be reacquainting myself with Claire's heady mix of showbiz savvy and wit.

'Wait for glam music to pass the way of the dance bands. Try and get her some TV work in Germany or, worse comes to worse, fucking Belgium. Shame. She really is amazing.'

Claire placed her hands behind her head and studied me.

'Long time no hear, or see, Elis. You look bloody terrible.'

'*Top of The Pops* party last night. And apologies. I should have called you sooner. I left it too long.'

'I don't know. We were all played out, weren't we? Tell me.'

'We still had a few good tunes left. Are you seeing anyone?'

'Nothing to write home about. You?'

'Nothing to write home about.'

She bit her thumb nail thoughtfully.

'Well, my dear, Elis. Unless you've changed your spots, how about us two leopards go across the road to the Westbury Hotel?'

'I didn't bring my toothbrush or my pyjamas,' I said.

'Don't get too excited. All I meant was for us to go to the bar. The company has now got an account there.'

'Am I not allowed to get a little excited?' I asked.

'Okay. A little. Just a little, for old times' sake.'

The faded grandeur of the Westbury Hotel catered for the landed gentry, scurrying maiden aunts and elderly Colonels from the pre-war Mayfair set. You had to wonder what they thought when they encountered those lascivious MAM boys stalking the racing green carpeted hallways. Claire led me to their new clubhouse, a ground floor bar that tried a little harder to be more with the times. On the wall, there were enormous snaps of various London landmarks blown up till all you could see was a fragmented fuzz of grainy dots, doing in photography I suppose what the IRA were trying to do with bombs. I kept my promise to Dave Cash and asked Claire to send Capital Radio an exclusive advance copy of Gilbert O'Sullivan's new single. When she refused indignantly, I didn't try and change her mind. In a situation where sides were going to be taken, it was always going to be Claire over Dave every time with me. Besides, a man in a waistcoat was serving us endless gin and tonics in tall, slender glasses with lots of ice cubes the size of matchboxes. Each sip was putting my head back together again. Claire was having the same effect on my soul. We soon forgot Gilbert O'Sullivan and Capital Radio and talked over old times, laughed at the stories that were worth laughing over, shook our heads at the way things had ended between us. I wished I could have stayed there all afternoon, enjoying her "tell it like it is" line in chat, running my finger down the cold glass and forgetting everything that had happened in the last week of my life. But hard as I tried, I couldn't stop Claire bringing to mind Penny, which made me remember Angie, which made me think about Molly and pretty soon I was back to playing at being a detective, trying to sleuth out another piece of the puzzle I had vowed to solve.

'My flat was broken into this week,' I said after a while, curious to see what she would say.

'Did they take anything valuable?' Claire asked.

'No. But I'm looking for the people who did it.'

'You're looking? Not the police? Elis, you've very much adopted a "for justice, against the law" view of the world, haven't you?'

'I think it's all to do with Apricus. Heard of them?'

'They're one of those religious cults, aren't they? Why? Did they break in? Are you behind with your subscription?'

'It's all linked. My break in. Angie Bright-Silver's murder. Turns out Angie was part of Apricus, along with Billy Coles and a call girl called Molly. There's a chance Penny Sands is mixed up in this as well.'

Claire calmly stared at me with her green eyes. 'Ah! Penny Sands. Was she the "nothing to write home about" you mentioned earlier? Or would that be the "call girl called Molly"?'

'Neither. Molly – Mary Shearer, to give her full name – was just someone I briefly knew. She died from an overdose.'

'Sorry to hear that. And don't I feel mean suddenly?'

'Don't. You had no way of knowing. And as for Penny, I should be apologising to you. I got things muddled up on her tour. I should have been more respectful to you, Claire. I wish things hadn't gone the way they had.'

'Mea culpa? You think that's the way to my heart?'

'If I knew what "mea culpa" means, then yes. If it helps.'

'It helps a little.'

Claire reached for one of my cigarettes and fired it up with the Zippo. 'I seem to remember Phil Fratton getting mixed up with Apricus?'

'They're the reason he moved to California and gave them

everything he owned.'

'Almost everything,' she corrected me. 'You are still in his flat, I take it.'

'I'm still there.'

'And then someone broke in?' Claire said distantly, mulling over the situation.

I reached into my back pocket. Alongside Penny's unopened record launch invitation was an Apricus pamphlet I had taken from Billy Coles' place.

'I want you to look at something.'

I was careful to pass her the right item for her inspection.

With keen eyes, Claire scanned the booklet, turning the pages quickly to get an immediate sense of what it was she was looking at. She then repeated her study at a much slower pace, carefully reading the text. Satisfied she'd reached an accurate assessment, Claire took a deep drag on her cigarette, allowing the smoke to curl from her mouth in a slow, protracted exhale.

'I thought this sort of stuff went out with Woodstock,' she said. 'See this? They are using the circumpunct. When I was a teenager, some of the other JFS sixth formers became interested in kabbalah, that is to say Jewish mysticism. They'd wear these circular amulets representing the *kether*, the topmost of the *sephirot* in the tree of life, "the most hidden of hidden things". All utter bollocks of course.'

Claire passed back the pamphlet.

'Whoever is behind this cult must have spent some time researching kabbalah ideas, I'd imagine. Cherry picking the bits they needed and fusing it with Inca sun worship, Hindu monism and God knows what else. Meanwhile, converts like Phil Fratton give over everything they own for the privilege of being brainwashed.'

'Enlightenment doesn't come cheap these days,' I added.

Claire sighed. 'Welcome to the Age of Aquarius, where spirituality is the new rock and roll, and just as lucrative.'

I downed my drink.

'Not so lucrative for the people being fleeced.'

'Or the people being murdered,' added Claire.

Twenty-Three

The crowd in South Molton Street were as silent as a chapel congregation. Each time the door opened, and plain clothes policemen came and went, the onlookers would peer and crane their necks, hoping for a peek inside the building, a clue or explanation as to what had happened. The open sign was turned to closed in the chemist shop to the left of the door. The shopgirls and pharmacist stood frozen like mannequins in the window, staring out at the coming and going.

I collared a nearby ambulance man, asking him what had happened, but he behaved as if he had not even heard me. Then I noticed his waxen skin, the speckles of vomit gruel that hung in the corners of his mouth and down the front of his sky-blue shirt. The three police cars and ambulance had already told me something big was going on. My first guess on arriving was that it was a drugs raid. The ambulance man's expression told me it was something more deadly, something more shocking.

I had been heading up to Bond Street tube after leaving the Westbury Hotel, sincere promises made by me and Claire to meet up one evening very soon. From Bond Street the plan had been to hop the tube to Holborn and then walk down Long Acre to meet Rick at *NME*'s offices. Even though South Molton Street would have been my quickest route to the tube, I had decided to walk a bit further down Brook Street and go north on Davies Street. I wanted to avoid passing anywhere near the studio; discovering

Angie's broken body was still too fresh in my mind. But my route still meant passing the bottom of South Molton Street and that's when I noticed the crowd spilling off the pavement and into the road, stopping the traffic. The commotion was outside the chemist shop at number sixty-four, outside the door that led upstairs to Ryemuse recording studio.

A mean-faced waiter from a nearby restaurant jostled past me to get to the front of the crowd.

'What do you reckon chum? Not another bleedin' murder, is it?'

I shrugged. 'Could be.'

'This place went to the bleedin' dogs when they let in all those pop stars with their rock and roll and drugs.'

'Don't forget their long hair,' I reminded him sarcastically.

'Too right. You don't know if they're girls or boys half the time.'

'It must be all very confusing for you,' I commiserated before moving on to find a phone box.

I rang Harry Baum from the box at the Davies Street entrance to Bond Street tube station. He promised to find out what had happened at Ryemuse within the hour, using the same source in the Metropolitan police as Terry Sporne used. I decided to wait out the time over a coffee or two at a café across the road before calling him back.

Greek owned, the drab café was somewhere I had walked past many times but never thought about entering. Their coffee tasted bitter and looked like mud, but it was strong, stronger than biker's sulphate, and made my heart pump, my nerve endings fizz. If they ever sold that stuff at Reading Festival, they would make a fortune.

Aside from the coffee, the owner was also good value, unwittingly entertaining me as he argued with his young English kitchen pot washer; football, and the underperforming West Ham United the topic.

'No, no, no,' the owner insisted, 'they play useless… is end of argument.'

'They're not useless, Mr Galanis. I can't understand how you could say that. I mean, fair's fair. What about the Pop Robson goal against Leicester last week!'

'But they only draw! Draw is no help to anyone. No good if them fuckers is not winning matches, playing shit all the time. And Bobby Moore! He is a joke, a comedian, make me laugh. He is no good for Hammers, no good for England. He let Poland win in the summer, giving the ball away, tackling like a pansy girl. Bang. Goal. And silly old England not in the World Cup.'

'We'll be great in the second leg. Home crowd cheering them on. We will qualify and we will win. Just you see.'

'No way!'

On and on they went, tussling it out, back and forth, neither finding anything they could agree upon. Finally, the pot washer lay down a challenge for his boss.

'Okay then. Name me one better midfielder playing in the league than the Hammers' Trevor Brooking…'

I left the café as the owner delivered his thorough response; each name ticked off with a digit on both his hands.

'…Johnny Giles, Steve Heighway, Ian Callaghan, Charlie Cooke, Stan Bowles, Gerry Francis, Liam Brady, Alan Ball, Ray Kennedy, Terry McDermott, Martin Peters…'

I crossed the road, my anticipation growing as to what I might find out from Harry. An hour earlier, the tube station had been quiet, almost deserted. Now it echoed to the clamour of rush hour, the sound of a thousand footsteps, excited people finishing work or heading home after shopping, their conversations rowdy and shrill. Once again, I made my call from the public phone box at the station entrance, watching the passing tide of humanity, straining to hear what Harry had found out.

'I got a pretty thorough heads up as to what happened there, Elisud. The police have opened a murder investigation...'

'Harry, I could have found that out from the evening paper.'

'...obviously, police have no forensics this early on. Scene of the crime report talks about the murder weapon being a long-bladed knife, possibly more than one assailant.'

'Who's the victim?' I asked.

Harry did not catch my question because I had to feed another coin in the phone. I searched my pockets, the 'da-da-da-da' phone pips screaming till I managed to find the final tuppence left over from the change for my coffees. I thought about Cannon, in his car, with a phone. I bet he didn't ever have to worry about tuppences.

The coin was fed into the slot and Harry came back on the line. '... our friend DI Simkins is up in arms apparently about there not having been a proper sweep of the first crime scene.'

'What do you mean?'

'No one knew about the room upstairs. It seems the uniformed officers never even bothered to go upstairs to the top floor. If they had...'

There was a commotion outside. Some kid tried to jump the barrier. The shouts of the ticket guard blocked out Harry for a moment.

'I missed that, Harry. Say it again.'

'...the producer and engineer thought at first it might be a dead rat under the floorboards. Happens, doesn't it? I remember the dead mouse I had...'

'Harry, I'm on my last tuppence...'

'...same thing is at Ryemuse. It's because the flesh was torn, the innards exposed, the body thrown against the radiator. All that makes a difference to the rot and the smell apparently. Also, it had been a few days. In the end, the smell was bad enough to make the studio people explore upstairs. The door leading to the attic room was locked. The studio engineer, Paul Richards, broke through and found him there. Jonesy, he had been tortured and stabbed multiple times, fifty or more. To the side of the body, a circle in blood was drawn on the floor, on the walls.'

'But who was it, Harry?'

'I imagine it was like one of those Manson killings…'

'Who was it?'

'…ritualistic…'

'Who was it?' I shouted.

There was a pause. Then Harry told me.

'Billy. Someone killed Billy Coles, Jonesy.'

The pips sounded again but I had run out of coins.

Twenty-Four

We met in Lee Wan Fooks, Chinatown. It was Rick's suggestion, not mine. A lot of music journalists and high-level Mayfair record company executives liked eating there, but I always thought it overpriced, the food overrated. Three doors down on Gerrard Street was Ming's, which was better, cheaper, and friendlier. That's where me and Peter Grant would go whenever we fancied a slap-up Chinese. But after the news of Billy Coles' murder, I was in no mood to argue with Rick's choice, and a slap-up celebration was the last thing on my mind. *NME*'s star journalist was on his way to a pub in Holloway to review an unknown band called Ducks Deluxe he had decided to champion. Rick was very, very excited, already writing his copy in a real time stream of consciousness, like a free jazz poet, like he had drunk a gallon of the same coffee I had been drinking earlier. Studying the menu, I tried feigning interest in what he was telling me, but really all I was thinking about was poor Billy and just how and when I could tell Rick about his death. I could see I would have to choose my moment.

'...popular music, as opposed to classical music, was created from the ground up, from the sidewalk, from the streets. Jazz: Louis Armstrong trammelled in a Storyville gutter lifts his head to the heavens and blows his horn. Blues: The chain gang working the railroad, the sharecroppers down in the dirt giving merciful expression to the human condition. Country: Appalachians farming the unforgiving soil sing atavistic songs that speak of dignity and endurance. Rock and Roll was, at its very best, a synthesis of all of these impolite, radical strands; pop becomes its eventual, inevitable refinement. But then something was lost. Genesis, Yes, ELP? Excuse me? Ground up? What particular street did that execrable tosh rise from? It's music that makes a hell of heaven.'

'Rick...' I said, trying to slow him down to the speed of, at the very least, a horse race commentator. There was no stopping him.

'This new scene is imbued with the smell of spilt pints of Fuller's and stale Rothman fags; undiscovered back rooms of pubs thrown open to the creative and uncomplicated, London's demimonde. No glitter, platform shoes or eye liner. Just guys who can really play their instruments and have something to say. That's what you have in a band like Ducks Deluxe!.'

He banged the table loudly.

'Are they signed to anyone?' I asked matter-of-factly.

'Here's the scoop. Do you remember that press officer guy who used to work for Tony Defries? One of your lot. The Welsh bloke. He's managing them! Word is he's already got them a deal at RCA. They're recording their first album later in the month.'

Rick might have hoped news about a fellow Welshman's success with an unknown band would go down well. It did not. Not one bit. Dai Davies, it seems, had just done exactly what I was wanting to do by successfully A&R'ing a band and getting them a juicy record deal. Anyway, he was not 'one of my lot', he was from Carmarthen, a whole different Wales to me. Bath was geographically nearer to Pontypridd than rural West Wales, and about as similar culturally. For a start they don't dig coal in Carmarthen. *'Pontypridd is Wales. Forget Snowden – Wales is about valleys, not mountains. Forget Carmarthen – Wales is about coal...'*

I could have launched into my father's speech, but Rick was already off again.

'The pub scene is going to be the next big thing, believe me. Ducks Deluxe are only the vanguard…'

I had no choice but to stop him in his tracks:

'Rick! They found Billy Coles dead today at Ryemuse. He was murdered.'

I had wanted to break the news a little more gently, but I just couldn't hold it in anymore.

'Shit!' Rick managed to say, after staring at me in disbelief for what seemed like a whole minute. However, his nose for a story eventually took over.

'Was he strangled in the studio like Angie?' Rick asked quietly.

'No. Billy was found in the attic room. He was tortured and stabbed. Stabbed repeatedly. Crazy stuff daubed on the floor in blood.'

'Like the Manson killings?'

'Just like the Manson killings.'

I then pretty much laid out everything I knew so far for Rick. I left out the bit about sleeping with the phony Gail Petters but everything else was on the table, including Penny Sands, Molly's overdose, my being hired to find Angie's killer (or killers) by Terry Sporne. I even told him I had a list of suspects that had at one time included his own name, but now, except for Penny Sands, all the names were ruled out. The tale's unfolding made Rick slack jawed, barely able to offer more than the odd gulp by way of comment. But when I finally finished, he reached into a duffel bag and brought out his notebook and the *NME* press clippings file on Angie.

'Angie Bright-Silver's life, the parts deemed worthy of reporting and saving. This file should be a lot thicker. That it isn't makes me sad. She was talented, beautiful, of the zeitgeist. I can't help thinking she deserved an awful lot more, Jonesy.'

'How thick is Billy's file?' I asked. 'Or mine. Or yours? At least she has a file.'

'Then let's not allow it to be her epitaph.' Rick said. 'Let's see if we are able to hear her speaking to us through these inky clippings, see if she can help "give sorrow words".'

'Give sorrow words?' I asked.

'Absolutely. The Bard warned: "the grief that does not speak knits up the o'er wrought heart and bids it break".'

'Grief? Bollocks to grief. That can wait. Let's find out what the fuck happened to Angie and Billy, first.'

With that we began working through the file, picking over our beef chow meins at the same time.

The cuttings were not arranged chronologically. Some were no more than thumbnail size, some half pages. I moved from a review of 'Little Girl's Dream', her last hit in 1969, to a mid-sixties photograph of Angie dancing with Anthony Newley at the Astor, to a gossip column claiming Angie had tried marijuana. The caption read, 'Angie Spliff-Silver?'.

After more searching, my frustration was growing. There was a nagging question that needed an answer:

'Have you come across anything to indicate when Angie could have been converted to Apricus?' I asked Rick.

'I don't think so.'

'It must have been when she was away from Sporne.'

'Unless they got to him as well?' Rick pointed out.

We both considered the idea for a moment before laughing out loud.

'Terry Sporne in a commune!' Rick said, shaking his head. 'There's an idea.'

Then it came to me. 'What about the film Angie did in Paris? That was only a few years ago, right?'

'1971,' Rick confirmed, riffling through the various clippings with his long, bony fingers.

'She must have been away from Sporne for weeks,' I said.

Rick dug out a small wadge of newspaper pieces. 'Here we are. The film was called *La Bestia Proibite e La Tentatrice*. Directed by Lucio Fulci. A French-Italian co-production starring Lino Capolicchio. The film disappeared without a trace. Angie only had a bit part. There's a press release from the film company. Shall I read it to you? "Stefano is a roughhouse kind of a guy who loves beautiful women, none more so than the highly sexed Florinda, the enigmatic neighbour in the flat above. As Stefano falls in love with the exotic temptress, he is pulled deeper into the complex web of lies and deceit that make him question his own sanity as one by one…"'

'Who played Florinda? Angie?'

'Nope, Angie played Stefano's wife. Someone called… Mary Shearer played Florina.'

I looked up in astonishment.

'Have you got any more photos from the film in your file?' I asked him slowly.

'We took the photo in my article from one of these.'

Rick passed over some cinema lobby cards showing stills from the film. 'Would you like to know how the story ends by the way?'

Rick resumed reading the press release.

'"…the complex web of lies and deceit… make him question his own sanity as, one by one, the many lovers he has encountered in his torrid past re-enter his life in the form of phantasmagorical she devils, lesbian vampires and sado-masochistic nymphomaniacs". Based on an Enid Blyton short story, I believe.'

Good as his joke was, in truth, I had already stopped listening, poleaxed by the two cinema cards before me. The first showed Angie standing alongside the woman I had known as Molly. Angie was dressed in a chaste, schoolteacher pleated skirt and ruffled shirt. Molly on the other hand was wearing a crazy PVC body suit with circular holes cut out to allow her breasts to be on show, a silver riding crop was held beneath Angie's chin, her intentions not entirely clear. The second card was what made me really draw breath. In this one – cropped for Rick's article – Angie was shown alongside an equally familiar face.

'What do we know about her?' I asked Rick, pointing to the blonde actress standing next to Angie.

He took a long look at the lobby card, then scanned the press release.

'Let's see. I think her name is… Linda Sonne. Sensational looking, isn't she? Why do you ask?'

'Because this Linda Sonne is the woman who pretended to be my neighbour. This is the phony Gail Petters who spun me the pretty tale and sent me on that wild goose chase to Staines. The woman who came back, possibly with some help, and ransacked my flat.'

'Looking for what?'

'The master tape Billy had taken from the studio.'

Rick scratched his head, trying to make sense of what I was saying. I tried my best to lay it out for him.

'This is what I think happened: Billy disappears with the tape after Angie is murdered. This woman, alone or with an accomplice, goes looking for it in the Marble Arch flat Billy has been staying in.'

'How did she get in?'

'She uses Angie's key – I found Angie's handbag and coat at the flat, taken from the studio. By chance, I ring up while this Linda Sonne is in the middle of turning Billy's room over. She does a cute South African accent, tells me she's the flat mate. When she doesn't find the tape, since she now knows I know Billy, she decides to search my place, getting me out of the flat by sending me off on a wild goose chase. Then, somehow, she discovers Billy is hiding out in the attic room above the studio, the same room he used to live in before sleeping on my sofa, before joining Apricus. My guess is Billy went up there on the very first night, taking the tape with him. Perhaps he first ran downstairs and left the front door open, so Linda Sonne thought he had done a runner. Anyway, someone eventually remembers about the flat, goes up there, and Billy is murdered. She gets the tape.'

Rick looked at the photograph of Linda Sonne.

'So, she's part of Apricus?'

'I think she's the one who converted Angie and Molly, probably when they were doing the film in Paris. Sometime later, she probably converted Billy as well. I think Billy was like some sort of caretaker for that flat in Marble Arch. It was where the new converts met – kind of like their temple – before being shipped off to California.'

'And you really think this woman killed Angie Bright-Silver? Killed Billy Coles?

'Yes, I do. If she didn't do it, she was not far away when it happened.'

'How are you going to find her?'

'I've got a few ideas, one of which would be to talk to Penny Sands. She certainly knows something. The band Angie was using to back her on the recordings were called Blank Verse. Penny acted so strangely when I asked her about them. Christ, she might even be part of Apricus.'

'You said she's been away on tour.'

I nodded, remembering the envelope with the invitation, still tucked away in my pocket.

'Do you know when she is coming back to London?' Rick asked.

'I'm not sure…'

I ripped open the letter and looked at the colourful invitation depicting a pirate ship. '…but I know where she'll be this coming

Monday, around seven thirty in the evening.'

'Where?' Rick asked.

'Westminster bridge.'

'Very precise. How can you be so sure?'

I passed Rick the launch party invitation.

'That's how.'

Twenty-Five

I decided to jump a cab with Rick up to the Lord Nelson on the Holloway Road to see the band he was so set on championing. After our talk about Angie and Billy's possible murderer, both of us were quiet during the journey. It felt like we would be dancing on graves to suddenly start enjoying ourselves and relax into the next phase of the evening. Still, Rick had a job to do, and I had my own reasons for making the journey. '*Some days you drift, some days you have a mission*,' I muttered to myself, thinking back to the night I last saw Billy, thinking about how he ended up, rotting in an attic. Harry Baum had said the studio people forced the locked door. Since Billy could not have locked the door after he was stabbed to death then the murder or murderers must have done it themselves. And since the door was not forced until the body was discovered, it follows that Billy let in the people who killed him, which means they were people he knew, people he trusted. That fact didn't quite fit with Linda Sonne. Wasn't she the one Billy was hiding from? And if he was hiding from her, didn't that mean she must have been around when Angie was murdered?

Rick suddenly leant forward, giving the taxi driver directions as the pub came into view.

'There's the pub. If you pull just by the front… just here… by the front…'

He was like a gig bloodhound, the scent of the venue in his nostrils, his only thought to pay the fare, track inside, and corner his prey. I had trouble keeping up with him, those long limbs generating a surprising amount of speed, his sharp elbows clearing an effective pathway through the busy pub.

The gig was in a large function room, clearly once a venue for bare-knuckle boxing matches and smokers in the past. The walls were covered with pictures of old fighters posing fists up, gazing fiercely at some invisible opponent. It all felt strangely familiar and I knew why. After the London ban on wrestling was lifted in the 1930's, a new circuit, under the so-called Admiral-Lord Mountevans rules, was created and included shit-hole pubs that looked just like this. A few, like the Merry Fiddler in Dagenham, were still on the circuit when I started. Tough old boozers with the same bare floorboards and ceilings stained caramel by decades of cigarette smoke. This was just like one of those places. Even without the canvas ring, it still felt gladiatorial.

The room was packed, standing room only, with a crowd I found hard to place. Teenyboppers had glam. Students had prog rock. Each had their distinctive uniforms of sorts. This audience's fashion influences appeared to be all over the place. There were Teddy Boys in Day-Glo drape suits and enormous brothel creepers, a look taking me straight back to the 'Ponty Teds' and Dai Perry starting trouble in the White Lion. A small group of skinheads stood nearby, although they weren't wearing the usual Doc. Martins and braces, but the same sort of terrible suits the Irish housebreaker had been wearing. A gang of serious bikers in greasy denim and studded leather jackets reeking of patchouli oil and petrol menaced the back of the room. The rest of the audience looked like the sort of blokes you would see on the football terraces, blinking and jerking from all the Mandrax in their system, relaxed and tense at the same time, ready to have a party but ready for a fight should the need ever arise. The age range was from sixteen up to early forties. There were a few women standing close against their boyfriends, a proprietorial arm encircling their waist, shoulder, or neck. But given this was a pub, understandably perhaps, it was a mostly male crowd.

The support band were already halfway through their set when Rick and I walked in. A four piece, they looked like they'd come straight from a railway arch lock-up after stashing their sawn-off shotguns used in a bank job. They played an odd, skittish type of R&B – every tune too fast, too frenetic and out of tune. The singer's hostility was what really surprised me. Glowering at the audience, falling-down drunk, the alcohol sweating out of him in great beads, he shouted rather than sang, his strong South London accent reducing his lyrics to nothing but vowel sounds.

'….aaaiii…aeeo…ooooaaa..auuuiii…iiiee…eee...'

I liked him and I liked the band.

'Who are they? I asked Rick.

'Uppity Daze,' he shouted back.

Great name, I thought.

The band finished their song to generous applause. The singer scowled, giving the impression clapping was the last thing he had wanted… or needed.

'Okay you lot. As an audience, you've been a fuckin' bunch of wankers. This is our last number, I Say Razor Blade, You Say Love...'

The announcement got a huge cheer. I wasn't sure if the crowd knew the number or just enjoyed being insulted. What would Angie have made of their lack of showbiz stage craft? How could her comeback ever have fitted into this new world? Hands turned out at her side, skipping from foot to foot wasn't going to cut it anymore. The same with her happy-clappy Apricus incense and circumpuncts. It was a long, long way from 'Little Girl's Dream' to 'I Say Razor Blade, You Say Love'.'

As they finished their set, I wondered about speaking to Uppity

Daze backstage, finding out if they had a manager, and, if not, offer my services as someone who could check out record label interest. But all that would have to wait. Thinking about Angie had reminded me what I needed to do next. It was time to leave anyway; Ducks Deluxe had taken to the stage. What seemed like another hundred people were trying to cram their way into the crowded back room. Much as I would like to hear Rick's favourite new band, I had only really come here because it was two stops away on the Piccadilly line from where Molly died of an overdose.

It was time to pay my respects.

The tube was deserted save for a few gangs of North London teenagers heading into the West End. Standing by the sliding doors, smoking what looked to be their first cigarette, gobbing their first gob, everything was a dare – we dare you to ask us to move, not swear, spit, have a ticket. They were match day hooligans without a match to go to. They would have enjoyed Uppity Daze at the Lord Nelson.

I jumped off at Caledonian Road and found my way to Molly's squat. Her road looked different by foot. It was darker; the deserted, boarded-up houses far more menacing up close, the corrugated iron panels even bleaker. In truth, the whole area was a demolition site, it was just that no one had bothered to tell the houses, though, by now, they must have had their suspicions. Since my last visit, a collection of skips were installed, dotted along the street, full of the gutted contents of these onetime homes. There was one outside Molly's place. The crew flattening the street had been busy.

Locating the loose corrugated iron panel, I made my way inside. It was easy. The windows were boarded up, but the front door was missing. I had my flickering Zippo flame to help me find my way. Wild shadows loomed and receded, the enveloping darkness making any attempts to get the geography of the house twice as difficult. For all that, I could see enough to know the whole house was rotting. There was a thick, thick smell of damp that went straight onto the chest and made you want to cover your mouth and nose. Rats had chewed through the wooden floorboards, leaving great holes that had to be avoided. Ingress, egress, as Francis O'Shea would have said, I thought to myself. Traces of both the squatters and the last rent paying occupants were evident everywhere, making for a curious mix. Green flowery wallpaper competed with a half-torn poster of Che Guevara; a Victorian wrought fireplace with empty bottles of Mateus Rosé on the mantlepiece. This was a house full of ghosts.

After a quick scan of the downstairs, I made my way upstairs, carefully navigating the mouldering staircase. Two rooms had been occupied it seemed. There were more posters on the walls, evidence of rudimentary furniture, candles in wine bottles and overflowing ashtrays. I established which one was Molly's room by the bedside table I had seen in Seabrook's photograph. Unfortunately, there was little else left. The room, like the others had mostly been stripped of belongings, either by the police, builders, or intruders.

I had seen enough. The thought of Molly, the struggling actress, falling into drugs and prostitution in this place was getting to me. If she was part of Apricus, why didn't she live at the swanky flat in Marble Arch? Was it because of her addiction? Whatever the reason, she deserved a whole lot better than a mattress on the floor of a derelict house. As I was making my way outside, it struck me I should check the skip just in case anything had been dumped there. I made my way past the corrugated iron fence and peered into the nearest skip. Amongst the mix of rubble and discarded floorboards were piles of old clothes and odd shoes. I found a long piece of wood and prodded around with one hand like a prospector. My other handheld the Zippo aloft for light. The first thing I found was the gold dress modelled first by Linda Sonne and then by Molly. It looked a whole lot less alluring buried in the dirt, sodden with rain. There were also panties and bras, make-up kits and toiletries scattered alongside photographs and paperbacks. A couple of titles caught my eye: *Clothed With The Sun* by Anna Kingsford and *1984* by George Orwell. Then I saw a Hugh Padley sci-fi novel, *The Ungulates of Venus*. Photographs were poking out of the top. I tilted my body deeper into the skip and tried to reach for the photographs. I had to use my fingertips – first and second finger –to pinch them out one at a time. I thought about those seaside arcade claw machines I'd play on holidays in Anglesey as a kid; steering the crane to where you could swoop down and try and grab a prize. This was a lot less easy, a lot less fun. The photographs were wet and slimy, making the job especially difficult. Inch by inch, I managed to rescue the nearest one. Holding it up to the lighter I could see it showed a smiling Molly standing next to a man, his face obscured by the dust and grit that had collected on the photograph. I wiped it clean down the arm of my jacket, then I took another look. It showed Molly standing next to Geoff Birch, bass player in Penny Sands' band, and one-time bass player in the Grass.

About to turn back to the skip, I felt a punch to my kidneys. It was hard but not hard enough to floor me, allowing me to stay on my feet. That was a big mistake on my attacker's part. Dropping the Zippo and photograph, I instinctively span around and connected with a shovel hook to his body, followed by a pivot jab to the face. The man collapsed like a felled tree, raising a cloud of dust from the skip overspill. I picked up the lighter and held it close to his face to see who had attacked me. Whoever it was, he had a big lump of a face and, courtesy of my jab, a freshly broken nose. Before I could ask him anything, I was under attack again, this time from a new assailant, and this time with a blow that did floor me. It was a hard kick to the ribs, followed by another to the head. The kicking was then repeated over and over. My head had become a football and Trevor Brooking was shooting on goal – or maybe it was Johnny Giles, Steve Heighway, Ian Callaghan, Charlie Cooke, Stan Bowles, Gerry Francis…

A policeman was standing over me when I came to. Somewhere off to the side, lost in my periphery, was the man whose nose I had broken, busy giving his side of the story.

'…you got to understand, since that junkie copped it, Thwaites Property have been paying me and my mate to stop squatters and vandals from coming down here. They don't want the aggravation, they don't want the publicity, not while they do their demolitions and clearances and whatnot.'

'You're nightwatchmen?' the policeman asked.

'That's what I've been saying. Nightwatchmen. Precisely. We caught this one red handed stealing wood and such from the skips.'

'Then he attacked you?

'Too bloody right. Unprovoked it was. I asked him politely what he was up to…'

'Not true,' I gasped, relieved to find I could still form words even though my eyesight was blurry.

The policeman cast a disinterested gaze my way, as if I were enquiring about yesterday's weather.

'Shut it, you,' he said pleasantly.

I tried again. This time whole sentences. 'I was attacked. It was self-defence, officer.'

The other 'nightwatchman', not the one with the broken nose, but the one with a great right foot suddenly piped up.

''Ark at that! Listen to the way he speaks, will you? He's not even from around here. He's a bloody Taff!'

'Not a criminal offence… not yet,' I suggested.

The policeman was uncertain how to proceed. 'Best thing is that I get a wagon to take him down the station then get a statement,' he said, thinking aloud.

'That's right!' the broken nose man exclaimed.

'You two will need to come along as well. Make a statement so we can charge him.'

'Now listen, we want what's fair, but we can't be leaving our posts. We'll get the sack.'

I stood up. My legs might have felt like jelly, but it was time to dig deep and take a grip here; try and find my persuasive powers.

'You can see I haven't taken anything,' I began. 'I was only looking in that skip. Curiosity isn't enough to charge me, especially if Burke and Hare here don't give a statement. You'll just get hell from the duty sergeant, officer. Besides, is it worth all that paperwork? Why don't we all just go our separate ways, each of us get on with what we have to do and make life easy for ourselves? There are real criminals out there. Of course there are. And you know I'm not one of those, accent or no accent.'

The policeman looked at the two men, gauging their response before reaching a decision.

'Fair enough,' one said.

'Alright with me,' said the other.

I reached into my pocket and found a pound note. 'You hit me. I hit you. We both got knocked around. Have a pint on me and no hard feelings.'

I passed the man with the broken nose the note. The policeman put away his notebook.

'It might be that it's as well to leave it at that,' he said.

You can always rely on the Met's finest to be lazy, I thought to myself.

'Here,' asked the man with the broken nose. 'Where'd you learn to punch like that?'

'Pontypridd, where we all speak like this,' I responded, walking away, keen to get going before the policeman changed his mind. Stopping at the skip, I bent down to pick up my Zippo lying on the road. I also pocketed the photograph of Molly and Geoff Birch. My day was starting and ending with the police. All in all, it had been a busy day but now it was time to go home. The tube would be closed by now, but it would be easy enough to grab a cab from King's Cross. One step at a time, nice and steady all the way to the taxi rank. Ignore the headache, the fuzzy vision, and the nausea. Nice. And. Steady.

INTERLUDE NO.6

July 26th, 1968: The Vesuvio Club

Her pupils were dilated to the size and shape of black olives.

I started to laugh uncontrollably.

'Your eyes!'

'Mirrors to yours!'

'What does that even mean?'

'We've travelled through the looking glass, Elis. This moment is happening. This instant is ours, and will always be ours, now. Don't you see? It's all so clear. Rockets and spaceships! We'll soon put one foot on the moon, establish life on another planet. We're all astronauts!'

I had no idea what Angie meant, but I'd never experienced such joy as in that moment. She was mine, and I was hers. Our love manifest. Perhaps she was saying what I believed, that everything in the universe had contrived to create our being together, sitting on the floor of a newly opened nightclub owned by Mick and Keith, higher than I'd ever been before on Marrakesh hash sold to me by dealer to the Rolling Stones, Tony Sanchez.

I looked around me. The guests were smiling. Beautiful, talented, dressed in vibrant colours, we were a rainbow, a tribe, a brotherhood, moving in slow motion, aside from time. We were joy. We were cwtch.

The euphoric happiness set in motion an unexpected explosion of earlier joyous memories. Out of these synaptic flashes came the recollection of seashells. It was suddenly very important I told Angie about the seashells.

'The seashells! Lying in the soil of an Anglesey campsite. As a child, from afternoon into evening I collected them in a bucket with my mother. "Each one once held a life," she told me. "Imagine! Scat-

tered across ocean floor, they were left here once the waters receded, creating this happy graveyard".'

Angie was smiling at me.

'A happy graveyard,' I repeated.

'Is there ever such a thing?' asked Angie.

'Yes. In a village called Llanfairpwllgwyngyllgogerychwyrndrob-wllllantysiliogogogoch.'

'A place that long and unpronounceable cannot possibly exist.'

'It has to exist. I went there once and collected seashells. Llan-fairpwllgwyngyll…gogerychwyrndrobwll...llantysiliogogogoch.'

'That's sounds so beautiful,' Angie responded dreamily. 'Will you teach it to me, one day?'

I noticed the room was reduced to a hush. A very famous person had entered the room. It took me a while to realise it was a Beatle holding a record under his arm.

'Hello, Paul' said Tony Sanchez, passing him a joint.

They went to the raised DJ booth. I was suddenly back at church. A sermon was to be delivered.

'It's the boys' new one,' McCartney said to the congregation.

'Hey Jude, don't make it bad...' a voice then sang from somewhere.

Twenty-Six

A throbbing head and dried blood on the pillowcase: It reminded me of waking up the day after a bout in the ring. The adrenalin would get you home, but you'd never be sure what you'd find swollen, twisted or broken the next morning. I checked my head for any signs of injury. There were no obvious cuts or wounds, meaning the blood came from the ear, meaning a likely skull fracture, if luck was really going my way. The rest of the morning was spent lying on the couch and thinking things through. The photograph of Molly with Geoff brought things even closer back to Penny. But what about Padley? Could he be involved in all this? Or was it just a coincidence that the photographs were inside one of his books?

Just off Piccadilly, the Albany was where the gentleman thief, Raffles, lived. I knew that because a real-life resident of the same Georgian apartment block – the celebrated sci-fi novelist, Hugh Padley – had once told me that little tidbit. This was back when we were recording Tony's Timepiece and Gracie was whispering his lyrics to great effect. Padley, it turns out, did his own bit of thieving when he stole Gracie from under Tony's nose and moved her into his penthouse apartment at the Albany. Thief he might have been, but Padley was no gentleman. He was the classic provincial grammar schoolboy done well. Through brains alone, he ended up at Trinity, Cambridge, following a spell of National Service in Malaya. His wealth came from a marriage to an American heiress. He was in a plane with her when it crashed in Mexico, but somehow managed to walk away without a scratch. Left with a considerable inheritance and a sense that he must have been spared for a reason, in 1965 he began writing his sci-fi novels and quickly became something of a hippies' favourite. This underground connection wasn't accidental. Like Tony, there had been a late conversion to drugs, which, again like Tony, Padley embraced wholeheartedly. The drug of choice was marijuana, and he really took a shine to it, adding his name to all manner of legalize cannabis campaigns, and appearing on television to advocate its use. Rumours were he'd moved onto opium, writing his novels in four days, puffing his way through a half ounce of the black tar to help get the words down. I could well believe it. I tried reading one of his books once. It might have worked for Coleridge, but Padley was certainly no Coleridge.

Arriving at the Albany, there was an idling taxi and a cabbie handling a set of suitcases on the front steps. Padley was nearby barking orders, clearly wanting to leave Mayfair in a hurry. My body tensed, the red mist descending. His guilt was now certain in my mind. It wasn't until I neared him, ready to stop him in his tracks with a punch, that I noticed he was paying over some notes to the driver.

He wasn't leaving after all. He'd just arrived.

'Jonesy! What a lovely surprise!'

His friendliness threw me. I never particularly liked Padley, and always felt I'd made that obvious. When did he decide we had become pals? Still trying to plan how I was going to handle asking him questions, I followed him inside the building with the cases and into the small wrought-iron lift, where we travelled up to the top floor.

Padley smiled over at me. He looked especially tired and drawn.

'Gracie went on ahead up to the apartment. Wanted to wash off the travel dirt in the shower while I sorted out the cabbie. She'll be delighted to see you again, though. Of that I'm certain.'

I said nothing. To be honest, I still wasn't sure how to navigate the situation. Padley took my silence as a reprimand. Key in lock, he paused and looked at me.

'You did hear about me and Gracie? I imagine you did. I suppose you think we behaved badly.'

'Not really, that is to say…' I muttered.

We entered the apartment; the hallway alone was the size of a tennis court. Recovering from seeing just how well Padley was doing, I returned to my original train of thought.

'…it's nothing to do with me, Hugh. But, I'll be honest. The way I see it, the upset it caused was the last thing Tony needed.'

'We had no way of knowing the news would break Tony like it did.'

'Wait. You think finding out about your affair caused his breakdown?'

'Of course, Jonesy. What else?'

'The fact he was digesting LSD all day, every day.'

'Oh! That! He'd already built up a resistance. Taking acid was like having a cup of tea to Tony.'

'No psychic death then?'

'No! Who have you been talking to? Psychic death? Tony's inner topography was unbreakable.'

The sound of rushing water from a shower intruded from a nearby room. Gracie, no doubt.

I cast a look around the apartment then back at Padley.

'Unbreakable "inner topography", eh? Shame his "inner" heart wasn't the same.'

'Yes. There you're not wrong, Jonesy. For all his talk of free love, Tony was a very conventional sort.'

'The sort who falls apart when his heart is broken. *Duw!* Who'd ever want to be conventional?'

'Don't be like that. Stick around a moment. Gracie will be joining us soon. Point of fact, we're just back from three months in Los Angeles and a celebration is in order. Hollywood has shown an interest in my Jupiter Belt trilogy. Kirk Douglas no less. He wants to play Captain Holt. I know what you're going to say: Kirk's not a good fit to play Holt.'

'I wasn't going to say that. I haven't read any of your books.'

'I see. Presumptuous of me to think you had. Sorry. Point is Kirk is all wrong. Hopeless. But when Hollywood comes calling, it's a case of take the money and run to the hills, or Mayfair in our case.'

'Do you know anything about Apricus?'

'That's something of a non sequitur.'

'It's just you were in Los Angeles; they're based in Los Angeles.'

Without my even noticing, Padley led me out onto a wide veranda circling the apartment. Mayfair was to one side, Green Park on the other. We were very high up. For a moment, part of me wondered if he was actually thinking of trying to throw me over the side.

'Wanted you to see the view, Jonesy,' he beamed.

'Very nice, too,' I affirmed. 'But getting back to Apricus?'

'They're loonies, I know that. Not thinking of joining are you?'

'Do you know any members? Linda Sonne, maybe? A girl called Molly?'

Padley rubbed his face, as if checking for stubble. He wasn't faking it. He looked exhausted.

'Don't know any of the members. I know the head guy, Abzari Afin, or to give his real name, Jonathan McCulloch. Hails from Bradford, though you'd never guess that now, hearing the way he speaks. He is, or was, a sci-fi writer. Very mediocre. Conceptually weak. Liked stories about astronauts landing on strange planets run by a master race of women, women with an insatiable sexual appetite. You know the sort of thing. Pathetic masturbatory stuff.

Not that there's anything wrong with pornography, just don't try and sell it as sci-fi. Certainly, that was my own, and many others in the community's, view of McCulloch, or, should I say, Abzari. You know what his new name means? Abzari?'

'Can't say I do.'

'It's Urdu. Means seeds or one who sows, a seedsman. Can't help thinking Johnny's still hung up on the sexual fantasy. I'm sure that's why he started his cult – thought it'd be a good way of getting laid.'

Padley put a hand on my shoulder and left it there.

'But enough of this. Where's my manners? Let's get you a drink. Or something more herbal. I've got a few jazz Woodbines somewhere.'

Ignoring his offer to follow him inside, I shook his hand off my shoulder.

'You must have been away when the news about Angie Bright-Silver broke,' I said.

'News? Why? What happened?'

'Someone murdered her.'

Processing the news, Padley looked out at the West End.

'Christ. That's tough to hear. Not that I knew her, or anything. Not personally. But as a pop star…'

'She was strangled, Hugh. They found the body at Ryemuse.'

'What the hell was she doing in that pigsty?'

'Recording a demo. That's the "what". As to the "why"? That's all a bit unexplained, right now.'

Hugh stiffened, a sudden thought coming to him.

'What about that engineer we used for Tony's Timepiece? Billy Coles? Does he still work there?'

'Did. Why'd you ask?'

'I wouldn't be surprised if was him. Gracie told me he touched her bum back when you were producing her demo there.'

‘Touched her bum? You mean he groped her?’

‘Something like that. And he was a thief. He asked Gracie if he could borrow the master recording of the Tony’s Timepiece demo to play to someone. She lent it to him. He still hasn’t returned it. I wouldn’t be surprised if he sold it.’

‘Doubtful. That tape was commercial poison.’

‘Harsh assessment, Jonesy! Very harsh. Anyway, we’re getting away from the point. Billy Coles was a pervert. He was handsy. You know the way some men can be. Lewd.’

‘You’re saying Billy Coles tried it on with Gracie, behind Tony’s back?’

‘That’s precisely what I’m saying.’

‘And that makes him a murderer suspect? Come on! I mean, after all, you also tried it on with Gracie behind Tony’s back. Does that make you a murder suspect?’

‘No, because I wouldn’t demean what happened between me and Gracie to the level of “trying it on”. And even if you insist on characterising my actions as “trying it on”, there is a crucial difference.’

‘And what’s that?’

‘I was successful.’

A few hours later, I was back in my flat. I hadn’t bothered waiting for Gracie to come out of the shower. I hadn’t even taken up Padley’s offer of a drink, or a ‘jazz Woodbine’. I wanted to lie down on my couch and think everything through.

It would take me a while to forget that view from the top of the Albany. If a view can ever be smug, there was a clear example. And meanwhile, Hugh Padley just kept getting the rub of the green. A huge inheritance, a penthouse apartment, bestselling novels, now a film and a literary muse who looked good on his arm, until the inevitable moment came when he would tire of her and seek inspiration elsewhere. Maybe that was being harsh on Padley. Maybe I only felt that way because I still felt sorry for Tony and I wanted a villain. Who knows? I was beyond caring for now. Hugh and Gracie were a false lead. I had only my instincts to go on to make this assertion. But what else was I going to do? Beat the truth out of them to make sure?

Spread out, boots off, lying on the couch, I wanted to work through what I did know: It was about connections. With Padley off the suspects' list, my Happy Families game now went like this: Geoff knew Molly, who knew Linda, who knew Billy, and Angie. Billy knew Angie, Penny, and Linda, who knew Molly, who knew Geoff. Billy disappeared with one tape which he tried to sell, and if Hugh Padley was to be believed, did the same with another tape… I had to stop.

My brain was hurting. This was no puzzle for someone with a possible skull fracture. I rang Claire instead.

'What are you doing tonight?' I asked her.

'I have plans.'

'Nothing to write home about plans? Or something a bit more serious?'

There was a pause.

'Why do you ask?'

'Because I got hit on the head last night. It might be nothing, but I need someone here to ring the ambulance if I pass out. You're the first, the only person I've tried. You should be flattered.'

There was a peal of pretty laughter.

'That has to be the worst excuse you've ever come up with. We might not be seeing each other anymore, but if you want to fuck, just come out and say it.'

As it turns out, Claire did watch over me. I didn't pass out, but we did fuck. A lot. Catching up on lost time, I guess. Not bad for a man with a head injury.

Twenty-Seven

Sundays in West London always made me edgy. The streets were too quiet. Danny's description of the Grapes Tavern said it all: 'not enough buzz'. That summed up Teen Avenue's Sabbath. Something felt different though that Sunday as Claire and I took a walk through a sunny, empty Mayfair. Arm in arm, our intimacy fresh, Teen Avenue felt good – no buzz, but still good, nevertheless. All the same, I knew by taking this romantic stroll, by getting together with her the night before, I was prompting "the moment'. The conversation would bounce and skip like a pebble across a pond but eventually it would land and there would be ripples coming back to shore. "The moment" would require us to talk about our emotions, our feelings, our future. That was something we had always been so bad at doing in the past, both of us mumbling and fudging our way to incomplete answers and unsatisfactory conclusions. That's why Claire so surprised me when she began talking the way she did.

'I'll be twenty-seven in a few weeks' time, Elis. Not that I feel old. But a birthday makes you think about things, makes you think about the direction your life is taking. You can understand that? Thing is, I'm starting to feel out of place working for an industry that is so concerned about selling a product to the young. It feels like a long time ago since I was a teenager.'

'You think I don't?'

'It's different for men. No one judges.'

'Who's judging?'

Claire nestled against me.

'Elis, I lied to you the other day. There is someone else. An old flame. You don't know him. We were students together at Cambridge. Over the summer, we met up again. Now he's asked me to marry him.'

'Is he okay?'

'Okay?'

'I mean. Is he a good man? Trustworthy?'

'He's asked me to marry him, not lend him a fiver.'

'Point taken.'

But what was the point? Was I supposed to drop to one knee and propose to her instead?

'The thing is, Elis. You and I are sort of even now. There's someone else in my life. Just like there's someone else in yours.'

'Claire, if this is about Penny Sands…'

'I'm not talking about Penny. You know who I'm talking about, Elis. There's a quote I always liked. It makes me think of you. "We love only once and on how that great love affair shapes itself determines the pattern of our lives". I suppose my question is just how much Angie's death changes things for you… changes the pattern of your life… and your ability to ever love another.'

I stopped in my tracks and turned to Claire. Her words had been as powerful as the blow to my head a few days earlier and I was reeling.

'What's his name?' It was all I could think to ask.

'The person the quote came from?'

'No, the guy who proposed to you.'

'Marcus.'

'I think… I think… you should say yes to Marcus.'

'That's what I thought you'd say.'

She wanted to leave there and then. I pleaded with her to stay.

'I haven't finished making my point, Claire. Don't go off tamping!'

'Tamping? What the hell does that mean?'

'It means going off in a strop, with a cob on.'

'At least allow me my moment of walking away, Elis? Grant me the whole woman proud and defiant, uncertain of her future, but certain of her decision as she walks towards a new horizon…'

'Is that something you want?' I asked.

'It is, Elis. It's exactly how I want this scene to end.'

'That's the point, isn't it? We're not actors in a film, or on stage. We're two people with bucket loads of steaming crap that we have to carry around with us like everyone else on this planet: The stuff that happened to us, the stuff that is happening to us right now. I changed my life around when I decided to move to Mayfair, three years ago. It hit me the way it's hitting you now. If you think it's time to make changes, it's time you made changes. You won't get any argument from me on why you should respect those feelings. Working in the music business? Yes, Claire. Without doubt, you are too smart to be doing that. As for your age? There's plenty of people running Teen Avenue who haven't been teens for a lot longer than you. And if it's marriage you want, then go get married. Right now, I'm not your man for that. But that doesn't mean I don't care for you or have feelings.'

I was surprising myself. This was the most heartfelt I'd ever been in front of Claire, in front of anyone. And I was still not done.

'Claire, I don't know about you, but I feel better at dealing with all the bollocks life throws up when I'm with you, than when I'm not. Marry Marcus if that's also part of the changes you need. But know this: I'd be happier if you didn't.'

A silence fell between us.

Then she asked: 'You still got that bottle of hock I bought you for Christmas?'

Nodding, I answered: 'Of course. I told you at the time...'

'...German wine tastes like hamster piss!'

'That's right.'

'It's just perhaps we should toast your newfound loquacity,' she smirked.

'Like I said, you are way too smart to be working in the music business, Claire.'

They were standing outside 9 Curzon Place, pressing my button on the door intercom when we appeared, having strolled back from our walk. Expensively dressed, made up like a model, Gracie was unrecognisable. If she hadn't been with Hugh Padley, I would never have made the connection. She looked like a successful Hollywood actress, not a former acid-dropping hippy with a fondness for stripping. Padley must have brought out these dramatic changes in her. I suppose the prospect of hanging out with Kirk Douglas in LA had required a rethink.

'Jonesy?' Padley greeted me, as we appeared. 'Just seen Keith Moon coming out of here. Did you know he lived in your building?'

Invited in, more by Claire than myself, Hugh and Gracie sat on the repaired couch in my flat. I performed the host's duties and poured each of us a glass of wine. For a moment I worried my head injury had been a lot more serious. Did I actually invite them over the day before? Then I remembered Padley showing me the smug view of London from his apartment terrace, my walking out. It made them being here now seem even stranger.

Gracie took a dainty sip of wine before getting to what was on her mind. Padley offered her an encouraging rub of her back at the same time, making me think they had rehearsed this moment.

'Hugh didn't know about all this. Not until yesterday. Thing is, I've been keeping in touch with the hospital since Tony was sectioned. Whenever I get the chance, I pop down there to see him. Sometimes he's too zonked to even know I'm sitting there. Sometimes he shouts at me. More often, he just sits there, listening to me talk. That's the worst of all, in a way. At least when he's screaming and bawling you know someone is in there. It takes a lot out of me, those visits. Even so, it feels important to me that I go. I need to know he's alright. I know how it must have looked to you, Jonesy. It would be easy to judge how things happened. Hugh and I getting together. It must all seem a bit underhand. Trouble is love is love. You can't help who you fall for, can you?'

She cast a look over at Claire, then back at me; taking our apparent domestic situation as confirmation of her proposition. I found myself thinking about Hein Van Clojt's, 'Lovely Love Is Lovely', for some reason.

'I was sorry to have missed you, yesterday,' Gracie continued. 'I'm not sure if Hugh mentioned, but I was in the shower. I'm not used to this flying lark. Makes me feel stale and dried out. Truth be told, until a year ago I'd only ever had baths, never showers. It still feels luxurious. I feel very fortunate.'

She looked at Hugh to see if he understood the point she was making. His indulgent smile surprised me. It seemed like kindness itself.

'The point is: We were only just back. We hadn't had chance to check our mail. When we did there was a letter from the hospital. Tony's doctor had been concerned about some unpleasant visitors the week before. He wanted to know if I knew anything about it.'

'Which you didn't?' I asked. 'Either of you?'

'Not a thing. As far as I knew I was his only ever visitor, other than you, and that was when Tony first went in.'

'Did the doctor say how these mystery visitors had upset Tony?'

'Not in the letter. But I rang the hospital later and spoke to a nurse. A man and a woman came to see Tony last week. They searched his room, and asked him lots of questions, she said. It unsettled Tony and he tried to commit suicide. That really upset me. I'm not sure exactly why I wanted to tell you all this. I suppose I still think of you managing the band, managing Tony. I just thought you should know. When I told Hugh about what the hospital had said, he agreed. He mentioned what you two talked about when you visited. About Billy Coles? I don't want to stir trouble and he might not even be connected to all this. All the same, maybe you could find out what is going on. Please.'

Without her hippy idioms and hallucinogenic drawl, Gracie was a straightforward, polite South London girl. I was warming to her in a way I never had before. Besides, the mention of a man and a woman visiting someone Billy Coles knew was piquing my curiosity.

'I'm glad you came to me, Gracie. I think I should go down to the hospital later today and find out what it's all about.'

'That would be kind. There's been a lot of water under the bridge and all that other cobblers. Tony's Timepiece seems like a long time ago. Me and Tony getting together seems a long time ago. I suppose I just want to feel Tony is safe and getting the best care he can. I suppose I want you to help to see that he does. We all owe him that.'

Hugh waited for her words to settle before he turned to me.

'If you're going today, maybe I can help. I have a car. I could drive down with you, if you like. Keep you company.'

Twenty-Eight

He drove a Triumph Stag and wore leather driving gloves. It struck me as the perfect look for Hugh Padley – the sporty gent about town. Those few years he had on me showed. Unlike Tony Carter, Padley had always stayed loyal to the decade in which he reached adulthood, and served in the army. He embraced the sixties, appreciated the new decade, yet I always suspected there was a big part of Padley that missed the grey, rationed fifties, the chilly wind across the parade ground, Cowdrey scores a century at Edgbaston. That whole time. That whole crappy era. Both of us lived in Mayfair, both of us bearded with long shaggy black hair – anyone watching us zoom past in the car might have taken us for brothers – nevertheless Padley, deep down, was a conventional man. It struck me his insane marijuana use was an attempt to offset that nature. The very proper Padley was trying to drug away his upbringing.

'Louis Armstrong reckoned this stuff allows you to see around corners,' he said, lighting an enormous spliff on the drive through Chelsea towards the river. High, smiling, he managed to maintain a steady fifty miles an hour, swerving and overtaking the afternoon traffic, with little regard for the Highway Code. Traffic lights were the only thing to slow us down… when he chose to obey them.

'Satchmo was right!' he declared outside Croydon.

'Didn't I hear somewhere opium was your thing these days?'

It was an unnecessarily mean dig at Padley, given he was providing me with a lift. However, he seemed to take it all in good humour.

'Opium? No, not at all. That rumour all started after I did an interview with a German newspaper. Something got lost in the translation. I think it was because I was twittering on about an ancient settlement called Kortik-Tepe in Southern Turkey. They found poppy seeds there dating back eleven thousand years before Christ was born. I was probably just saying humans have enjoyed getting high for an awfully long time.'

Against my better judgement, I took a few tokes of the joint he offered me. It was so strong it might as well have been opium. Pretty soon I was feeling what Padley was feeling, his way of manoeuvring through the traffic suddenly making sense. In this manner, it took us no time to reach Downview Hospital in Banstead. Padley raced up the narrow road to the main building, before parking the car, and turning to me.

'I'm not sure the old noodle is up to this,' he declared. 'I haven't seen Tony since it all went a bit wrong for him. And all went a bit right for me.'

Leaning back in his seat, he rubbed his bloodshot eyes.

'You might have to go in and fly solo,' he muttered, 'I'm off my tits.'

Casting a look up at the high, Hammer Horror tower that dominated the hospital, I started to feel the same way. If ever there was a place to set off a drug induced paranoia it was here.

'You should stay in the car,' I advised. 'Seeing me might be enough of a shock for Tony. He doesn't need to see you as well.'

'I suppose I imagined it might have been an opportunity to apologise to the man.'

What had Claire called it? Mea Culpa? It surprised me hearing it coming from Padley. I lit a cigarette and tried to find the centre to things once more. I was here because Gracie had appealed to a better nature I had told Dave Cash I didn't possess. I was here because I was Tony's Timepiece's former manager, and the group's founder, Tony Carter, needed someone checking in on him. Those two things were true. There was also another reason. Gracie mentioning the two visitors searching for 'something' had got my curiosity going. Not even Padley's extra strong grass could dull that. It had struck me earlier, sitting on my torn and shredded sofa, that there had been a lot of searching for 'something' recently. Two ransacked flats were evidence of that. So the obvious question arose. Could this all be related?

'I'm going to go inside and try and have a chat with Tony,' I told Hugh. 'If I don't come out, try and find me. Just in case I've been sectioned.'

A hospital providing therapy. That's the gist of what the sign said at the entrance. The therapy began when you walked through the door, whether intentional or not. It was a sort of childhood regression therapy. Associative memory, or something like that – at least, it was for me. All the corridors – and it seemed every other surface – were painted the same pale blue-grey as the underwings of a Spitfire. Fighter planes: That was my thing, when I was a kid. Painting little model kits and hanging them in my room on cotton threads, the underwings were the hardest thing to get right. All the illustrations in the *Eagle* comic book were from above. An aerial display of Spitfires and Hurricanes in Anglesey finally revealed to me what the colour should be. It was blindingly obvious really. The point was not to be seen. Hide in the sky and disappear. Blue/grey. That made sense for a fighter plane. But what was the thinking in a mental hospital? Then again, 'hide in the sky and disappear' seemed a good description of the inmates I encountered. They all moved around the corridors with the same purpose as clouds. Vague, unfathomable, they looked everywhere but at each other. Since I wasn't wearing the patients' starch white trousers and jacket uniform it was easy for these clouds to spot me as an outsider, a visitor. Through stolen, furtive glances I was immediately established as someone beyond the institution, someone from the world they had been deliberately removed from, whether by choice or by force. Their curiosity seemed to be more concerned with who I was visiting, not who I might be back in a reality that existed beyond Downview Hospital.

'Are you here to see George? I know you are. Have you tried to find the rope? I've already explained to him. No rope in the world exists that can produce the Indian rope trick to the specifications George describes, so tell him, and give us all a break. You are seeing George, today? Tell me!'

The "cloud" talking to me was addressing a space about a foot above my head, some sort of imagined floating third eye. Her hair was cut very short, pixie style. In other circumstances, given her relative youth, she might draw comparisons to Jean Seberg. In a place like this, fashion sense – or style of any sort – seemed a grotesque, cruel criteria to apply to the people you met. Jean Seberg's double was a perfect example. Her hair was short for one reason: To assist the electric shock treatments she received. And there must have been plenty. Her eyes had fused and were incapable of switching focus. Everything was middle distance.

An orderly was taking me to Tony. This guide moved me on past Jean Seberg by placing a gentle hand on my shoulder, advancing me like I'd already seen him do with the clouds drifting about the place. Gravity didn't seem to operate. Everyone could float. The orderlies were merely here to stop us bumping into each other.

'Don't worry about Heather,' my guide advised me.

He was dressed in a puke green uniform. Bald, heavily built, he could have been one of Terry Sporne's heavies, if not for his gentleness. Should Hare Krishna ever decide to go into the protection business, this guy would fit right in.

'How long has she been in here?' I asked him politely.

'Who?'

'The woman talking about the rope. Heather.'

'She's been in here ten or so years. Before I came here, anyway. I think it was a lost baby that tipped her over the edge, maybe something of that order. Hard not to feel sorry, isn't it?'

Especially when she was led away once a week like a little lamb to be zapped with 120 volts, I thought to myself.

'I think I remember you from last time,' said the orderly. 'He doesn't get many visitors, so we tend to remember.'

'It would be helpful if you could tell me who else has been visiting.'

'Helpful to whom?'

I looked at him, trying to read his expression. Perhaps he was suggesting money needed to pass hands before we could get to what I really wanted to know. I cooked up some bullshit.

'I used to manage the band Tony was in. If people other than his family – like disgruntled bandmates – are pestering him, I need to know. It's part of my responsibilities.'

'Are his bandmates disgruntled?'

'I don't know. But they might be. I hear there was a scene last week.'

'Yes! I heard that too! What was that to do with?'

'It's probably to do with song copyrights, royalty residuals. They're probably trying to screw him out of money. That's why I need to know who came to see him. Do you get my drift?'

'Of course, I do. Nobody should take advantage of a person when they're broken, don't you agree?'

I was about to answer when a doctor hurried over.

'Sorry, I was delayed, Mr Jones. Reception said you'd already set off.'

He turned to the orderly.

'Thank you, Ralph. I'll take it from here.'

Ralph nodded and made his way back the way he came, gently moving away the clouds in the corridor blocking his passage.

'Did he ask you for drugs?' The doctor asked.

'Who?'

'Ralph! It's like a prison in here. Even though everyone is on some sort of drug, drugs are still the currency. They take stuff to counteract whatever we give them. Uppers, if we give them downers. Downers, if we give them uppers.'

'You could just give them the drug they wanted.'

The doctor laughed, taking my comment to be a joke, before continuing. 'We do our best to stop it, but everyone has their own favourite chemically perceived reality, and that is going to win out every time. Ralph and the others help facilitate that. It's very disappointing.'

'If he's selling drugs to the patients, you should sack him. Why don't you sack him?'

'Because he's a patient here as well. All the orderly nurses are. Sorry. I thought you would have known from last time you visited.'

'That detail must have escaped my attention.'

'No matter. Tony is in the day room. I suggest no more than ten minutes with him, but it is only a suggestion.'

'How is he doing?'

'We like to do a thing here which is to ask: 'what is he not doing anymore?'.'

'Okay. Doctor. What is Tony not doing anymore?'

'The things he did last week: Screaming. Attacking the staff. Attempting self-defenestration.'

'Self… what?'

'He tried to throw himself out of a window. Did it a lot before.

Did it again last week. This week, no. Like I said, it's all about what he's not doing.'

We approached a bright room at the end of the corridor, full of late afternoon sunshine.

'Doctor, I was trying to explain to Ralph. The other people visiting him, it would be helpful to know. As his manager there are legal reasons and…'

'Fine. Everyone signs in, just like you did earlier. Collect a list from me on the way out. Now, remember, no more than ten minutes, ideally.'

Tony was sitting in a wicker chair looking out at the garden. He was napping in a shaft of bright sunlight. It looked almost as if he was taking a luminescent shower.

'Tony?' I asked, entering the room. 'Any chance we could have a natter?'

I felt stupid, phrasing it like that. Something of Ralph, the orderly's gentleness, had rubbed off on me.

Tony opened his damaged, rolling eyes.

'It's really a question of crotchet triplets or sixteenth notes. Missing out notes in a triplet pattern gives you jazz. Missing out notes in eighth notes gives you soul music. Listen.'

He started tapping his feet and clapping his hands. It sounded like he was building a shed. There was no rhythm to discern whatsoever. I lay a hand on his, to stop the arhythmic beating.

'I'm glad you're thinking of music again, Tony. I would like to hear you play your drums later. First, I'd like to have a chat. It's Jonesy here. Elis. Taffy. You remember me? Right?'

'I remember playing with Tubby Hayes. I remember playing with Joe Harriot. Then, I don't remember so good. What do you play? By your voice I'd say double bass.'

'I'm not a jazz musician, Tony. I used to manage your band, Tony's Timepiece. We recorded a demo.'

'A demo? Not quite an album, is it?'

'No, not quite an album. We went to a studio called Ryemuse to record three tracks. Three long tracks, mind. One was called 'Augean Master'.'

There was a silence as Tony moved his head from side to side, as if trying to land the right marble in the right hole.

Suddenly he started drumming on his thighs and singing again. His strained voice reminded me of the lead singer in Uppity Daze, though the strangled vowels did allow some familiar lyrics to emerge.

'Through the power of a demiurge, we cleanse the path to luminosity, our votive offerings a gift to the Augean master governing us all.'

'You remember the song! 'Augean Master'!'

'Of course I do. I wrote it. I mean, I wrote the music. The guy fucking my bird wrote the lyrics. Hugh Pain-In-The-Arse. What you reckon to that? I brought him into the fold, so to speak. Cuckoo in the nest. Gracie warned me he was trouble. But he had all the words and I wanted words. Hugh Padley had all the words, alright. Charmed his way into Gracie's knickers, while he was at it. My back wasn't even turned. I was blind to it, even though I was watching all the while. And I'm not speaking in metaphors like that slippery, two-faced bastard.'

The drumming was getting dangerously manic.

'Can I hear some more lyrics, Tony. Maybe without the drumming?'

Tony paused his tapping and intoned tunelessly.

'Foreshortened orbits, a space craft in a solar current, Venus calls all before her, resplendent is the orphic, mighty is our liege.'

I was no longer sure if he was singing a real song lyric. It sounded like something Gracie would have sung, but it also sounded nonsensical, even for sci-fi's master of the nonsensical,

Hugh Padley. Tony rolled his head, trying to place those marbles again. It was no longer working.

'I don't remember the rest. They're not the easiest lyrics to remember. Not like, "she loves you, yeah, yeah, yeah"! Still, I hear it's going to be a big hit.'

'"She Loves You"?'

'No. 'Augean Master.''

'Who told you that?'

'The record label. When they took the tape away. Not sure I'm ready to have a big hit. Not unless *Top of The Pops* would come and film me here. Do you think they would? There's also the question of getting the band together. Rehearsing? That might be difficult on account of my mental state. I tried telling them all that, but they pushed and pushed and so I gave in. Tell Billy I didn't want to hand it over. Tell him I didn't have any choice. Record labels run the world.'

'What record label could it have been?' Padley asked.

We were heading back to London at a more sensible speed. Padley had slowed the car right down to hear my reply.

'A label that doesn't exist!' I explained, exasperated. 'Look, Hugh. The story goes like this. Two people…'

I read the names I'd written down and copied from the hospital signing-in book.

'…Johnny Holt and Frodra Brecht…'

Hugh Padley nearly swerved the car. 'Hey! They're characters from my book!'

'*The Ungulates of Venus*, by any chance?'

'Yes, but I didn't think you'd read my books.'

'I haven't, but Linda Sonne has. I found a copy in a skip outside her squat.'

'A skip? Outside a squat?'

'Don't take it personally, Hugh. I'm sure she loved the book. Enough to remember two of the characters' names.'

Padley was pleased with that insight. I continued laying out what I had uncovered.

'Linda Sonne and a man, I'm guessing Geoff – they said he was tall and thin – claimed to be from a Mayfair record label when they spoke to Tony. They said the three tracks on the Timepiece demo were now going to be released as part of an exciting new album. They gave him the full Teen Avenue bullshit, by the sounds of it. They told him the album had hit written all over it, and the money was going to roll in, enough to get him out of hospital. The trouble was, so they said, the engineer on the original session, Billy Coles, was trying to stop it being released. These record company executives wondered if Tony knew where the tape was? Had Billy been to see him? And if he had, did he leave anything with him to look after? Tony became upset. He's not just been treated in that hospital; he's hiding from a world that terrifies him. Last thing he wants is a hit. He lied to them, pretended not to have the tape. Seems they did a little searching of his room just to make sure and found it in no time – a quarter inch reel of Tony's Timepiece that now had Angie Bright-Silver's voice all over it.'

Padley was straining to keep up. 'Not Gracie?'

'No, Angie Bright-Silver. I think Billy redid those original Timepiece tracks, cut them down and made up some backing tracks for Angie. Each of the original pieces were at least twenty minutes long, with lots of different sections. Billy could have trimmed them to form basic rhythm tracks that Phil and Geoff could work up as the basis of songs. Angie would then have come in and sung the top line. Only no "Whispering Wendy", no "Acid Gilberto". The vocalist singing on these new tracks would have been Angie Bright-Silver.'

'It sort of makes me want to hear it.'

'Hugh, these are the people who killed Angie!'

'Yes, I was forgetting.'

'The plan went wrong when Billy Coles ran off with the tape, so they tried everything. They tried searching his flat, my flat, and then worked their way backwards through Billy's old contacts, ending with Tony.'

'Why didn't they try my place?'

'I think they were planning to do just that, but then someone remembered the attic room at Ryemuse. They went over there, knives out, found Billy, then tortured him till he told them where the tapes were.'

'Hidden with Tony!'

I referred to the piece of paper I used to record details from the hospital signing in book.

'Two days before Johnny Holt and Frodra Brecht visited Tony, there was another visitor. Someone by the name of William Coleman. I think we can assume that was Billy. I like to think that he wasn't just hiding the tape by going to Tony, but also trying to tidy up the terrible mistake he had made. Newly recruited to Apricus, and keen to make an impression, he agrees to help with the crazy plan to record Angie. Problem is there's no money, no budget. Billy has a brainwave: Use an existing backing track. He goes to Gracie, asks to borrow the old Timepiece demo and gets to work. Then, when he sees sense, when Angie is killed, he returns the tape to Tony, the rightful owner in Billy's confused, upset mind.'

'And where is Billy now?' Padley wondered.

'Sliced up on a morgue slab.'

Padley stared at me. It was time to give him the last part of the sorry saga.

'Once Billy coughed up the information, they tortured him some more I imagine – just for fun – until bored, they finally put him out of his misery and killed him.'

'Billy Coles is dead?'

'I should have told you that part before. Sorry, Hugh.'

Hugh Padley looked genuinely shaken by the news. He started crying. We drove in silence for a while, before he turned to me.

'Hearing about people dying before their time triggers something in me, Jonesy. Takes me back to Chloë.'

'Chloë?'

'My first wife. She died in a plane crash. Terrible business. Absolutely bloody awful. Did you not know?'

I did know. It was more a case of not ever having allowed Padley the understandable grief he must have felt when his wife was killed. Just because you don't like someone doesn't mean they don't feel, I reminded myself. Was I guilty of making that same mistake with Terry Sporne?

We got back to Mayfair around seven in the evening. Padley dropped me off in front of my flat. I was pretty sure Claire had headed back to her place. I was looking forward to resting up and crashing out. Out of the car, almost at the front door of the building, Padley called me back.

'Jonesy! You don't think anyone will be pestering Tony again, do you?'

I thought back to Tony sitting in the day room. He might have not felt any emotions after my visit. He might have gone back to bathing his face in the sunlight with thoughts of triplets and eighth notes consoling him. He might. Seeing him earlier had shaken me, though.

'No one will pester Tony again. Not anymore. Tell Gracie: Tony will be looked after.'

'Elis, the thing I said about Billy Coles being a murderer, yesterday. I feel a bit bad about it now. Speaking ill of the dead isn't my usual style.'

'No, you're alright, Hugh. I should have told you when I was in your flat. That was bad of me. I was taking Tony's side of things, bearing you and Gracie a grudge. That was stupid and wrong of me. Hey! Ever heard of a song called Lovely Love Is Lovely?'

'Can't say that I have. Is it important?'

'Not really. It's just the reason I shouldn't have had that grudge. I tell you something else, it's the reason I make a mess of things time and time again.'

INTERLUDE NO.7

February 13th, 1969: Post Office Tower

The restaurant was revolving; a full circle taking in the London skyline every twenty-two minutes. Apple were launching Mary Hopkin's new album, Postcard. *It was the must go to party of the winter, everyone was there. Not me though, at least not for much longer. I had made my appearance, now it was time to go.*

Dressed in white, her hair and makeup different, Angie caught up with me just as I was leaving.

'No hello, no goodbye?'

'It's been… a tough day,' I explained.

'Terry wants you to talk to Mickie Most, find out if he might have a good song for me,' she said.

'Why doesn't Terry ask him?'

'They fell out.'

'Then why don't you ask him?'

'What if he said "no"? I don't know if I could bear it right now, Elis. My latest, 'Silk Purse Polka', didn't set the world on fire, did it? I need your help.'

I stared at Angie, wanting nothing more than to take her in my arms. Better still, grab her by her hand and lead her away from this… revolving hollowness. But where would we go? Where could we ever go?

'I'll ask Mickie,' I finally said, 'but you deserve better than Lulu's cast offs. A lot better.'

It came out wrong. I was too sharp with her, too angry.

She said: 'Tell me what's going on with you tonight.'

'Angie…'

'Please. Just tell me what's going on.'

I hesitated. Then:

'...a friend of mine, Phil Fratton, nearly died of a heroin overdose today.'

'What did you... did you take him to hospital?'

'No. A private clinic I know about in Raynes Park, one that doesn't report junkies.'

'Will they cure his addiction?'

'No. They just stop him dying. I'm picking him up tomorrow and taking him back to his flat. I'll look after him while he goes cold turkey.'

'Where is his flat?

'Somewhere in Mayfair.'

'Mayfair?'

She spoke the word as if it would cast spells. I noticed her eyes were moist with tears.

'Elis...?'

'Yes?'

'He's lucky to have you as a friend... we both are.'

Twenty-Nine

Baum & Associates were in Chesterfield Hill, just before the turn into May's Hill Mews. The place names were misleading. There wasn't much of a hill and there wasn't much of a mews. As for the name of the law firm itself, that too was inaccurate. Harry preferred to run the place as a one-man operation. There hadn't been any associates there for over twenty years. As if intentionally matching these discrepancies, there was a striking oddness about the interior of Baum & Associates. Given Harry's age and his crumpled suit, soup-stained tie look, it would be easy to imagine his office to be an old-worldly, tumbled down, dusty museum. Not so. It was contemporary, light and airy – the sort of place you'd expect to see Jean-Luc Godard sipping on an espresso. Everything was white, from the carpets to the walls, to the Italian leather sofas the length of a test match cricket crease. Bold abstract art (courtesy of Michael Herlighey's gallery) assaulted the eyes. All this style was down to a case Harry handled a few years back when he had represented a French interior designer on a fraud charge and won. Harry waived his fee for an office makeover, and the designer went at it with a vengeance.

Although there was just Harry and two secretaries, the law firm occupied the whole ground floor. Harry's own office was at the front looking out on the road. As I approached, I could see him at the window, the white venetian blind raised. It had taken twenty minutes for me to arrive at his office from the phone call to my flat first thing that morning. Harry looked like he'd been standing there waiting for me the whole twenty minutes.

'It's getting messy, Jonesy,' Harry began, as we sat on his Italian sofa. I leant back into the leather folds. It was like falling into a soft snow drift. Harry remained perched on the edge, denying himself any comfort. He wanted to remain focused.

'Two murders,' he continued, 'the Met want their collar.'

'So do I.'

'Yes, but you want the real murderer.'

'What do you mean?' I asked.

'Elisud, do you trust me?'

'Sure I do, Harry.'

'I mean if there was any other way, I would suggest it. But I don't think there is.'

'What way are we talking about then?'

'I want you to make yourself comfortable. I'll leave it a few hours until the next shift takes over and then I'll make the phone call.'

'To?'

'The police. What did you think I was talking about?'

Now I sat up, joining him on the edge of the sofa, matching his focus.

'You can't run away from this,' he continued, 'that'd be stupid. And if you stay in Mayfair, they'll track you down. Better you hand yourself in and when you do, I'll be here to make sure the arrest goes smoothly.'

'You're kidding me, Harry.'

'About the arrest, or about it going smoothly?'

'Let's start with the arrest.'

'What do you want me to say, Jonesy? The Met are desperate. They know you're not their man, they know they haven't got a case, but charging you gets all the heat off them for a while. You'll be acquitted, there's no doubt about that. But it might take a while.

You will be on remand.'

'I go to prison?'

'You do.'

'Those bloody bastards Seabrook and Simpkins!'

'It's not them, Jonesy. It is coming from higher up. Much higher up. The very top. Seabrook and Simkins are against arresting you, point of fact.'

'But they're happy to go ahead and still do it?'

'You think they're ready to disobey a direct order for you?' Harry chortled.

'Where are you hearing this?'

'The same source who told me all the details on Billy Coles. She's reliable.'

'She? The Met's mole? A "she", Harry? You have your own Mata Hari?'

'This facetiousness will be the undoing of you, Jonesy. "She" is my cousin Perry's daughter, and I trust whatever "she" tells me completely. The arrest warrant has been already issued. All I can say is that you should be thanking the IRA. It's down to them that you haven't already been picked up. Manpower: a lot of police resources have been switched in the last few weeks. Chances are they'll put uniform onto arresting you, and you know what that means. Those goons like hurting people.'

'If they catch me.'

'When they catch you.'

'Sounds like I've still got time to duck and dive.'

'Hours. At best. But it's what I said before. Habeas Corpus has gone out of the window. Uniform officers are even using plain vans now Jonesy. I wouldn't like to see you picked up off the street and thrown in the back of one of those. Do me this favour and do it my way. There would be an anonymous tip off to Seabrook and Simpkins…'

'From Mata Hari…'

'…telling the police you were here. They'll arrive and things will be done orderly, legally. You wouldn't have to confess to anything. What do you reckon? I'm too fond of you to see you duffed up or worse.'

I looked through the window out onto the road. Everything Harry was saying made sense. I just couldn't find it in myself to go along with his suggestion. Not when I was so close to finding Angie's killer.

'I appreciate you thinking of me, Harry. I can see the wisdom of your course of action.'

'Good.'

'But I think I'll have to decline.'

'Jonesy! This is crazy.'

'Harry, I'm looking for the killer of Angie and Billy Coles. That's two people I happened to care about. It's not just any job I've been hired to do. This isn't minding film stars or keeping musicians in order on a provincial tour. This isn't paying a disc jockey a ton to play the latest single from a record label. This isn't even a job. It's too personal to call it that.'

'You're just going to walk out of my office? After everything I've said to you?'

'I am. So, *wela I chi wedyn*, as we used to say in chapel.'

'Where will you go?'

'Not sure but I've got to catch a boat this evening.'

Harry put his head in his hands.

'A boat?'

'Yes, Harry, a boat.'

Thirty

Me and all the other liggers – the journalists, record label suits, friends, and musicians – stood in a huddle on the darkening quay alongside Westminster Bridge at the agreed time. Chas Parker's quip about the lifejacket now made sense. Island Records had hired a boat to go up and down the Thames for Penny's album launch. The mood was one of eager anticipation, like a school field trip or a stag do. Sharing this excitement, the Island Records' team, including Chas, were dressed as pirates, while the waitresses serving canapes were dressed as mermaids. Unprompted, Leo Sayer produced a ukulele from somewhere and began singing and playing "On a Slow Boat To China". Not everyone though was feeling the party spirit. Radio One DJ John Peel sidled over to me.

'Jonesy, if I gave you a fiver, would you smash that fucking ukulele over his head?' he enquired mildly.

Penny was nowhere to be seen on the quayside, a fact that was worrying many of the music journalists. Very much taking on the role of holiday camp entertainer, Chas Parker explained that she was waiting on the boat. Anyone wanting interviews should put their name on the list, he suggested. I went over to Chas and asked for an interview slot.

'Which paper are you writing for?' he asked me warily.

'I'm freelance.'

'Come on, Jonesy. Be cool. You're no more a freelance journalist than I'm a pirate. Is this all about what happened to you two on her tour? Not that it's any of my business, but seriously, tonight is not the night to be raking over the coals. There's a lot of pressure on Penny. Enjoy yourself, get smashed courtesy of Chris Blackwell and Island Records, but keep your distance, eh?'

A tinny whistle sounded as the boat, a sizeable river cruiser, approached. A marquee and bar were set up on the forward deck. Loud folk music – Penny's new album presumably – pumped out of the impressive sound system and hung like mist over the water.

'Ahoy, landlubbers,' Chas shouted. 'Shiver my timbers if it ain't the Jolly Roger, ready to press gang you all on a voyage to meet the Queen of the pirates herself, Ms Penny Sands.'

Everyone cheered. A chorus of 'Aargh, Jim lad' rang out. The fact that Penny's album had nothing to do with pirates, boats or rivers didn't seem to bother anyone, especially Island Records. It was just like Claire had said. 'All publicity is bullshit.' Here was the proof.

We set sail into a stiff breeze, the smell of diesel, bilge and churned Thames water blowing into our faces. The choice of alcohol was white wine, champagne, or rum, served by circulating mermaids. People would grab whatever was on offer, alternating between the different drinks, which only heightened the speed of inebriation. By the time the boat had reached Waterloo Bridge, the guests were already very pissed. Penny was below deck doing interviews, but there was no sign of Geoff Birch. I wasn't even sure he was onboard. I did spot Malcolm Morton, the chubby drummer from Penny's band. A lugubrious Geordie at the best of times, Malcolm looked particularly unhappy tonight.

'Hey Malcolm, how's things?' I asked.

'I'm not liking the boat. I get seasick, you see.'

'Sorry to hear that. How was the tour?'

'Hard going. The dep' bass player wasn't much cop. Some bloody jazzer noodlin' about like he was Charles Mingus. We needed you there to knock us into…'

'Wait. Wasn't Geoff with you?'

'Nah! I assumed you arranged his replacement.'

'Nothing to do with me, Malcolm. Why wasn't Geoff playing in the band?'

'Penny and him have had another bust up. Serious this time. She's a total bloody wreck.'

I patted him on the arm.

'Keep your eye on the furthest point on the horizon,' I told him, 'it'll stop you feeling seasick… and stay off the rum. You'll be alright.'

'Thanks, Jonesy.'

I left Malcolm and went to the lower deck, following the signs saying, 'Press Room', hoping there was a way I could talk to Penny. Most of the big music papers had already done their interviews, but a pair of journalists were still milling about in the corridor leading to the deserted aft seating lounge. Peering through, I could see Penny in earnest conversation with Jerry Gilbert, folk correspondent for *Melody Maker*. The lounge had rows of seating alongside tall viewing windows steamed by condensation.

'Which one of you is next?' I asked the journalists.

One of them put up his hand. Balding and wearing John Lennon glasses, my instincts told me he was foreign.

'It is me that is next. Not good a situation, this journalist's interview is making me wait a long time over.'

I was right about him being foreign, probably Dutch or German by the sounds of it. The other journalist, dressed in a yellow corduroy suit, piped up, his American twang immediately apparent.

'He's right. We've been waiting a "long time over". *Melody Maker*'s wedged in like a barnacle.'

'Sounds like Jerry Gilbert,' I agreed. 'Those two will be

reminiscing about old Durham mining disaster songs for hours.'

The Yank offered me his hand.

'Haven't had the pleasure. Frank Ricotta, London correspondent for *Rolling Stone*.'

'Elisud Jones,' I said. 'And I don't mind waiting, to be honest. I just this minute bagged an interview with George Harrison. Still getting over it.'

'George Harrison is aboard the ship?' the Dutch or German journalist asked.

'Yeah, and he's pretty happy to talk to the press. He was telling me about a new project he is planning on doing with Eric Clapton.'

The two journalists exchanged the briefest of glances before slowly edging their way down the corridor and towards the staircase leading to the upper decks.

The Yank threw me a winning smile. 'Why don't you go in before me buddy. I'll come back down in a while.'

Off they hurried.

With the two of them gone, I was now at the head of the queue. Even so, I wasn't prepared to wait for Jerry to finally get around to asking Penny a question.

'Jerry,' I shouted. 'Sorry to do this to you. I have a message from Linda Sonne for Penny I need to convey.'

Penny looked up, startled on hearing the name Linda Sonne and confused on seeing me heading into the lounge.

Jerry held up his hands, palms facing me like he was surrendering. 'No sweat, Jonesy.'

He remained where he was.

'It's a confidential message, Jerry.'

'Oh. No sweat.'

Jerry gathered up his tape recorder, his Native American bead satchel, and left the lounge. I immediately took the seat he had vacated, smiling at Penny.

'"I'd love to get you on a slow boat to China… all by myself, alone".'

An anxious Penny frowned.

'It's from the old standard,' I explained. 'Leo Sayer was singing it at the quayside.'

She was a mess. Dark rings under her eyes. The folk pixie had become a Tolkien wraith.

'I was going to ring you when I got back but…' she began.

'I've had quite a week since I last saw you. My guess is that maybe you have as well. Care to tell me about it?'

'I don't know what happened to Angie,' she blurted.

'But Geoff does? Is that why he's not here. Is he hiding out?'

'He's not hiding. He's in the studio.'

'With Angie's recording? Is he doing a mix down?'

Penny nodded.

'Where?' I asked. 'Where is he doing the mixing?'

'I don't know… it… he moves around,' she offered vaguely.

'And Blank Verse?'

'Just the cover name for the sessions. After we talked in the Guinea, Geoff wanted to warn Angie that you were suspicious about Blank Verse.'

'I was curious, not suspicious,' I clarified.

'We were… everyone was ultraparanoid. Geoff knew about your links with Terry Sporne… he was concerned. That's why he went back to Ryemuse when we left the pub.'

'You didn't go back with him?'

'No. I waited for him at my place. When he came back, he said there had been an accident. Angie was hurt.'

'An accident?'

'That's what he told me. That's all he told me. Then the papers the next day said Angie had been murdered. I didn't know what to do, so I rang you.'

'Where were you when you made that call?' I pressed.

'The Island office. I was hiding out there till I left for the tour. Geoff found me.'

'When he did, he asked you to help him find Billy Coles?'

She nodded again.

'Was Linda Sonne with him?'

'Yes. I told her we were going on tour and I couldn't help. That's when Geoff told me he was staying in London and not coming with me to Scandinavia. I had to ring around and find a bass player there and then.'

'Was it you who told Linda Sonne all about me so she would be primed when she came round to my place the next day?'

'No. I didn't tell her anything. In fact, she seemed to already know you well. I assumed you were once lovers.'

Lovers? What did she think this was? A Noel Coward play? I lit a cigarette and took stock before going another round.

'How did Geoff get involved with the recording for Angie?' I asked her.

'It was Billy who contacted him. I told him he shouldn't have anything to do with Angie Bright-Silver. I remember what you told me about Terry Sporne and the way he operated. Geoff wanted me to do background vocals and I told him I wasn't putting one foot in Ryemuse, let alone sing on the sessions. Now Angie's dead. Now Billy's dead...'

'And they had to stab him over fifty times to make sure.'

Penny flinched, but I carried on asking her questions.

'Is Geoff part of Apricus, Penny?'

'Not at first. Then, he suddenly became interested. Really interested. That Linda Sonne did a number on him, Jonesy.'

'I bet she did. And what about you? Were you ever part of Apricus? That album title –The Sun, Stars and the Moon. The sun bit had me thinking you were.'

Penny was shaking by now, overtaken by heavy sobs.

'Almost, but in the end… I wanted them out of my life,' she cried.

'Where's Geoff? Tell me, Penny. Which studio have they gone to? Which studio…?'

An angry Chas Parker appeared, still wearing his pirate costume, his cheeks a 'yo-ho-ho and a bottle of rum' shade of rosy.

'Jonesy! What are you doing bothering Penny? Can't you see she is upset, mate? I'm afraid I'm going to have to ask you to leave.'

'What are you going to do? Make me walk the plank?'

He pushed my shoulder. 'I'm not bloody scared of you, boyo!'

Then he pushed me again.

'Well, you should be,' I said, as I leapt to my feet and squared up to him. Flinching, he lost his balance and fell back, hitting his head on a chair. There was blood, not much but some. Penny ran away screaming. Some big guys were called downstairs, and I was asked to leave the boat at the next convenient stop, which turned out to be Southwark Bridge, on the south side of the river. Before that could happen, I managed to negotiate a quiet drink in the upstairs bar until I had to jump ship. Nursing a hefty half pint of rum, I was joined by the *Rolling Stone* journalist, Frank Ricotta.

'From what I hear, you should be the one wearing the pirate costume,' he quipped. 'By the way, jumping the queue with that George Harrison line was a pretty low trick.'

'Sorry.'

'You English have got an attitude problem.'

'Not me. I'm Welsh.'

'Who the hell do you write for?'

'Antisocial Monthly,' I replied. 'Freelance, of course.'

Ricotta roared with laughter. 'Freelance, eh? Best way to be…'

He helped himself to the champagne by drinking straight out of the nearest bottle, no glass.

'...I mean, like, I'm a staff writer. However I write up this story my editor will chop and change it to what suits the magazine's policy.'

'What is Rolling Stone's policy on Penny Sands?' I asked him.

'Great voice. Terrible music. Folk music to most of us American rock journalists is like blues for you lot. It's the thing that came before rock, not after. It's yesterday's news.'

Ricotta was growing on me. I could detect a kindred spirit. The champagne bottle move, the yellow suit, the dry wit. I liked the whole ensemble.

'Tell me something,' I asked. 'What do you know about Apricus?'

'A ton of stuff. *Rolling Stone* has wanted to do all kinds of articles on them. Legals nixed us every time. Apricus are seriously weird, seriously dangerous dudes, man.'

'How so?'

'They target people in the public eye – they have to be young. That might mean movie actors or sports people, but rock musicians are their speciality. The unhappier they are, the better. Apricus flatter their ego, help them quit drink or drugs or gambling, pair them up with what's called an "astral guide" – like a marriage – then take their money. All new recruits eventually go through a "purification" at their compound near Los Angeles to become "circles of light". They run that place like a Maoist Cultural Revolution boot camp. There's no drink, no drugs, no sex except for the very top guy, Abzari Afin, who visits once a week from a luxury penthouse apartment in Bel Air and takes his pick of the hottest women. After the "circles of light" purification comes "the enrol". That's where the new couples – Mr and Mrs Wacko – go back into the world and set about recruiting other people in the public eye. If they recruit a well-known star, it's like passing go, and they can rise up a level, which is seriously advisable, unless you want to go back to boot camp cleaning latrines and peeling potatoes forever.

'Do people ever leave Apricus?'

'Are you kidding? No way! They hunt down deserters like they do in the French Foreign Legion. You can never leave, not out of choice. On the other hand, you can be kicked out.'

'Why would they kick someone out?'

'For screwing around, or taking drugs, or breaking any one of their thousand crazy rules. And once you're out, it takes a lot to get back in. You don't cross Apricus.'

The boat slowed in a series of stuttering jolts as we reached my Southwark drop off.

'I think this is where I get chucked overboard,' I said.

Ricotta nodded. 'Maritime law's a bitch. Sorry you got to go.'

'Don't worry,' I said, downing my rum and turning to leave. 'I've been thrown out of better parties than this one. Hey, do me a favour. Give Penny a nice write up. You never know, you might change your editor's mind.'

Ricotta gave me a grin. 'Sure. Why not? It's worth a try.'

I stepped off the boat at a jetty alongside Bankside Power Station, my departure accompanied by a liggers' chorus of drunken cat calls, cheers, jeers and, in Leo Sayer's case, a rendition of Peter Cook and Dudley Moore's 'Goodbye'.

I really should have broken that ukulele over his head when I had the chance.

Looking back at the lower deck of the boat, I could see the indistinct image of Penny at a misted-up window. She looked my way before writing three large letters in the condensation that read: l.m.s.

The boat moved off and soon I was left alone in Southwark, staring at the dome of St Paul's Cathedral illuminated across the river, having figured out what she meant with that writing on the window and wondering how the hell I was going to get home.

Thirty-One

Home then. Home to Wales, charging down the M4, revenge and retribution on my mind, Montgomeryshire the destination. Rain was falling, slickening the concrete lanes, rendering the route ahead a polished coat of silver. What traffic there was meekly hugged the first two lanes, allowing me to favour the outside lane and use the incredible power of RAK's Jaguar to maintain a steady ninety as I carved and sprayed through outer London. I was listening to the new commercial radio station, Capital Radio. It was too early for Dave Cash, but another old Radio One DJ, David Symonds, was bedding in nicely holding down the breakfast slot. He'd just cued up the Kinks' "Waterloo Sunset" as part of his 'memory lane' feature. For him to play that song, in this moment, felt like a sick joke, a mocking coincidence, full of irony. It had always made me think of Angie, ever since it first came out in the summer of '67. The well-known story had it that the 'Terry meets Julie' part of the lyric – the couple described crossing the river – was originally going to be Terry meets *Angie*, until Larry Page, the band's manager, told Ray Davies he had to change the lyric. Terry Sporne had found out about the reference and was not happy. Someone it seems told him, possibly Ray's brother, Dave, that the song was all about a pervert 'looking at the world' from his window, supposedly having a wank as people left Waterloo Station'. Terry didn't like that. Not one bit. Davies did what he was told, Angie became Julie, and posterity went on to assume the couple blessed by a Waterloo sunset referred to Terence Stamp and Julie Christie. Angie Bright-Silver lost out on being name checked in the best song from the sixties. That was the story, and it always made hearing the song poignant. Now there was a new poignancy. Waterloo Station was where Billy planned to sell Dave Cash the tapes before he was murdered. Capital Radio didn't know it but they'd provided me the perfect soundtrack for driving to Wales to confront Billy and Angie's killers.

Borrowing the RAK car had been easy. I simply told Dick Leahy I wanted to impress a girlfriend by taking her for a spin. The idea appealed to him greatly, just as I knew it would. He even suggested a pub in Wimbledon called the Crooked Billet as a good place to have a drink. He came over wistful, making me think it had romantic connotations for him from a time before his marriage.

'It's a Young's pub. They keep a good cellar. Lovely pint. You can have a drink on the small green outside, then wander over to the common to do the necessaries alfresco style. Bloody marvellous!'

I told him that all sounded like a jolly good idea and thanked him. Ten minutes later I left Mayfair and was on the road, making headway past Heathrow within the hour. I estimated my journey time to be about five hours.

The pieces all came together for me when I saw Penny trace l-m-s on the window. LMS was the acronym for the Lane Mobile Studio, set up last year by Ronnie Lane. Taking a twenty-foot converted silver Airstream caravan, Ronnie, installed a state of the art eight track and somehow even managed to squeeze in a small recording area at the back. Musicians immediately started raving about his mobile studio. Eric Clapton had used it to record his comeback gig at the Rainbow Theatre at the beginning of the year. The Who's *Quadrophenia* was recorded with the LMS over the summer. But when not in use, Ronnie kept the mobile on his farm in a tiny village right on the Wales-England border. It was clear that the LMS was tied up with the whole Angie Bright-Silver business. The last time I saw Billy he was telling me about doing work for Ronnie at his mobile studio. My fake Gail Petters, brilliant actress though she was, had already proven her tendency to draw closely on real life for her improvisations with the whole Vigo Street, theatrical costumier's slip. She had also mentioned Montgomeryshire when she talked about being evacuated there as a child in the war. Add to that, Penny telling me Geoff was 'moving around' to work on Angie's album, before coming clean, and writing the letters in the window. Even though I was new to this whole finding clues business, it seemed like I had enough there to warrant driving to Wales. I was now certain who I was going to find there as well – Geoff Birch, and my phony Gail Petters, Linda Sonne, busy mixing down the recording ready for mastering. They killed Billy and got the tape less than a week ago, not enough time to get a whole album mastered. I still had time to catch them and if I did… and if I did.

I played the two choices over and over in my mind – call the police or call Terry Sporne. The first call would see them go to prison, and me off the hook. The second phone call would get them killed. In the end though, the choice was really about what kind of person I wanted to be. Was I for the law or for justice? I stopped working for Terry Sporne in the sixties because of the violence, because of the darkness he brought out in me. That wasn't the kind of person I wanted to be, so I moved to Mayfair to start over. Okay, a dog's body for record labels wasn't everybody's idea of a great job, but it suited me a whole lot better than what I had to do in Soho and do for Terry Sporne. But then I thought about Angie and Billy. Shouldn't Linda Sonne and Geoff Birch pay for what they did? An image came to me of Billy Coles, scared, hiding away in the attic room, planning his escape by selling the tapes. There is a knock at the door, a friendly voice, someone from the days of the Grass. Billy opens the door, relieved to see his old friend Geoff telling him not to worry. Within seconds, Billy is stabbed over and over again by Linda Sonne, maybe with Geoff's help, by now smitten with her, smitten with Apricus. Then they dip their fingers in his wounds, use his blood like paint and daub the room with circumpuncts. Wouldn't justice demand they suffer at the hands of Terry's specialist crew? Have their own blood spilt and daubed across the floor of some hellish Soho basement?

I stopped for petrol after turning off the M4 near Swindon, noticing the tabloid newspapers on the rack in the garage shop. Thankfully, there was no mention of me, but they all carried headlines about a raid on a 'Mayfair Vice Ring'. I didn't have to look too hard to know that the story was about Mr Samuels Junior and his assistant, Ms Ghisham. The days of hiring out "dresses" in Heddon Street were over. Simkins and Seabrook had taken my tip off and brought the whole thing crashing down. It still didn't feel like justice, not for Molly. Not even close. With that thought in mind, I gunned the engines and set off once more. The downpour continued as I took the A roads towards Gloucester then up to Leominster. From there, I was hugging the border on the A488, following the vague directions described by Rick Kempe on how to get to Ronnie's farm. He had driven there to interview Ron earlier in the year after the split from the Faces.

'The trouble about the bucolic is it's lovely for the people living in it, bloody inconvenient for anyone wanting to visit.' Rick had said.

Despite driving through the continuing deluge, I was still making good time. Well beyond Capital Radio's reach, the radio was now tuned to Johnny Walker on Radio One. Out of the blue, he played Lynsey's hit single from last year, 'Sugar Me'. It struck me that there was a touch of Gracie about Lynsey's soft, vibrato less delivery, totally hypnotic as it played against some imaginative drumming (even if the whole track did noticeably speed up). I found myself anticipating the cracked whip sound on the third beat of the bar, in between 'the baby, baby sugar me' chorus. The infectious beat was making me put my foot down on the accelerator, drum my fingers on the steering wheel, and nod my head in time. It was as if the song was helping to transport me all the way to the Welsh Marches. People said Lynsey's lyrics were about a kept woman, under the thumb of her sugar daddy. Others that it was about heroin withdrawal, or oral sex, or, given the whip sound, a song about a dominatrix. Driving to Ronnie Lane's farm, I now heard something different in the lyrics. What I now heard was a woman's cry for things to be settled. For a conclusion, a result.

This was a song about redemption.

Honey sweet and harmony. It was time to sugar me.

INTERLUDE NO.8

December 30th, 1969: Olympic Studios

Mickie Most knew his way around a studio. Eccentric as Joe Meek, precise as George Martin, those two influences made for a good combination. It was gold time for Silver, Angie Bright-Silver. Mickie's Midas touch. The Animals, Herman Hermits, Lulu, Jeff Beck, Donovan – they all owed their success to Mickie. Could he do the same for Angie?

Mickie's focus was currently on the guitar.

'It's the whip that drives the team of horses,' he explained to me.

Today, Jeff Beck was carving an extraordinary sound with his stripped Fifties Fender Strat. Through the glass, from the control room to the studio, I watched him beaming as the band ran down the arrangement. Forget Hendrix, this was a real genius at work.

Musicians rehearsing the songs; Mickie loved this stage in a recording.

'Experience has proven to me over the years that given a chance, and enough freedom, musicians will always land on something brilliant by happy accident. When a golden moment comes, I lean into the talkback microphone and make pronouncements like God. "That bit you just done before the middle eight? Keep it. It's another hook! Keep it!". That's how I get my gold nuggets, Jonesy.'

Sealed behind the glass, alongside Jeff Beck, other trusted faces were at work. Danny Thompson was on double-bass, Nicky Hopkins on piano, and Clem Cattini on drums. They took no time working up the jazzy bossa-nova groove and refining the basic shape of the thing.

'We are ready! We are ready! I'm hearing nuggets of gold, Jonesy.' Mickie grinned.

I was sitting next to him at the desk, in the best studio in London.

Angie was right behind us, alongside Terry on the control room's large sofa. My role was unclear. Mickie just asked me to be there to make sure, 'it all went smoothly.'

So far it was. We could have a finished take laid down by lunch-time.

Then Terry Sporne piped up.

'Not sure about these lyrics, Mickie,' he scowled, looking over a typed sheet.

'What's not to fucking like, Tel?'

Only Mickie had the balls to call Terry Sporne, 'Tel'. Sporne didn't seem to notice. Or maybe he did and he just had to swallow his pride. He knew he couldn't blow this for Angie. All the same, he wanted to flex his muscles by passing comment on the song we were recording, 'Little Girl's Dream'.

'"Holy men, princes, vagabonds and thieves, schemers and crooked men, promising you grief". I mean it's all a load of shit. Am I right, Taffy?'

I turned my chair to face Terry Sporne. 'The thing is you have to follow trends. This is more like Dylan, than Burt Bacharach. More Donovan than Dave Clark Five.'

I didn't work for Sporne anymore. I worked for Mickie. I might not have been brave enough to call him 'Tel' but I wasn't going to back him when I knew he was wrong. Angie agreed with me.

'Elis is right, Terry.'

Sporne was not going to let it rest.

'We tried to be fashionable before and all that happened was that you got saddled with that hippy crap, 'Sitar Sam'.'

'I loved 'Sitar Sam',' Mickie beamed.

'You must have been the only one. That song killed Angie's career.'

I could see Angie's face dropping. The confidence was already lacking when she arrived that morning. Others might not have noticed, but I did. Sporne wasn't helping. It seemed a good idea to get Angie out of the control room and into the studio, away from him.

Angie followed me down the steep staircase leading from the control room into the studio.

'I'm nervous, Elis. There's such a lot riding on this. Do you think I'm up to it?'

'I think you're going to be fantastic.'

Making our way to the vocal booth, we were hidden from sight behind the large baffles set up to create separation. The sound was dead. No reverb, no acoustics whatever. Without the air around it, her voice sounded strange.

'There's a New Year's Eve party in Barnes tomorrow, Elis. Promise you'll come. I want to start the new decade with you.'

'Where's Terry going to be?'

'At the Astor.'

'And you don't fancy that?'

'Like I say, I'd like to start the new decade with you.'

She leaned in and kissed me. It was no more than a grazing, a soft brush of lips, but it felt like a bee sting to me.

'I'll leave the address with Mickie. Terry will never know.'

It took just two takes for Angie to get a performance Mickie was happy with. We were separated by that sheet of glass between the studio and the control room. It made no difference. I knew. She was singing the song for me.

Thirty-Two

'Ronnie's down the pub,' the beautiful gypsy woman told me.

She was boiling a ham in a giant pot on a camping stove, a pair of young children shyly peeking out from behind the folds of her hippy dress. Coal black hair fell in long curls, framing her proud face and eyes green like a tabby cat. I guessed her to be Ronnie's new wife, Kate. She couldn't really be anyone else.

I had known and liked Ronnie's first wife, Sue, back when Don Arden was the 'rod of iron' manager of the Small Faces, and I was schlepping as his heavy. Sue kept Ronnie grounded for as long as she could, but it was a losing battle. Wagging tongues in Teen Avenue were convinced that the inevitable split from Sue and hooking up with Kate had messed with Ronnie's head. Kate was the Yoko Ono who made him quit his next band, the Faces, to go and live in a field in Wales. I knew different. It was nothing to do with Kate or leaving Sue. Ronnie had been talking about 'going back to nature' almost from the time I first met him. When he became a disciple of the mystic Meher Baba, that idea only grew and grew. Once he was with Kate, he finally delivered on those many drunken promises and bought a hundred-acre farm nestled in the undulating Montgomeryshire countryside. It was a nice spot. And would be a lovely place to live and bring up a family… one day. Just not yet. To call Fishpool Farm, in its current state, a hovel would be to oversell the place. As with Molly's Islington squat, the cottage was not only missing a roof, but also several windows and one whole wall in the general area where the improvised kitchen had been set up. The yard at the front was filled by three ruby red Scammell fairground vehicles in various states of disrepair. A pack of rabid dogs ran around barking at shadows as a brood of chickens picked away in the mud. Amongst all this chaos, one thing was notable by its absence – the mobile studio.

'He's not down the pub on his own, is he?' I asked Kate, keen to know if Geoff or Linda Sonne were with him.

She nodded. 'On his own. He's making some phone calls there. We don't have a phone yet.'

Or much else, I thought to myself. She seemed to read my thoughts.

'The concrete floor is being laid next week though. And Ronnie's starting on the roof soon.'

'What time does the pub close?'

'I'm not sure it ever closes,' she answered, prodding at the ham.

The Miner's Arms was to be found two miles from Ronnie's farm, down twisting narrow lanes and through tree tunnels of birch bordered by high hawthorn hedges. On the ten-minute drive, I only passed three farms, saw no other cars, and no sign of any other farmers working the fields or tending the sheep. Ronnie had really found somewhere in the middle of nowhere. I parked the Jag in the surprisingly full pub car park, the sleek lines of the RAK sports car out of place alongside the mud splattered Land Rovers and battered Bedford vans. Opening the door, a warm fug of smoke and hoppy ale hit me like a wall. The reception from the locals was a lot cooler. Walking in, some smirked at me as they held eye contact longer than felt normal. Others shook their head. I understood. They didn't know me; I wasn't one of them and that's all that mattered.

Ronnie was sitting by the roaring fireplace playing dominoes.

I'd forgotten how small he was, almost like a hobbit. Fully embracing the farming life, Ronnie was dressed in heavy brown cords, a white shirt, red neckerchief, and the sort of heavy boots navvies wear to dig ditches. Out of the two of us, I looked more like a rock star.

'Hello Ronnie,' I said, approaching the table.

'Jonesy?' he drawled. 'Of all the bars in all the world… What the fuck are you doing here? That hooligan Don Arden hasn't sent you, has he?'

I didn't want to get into who had sent me, not straight away, at least. 'What are you drinking?' I asked instead.

'A pint of best and get one in for my friend, Bryn, while you're at it, ta very much.'

Bryn, a silver haired old timer, was his dominoes opponent. He gave a grateful nod in my direction before turning back to the game.

I ordered the drinks knowing my Rhondda accent would do little to soothe the standoffish locals. They would now pigeonhole me as a *hwntw*, the name people in the North called people from the South. It means 'beyond' or 'over there'. In South Wales, we dismissed the Northerners as *gogs* (from the word *gogledd* – of the North). So much for the Celtic brotherhood. Still, at least I wasn't English, and I knew Ronnie, so I was tolerated a little better than some poor lost tourist who had the misfortune of straying this way hoping to experience some of the local hospitality. It was typical of Ronnie that he had managed to win over the locals in no time. But then Ronnie was one of those people you just liked straight away.

The drinks served, I carried them over to the fireplace and settled at the table next to Ronnie, watching the game of dominoes unfold.

'Met Kate, did you?' Ronnie asked.

'I did, Ronnie.'

'She's lovely, isn't she? Farm's a bit of a dump, but we're getting there. Bryn 'ere is going to give me a hand with the sheep.'

Bryn eagerly confirmed this arrangement. 'That's right. With the sheep, like. Sort them out. Give Ronnie a hand.'

They each played a few more tiles, their concentration fierce as the game reached its conclusion. I was happy to wait. The fire was warming me nicely and the beer tasted good. There was a sharp rap as Bryn tapped a knuckle on the table, a warning that he had one tile to go. On his next move he made good on that warning. Bryn was out. Ronnie had lost.

'Bollocks, you cunt,' he laughed.

Bryn gave a sly grin before staring off into the mid-distance, his way of allowing us to talk about what we needed to talk about, just as if he weren't there.

'Haven't seen Billy Coles, have you?' Ronnie asked, slurping on his pint.

'That's sort of why I'm here.'

Ronnie nodded.

'In a breaking his arms sort of way?'

'I don't go in for that much these days.'

'You're a reformed character,' he laughed. 'I forgot. Pity.'

I had the impression Ronnie was unaware of Billy's death. I decided to hold off from saying anything till I learnt a bit more.

'Is Geoff Birch also why you're here?' Ronnie asked suddenly.

'He is. And that's the second question you asked that I was going to ask you.'

'Beat you to it then, didn't I?'

Ronnie had almost finished his pint. I gestured over to the barman and suggested 'the same again' by tapping on my pint glass.

Ronnie stared at the fire. 'I moved here to get away from all that London muso bullshit. People not doing what they say they are going to, not showing up when they say they're going to show up – drove me mad!'

'Is that what happened with Billy and Geoff? Not showing up?'

Ronnie scowled at me. 'Billy Coles booked my mobile studio for last month, then they never showed up. The singer got stage fright or some bollocks. Next thing I know, Geoff appears with some American bint in the end of last week, expecting to use the effing thing to mix down a tape they went and done in London. I told him, the studio's not here, ya cunt. It's getting set up ready for Black Sabbath. I told him to see if he could fit around them. They rang Ozzy Osbourne from the phone here. I don't know how they did it, but they got a week's grace before the boys started their album. That's the last I heard. Incidentally, I know, as a fellow bass player, I should stay true to the union, but isn't Geoff Birch fuckin' hopeless?'

I collected the fresh pints from the bar and sat down again.

'Where are Sabbath going to be recording with the mobile?' I asked.

'Forest of Dean. Ever been there?'

I remembered the book I had found in Billy's flat. 'No, but I've heard of it.'

'Good, I'll write down the address. By the way, tell Geoff to fuck off when you see him.'

'With pleasure,' I smiled.

Thirty-Three

He sounded like he was a thousand miles away.

'Where the fuck did you say?'

'Clearwell Castle. It's in the Forest of Dean.'

'What are they doing in a castle?'

'It's hired out to bands to record and rehearse. Badfinger lived there for a while. Deep Purple were rehearsing their new singer there last month, I heard.'

Sporne was still finding it hard to process. 'But a castle? A castle? And they're definitely there?'

'As certain as I can be.'

'Here's what's going to happen, Jonesy. I'm sending Cliff and a few of the boys. They'll bring them back to London. You get yourself to this Clearwell and keep an eye on those scum in case they do a runner.'

'Will do, Mr Sporne.'

In the end it hadn't been a difficult decision to ring my old boss rather than Seabrook and Simkins. Just like the old days, Sporne had paid me to do a job. And just like the old days I was delivering.

'Jonesy?'

Sporne paused, leaving only the static on the line.

'I won't forget this,' he said.

I had estimated a two-hour journey time to Clearwell from Ronnie's farm. The travel time from London would be four hours.

Since I had rung Sporne from a service station outside Hereford, roughly halfway into my journey, it meant a three hour wait at least once I reached Clearwell before the cavalry arrived. I laughed aloud as I did the mental calculation, realising it sounded like one of those maths questions we would get at school:

A villain's hit man is travelling from London at an average speed of 60mph, his former bagman is travelling at a speed of 50mph...

Anyway, my reasoning was sound. I reckoned I could spare an hour or so to have something to eat, maybe even a loosener before meeting up with Cliff. The nearest town of any size was Monmouth, a few miles away from Clearwell on the Welsh side of the River Wye. That sounded like a good enough place to hold up and recharge. In due course, I could then make my way to the castle and wait, killing time rather than killing Geoff and Linda, something which would happen if I went in there on my own. I would wait because Terry Sporne wanted them alive, alive so he could torture them to death. I would wait because I didn't want to deny him that pleasure.

It was early evening by the time I arrived in the county town of Monmouth, or 'historic Monmouth' as the town signs insisted. 'Historic' turned out to be code for creepy and ominous. There was a distinct absence of people, with no indication of any of the higgledy-piggledy houses even being inhabited. A feeling that this might be a ghost town was further encouraged by a thick mist rising from the rivers Monnow and Wye on either side. Streetlights were muted, sounds deadened by the damp cloud like covering. I thought about Billy Coles' book, *The Paranormal and The Forest of Dean*. Someone should write a sequel featuring Monmouth, or should I say, 'historic' Monmouth.

Parking up near the county hall, I went into The Beaufort Arms Hotel to see if I could find anything warm to eat. The landlord seemed happy to see me, guiding me into a restaurant area.

I was the only customer. Eating out was not a big thing in Monmouth, it would seem. The dining room was antiquated and busy with dark brown tables and chairs. A brass plaque on the wall indicated Nelson had once stayed in the hotel with his mistress, Lady Hamilton. They were probably the last people to eat in the restaurant as well. Mayfair had its own famous Nelson connection, of course. The esteemed Admiral bought a town house in Savile Row for his 'inamorata' Lady Hamilton. It was easy to see why Nelson reached his one good hand into his pocket, fetched out his wallet, and paid up. It must have made life a hell of a lot easier popping over to Mayfair than travelling all the way to Monmouth for his 'amative carnalities', to borrow a Dick Leahy phrase. A few hundred years later, the Beatles bought the same Mayfair town house as their Apple office, even playing their final concert there in January 1969, until the tailors next door complained about the noise. 'Get back to where you once belonged' was the last snatch of lyric McCartney ever sang live with the Beatles up on the building's windy rooftop. All alone, in a Monmouthshire hotel, I found myself humming the same melody, 'get back... get back.'

A nagging, incessant feeling of unease steadily grew, continuing even when my meal – a lukewarm steak pie with a pint as thin as dishwater – finally arrived. As far as I could tell, I had my suspects cornered, ready to be dealt with by a bunch of Soho sadists. I should have been feeling pleased with myself, instead of fretting. And yet, there was a few wrinkles in all this that I just couldn't smooth out, no matter how hard I tried. I mean, I understood why Billy might have been killed cult style after stealing the tape. But why was Angie killed in the first instance? And strangled? What was the motive for her murder? Then the business of Billy seeing a friendly face. I was working on the assumption it was Geoff. But Geoff would have already shown his hand in the lead up to the Angie's murder. Billy, Linda *and* Geoff had planned the recording.

In what way was Geoff a friendly face? With all these troubling questions rattling around inside my head like a bag of marbles, I decided to go across the border and scout out Clearwell Castle before Cliff arrived. By now it was nine o'clock. Sporne's goons would be there by eleven. I had two hours to check out the lay of the land and get a clearer idea about which part of the castle Geoff and Linda might be hiding. And if I did see them, I would just have to fight hard any temptation that might overtake me to kill the pair.

The bible black, starless night and narrow lanes winding deep into the Forest of Dean meant I had to take the speed right down, the Jaguar's engine growling loudly in resentment at being curbed and restrained. It made me think that I should do the last half a mile on foot so as not to alert anyone. Monmouth felt like New York compared to the sleepy hamlet of Clearwell. A loud sports car was only going to draw unwanted attention. Better to play it safe.

I found a good spot to park near a T-junction, the beams from my car illuminating a nearby war memorial honouring the local men who had given their lives in the First World War. I gazed at the stone monument a while. Two soldiers stood guard, with heads bowed and bayonetted rifles at their side, battle ready.

I climbed out of the car and waited for my eyes to adjust to the darkness before setting off. A leaflet about Clearwell picked up in the hotel served as my guide. Brief and to the point, it advertised Clearwell Caves, the one possible tourist attraction to be found in the tiny village. The caves were a result of several thousand years of ochre and iron ore excavation, which explained why the small narrow cottages adjacent seemed so familiar. This was once a mining village; those sunken shafts would have required a tribe of tough men with strong backs like my father. For Clearwell, all that digging in the dirt was a memory now, nothing more than an underground museum to visit on a rainy afternoon. God help Pontypridd if that ever happened in the Rhondda, I thought.

There was another landmark on the leaflet. In an effort to show *something* other than just the caves, Clearwell Castle was featured on a sketched map. Although it was explained, with obvious regret, that the Castle was no longer open to the public, the map showed how it could be found on the opposite side of the village to the caves, half a mile up from the road junction. I made my way there in cautious, measured strides, keeping an eye out for anything suspicious or out of place. It felt good to be using my reflexes again, just like my days in the ring, anticipating, coiled and ready, prepared for action. It was nothing more than adrenalin, but it felt good all the same. I was also aware of my breathing. Without thinking, I was taking in and exhaling air through my nose, exactly the way wrestlers and boxers are taught. By not opening your jaw you risk less injury. Breathe slow, move fast. be battle ready.

A few minutes after setting off up the road, I spotted a high moss-covered crenelated wall either side of a large archway. I crept nearer and peered through. A narrow path led to another crenelated wall and gatehouse about fifty yards ahead. To get to the gatehouse, I would have to cross open ground, making me visible to anyone watching. There was no other choice but to risk it. It wasn't as if Linda Sonne would be standing on the ramparts armed with a crossbow, after all. I ran between the two walled sections and reached the gatehouse, the outline of the main house, or keep, now visible ahead. The heavy iron gates of the gatehouse were open, and I was able to step through into a bailey about the size of a football pitch. Being careful to stay in the shadows, I glanced about, looking for signs of life. I didn't have to look far. Parked in the corner, against the wall of the keep and catching the pale moonlight, was Ronnie's silver Airstream mobile studio, cables spewing, lights on – all evidence of some sort of activity. As if to make the point, my haven of shadows was suddenly lost when the door to the mobile studio opened and a funnel of light spilled across the bailey. A tall man descended the set of steps from the Airstream and headed off towards the keep, his gait immediately familiar. A shuffle rather than a walk, he was rubbing his arms as if staving off the cold. I still wasn't totally sure until he opened his mouth and a plummy, aristocratic English accent escaped into the night air.

'...whatever you say, sure thing... I won't be a minute... I'll have a gypsy's kiss and I'll be back...'

It was now unmistakeable.

I was looking at Phil Fratton, the former guitarist of the Grass, my friend, the man whose life I had once saved and from whom I received a flat in Mayfair by way of thanks. Phil Fratton, who never made my list of suspects even though he was an obvious inclusion. Phil Fratton who should have been in California but was now standing in front of a castle in the Forest of Dean on a cold, dark autumn night. As my mind was whirling with these thoughts, a noise made me spin around. Linda Sonne was there, armed not with a crossbow, but a coal shovel which she then proceeded to use in a glancing blow right across the side of my head, just as if she were swatting a fly, and with the same cruel disregard of the consequences. I fell to my knees before passing out, 'Phil bloody Fratton,' my last words, I think.

Thirty-Four

When I came to, the debate seemed to be this: Kill me first, then transport me to the caves, or take me there first before killing me. Weighing up the options were Linda Sonne and Geoff Birch, busy restocking the fire from a coal shuttle, bickering all the while. A hellish red glow was the only light in the room.

Geoff aggressively stabbed at the embers with the same shovel that Linda had used to knock me out.

'If we kill him here, they'll be blood. Lots of blood… the police will know it was us. We have to take him to the cave.'

Taking up a position on the floor, Linda Sonne watched the fire burn as if it were an LA sunset, her head leaning back, eyes closed, enjoying the warmth. She looked amazing, her blonde hair, now braided, hung down her neck like threaded golden twine, her white robe giving her the appearance of an Aztec hand maiden.

'It's a question of efficiency, Geoff. Conserving our energies. The cave means a drive.'

Her natural voice was a lulling, emotionless, Californian purr. She must have been a hell of a mimic to pull off that cut glass, Gail Petters English accent.

'I'll drive him and do it there myself,' Geoff spat, his own agitation clear.

Linda continued to soothe. 'We can all do it here. I can help you carry him with Phil to the car afterwards. Isn't that the most practical course of action, Geoff?'

The debate rumbled on, giving me an opportunity to get my bearings.

I was lying on cold flagstones in a large baronial room, somewhere within the castle. My hands and legs were tied with gaffer tape. A steady warm trickle, probably blood, was making its way down the side of my head. In the background, the recording that cost Billy his life was playing. I listened as the coy, disembodied voice of Angie sang expertly over what had once been Tony's Timepiece demo tracks. Taking away Hugh Padley's sci-fi lyrics had robbed the music of its eccentric charm. In the same way, without Gracie's eerie whisper, the music was less haunting, just plain ordinary. Billy had done a good job cutting and splicing, but I could still spot the musical remains of the second section of 'Augean Master', complete with a terrible new Apricus inspired lyric and weak refrain planted on top.

'Circles roll. Circles spin. Love is nature's circling.'

It hurt me more than the wound to the head, listening to Angie singing such rubbish. Instead, I focused on her beautiful voice, remembering the time I heard it isolated on a pop record in Islington, the time I knew things would never be the same again.

'Lines are arrows, a sword, a blade. Lines are just the hate you made.'

I hadn't noticed Phil slumped in a nearby chair listening to the track, listening to Linda and Geoff bicker. His skin tone was an unhealthy mixture of alabaster and pickled dinosaur bone. His eyes looked enormous, bulging and unfocused. I'd seen that look before, back when Phil was a junkie. It was like staring at death.

'Phil…' I croaked.

He offered me a bashful wave of the hand. 'Hello Jonesy. Doesn't Angie sound heavenly? Billy did well building up those tracks. You must be delighted your Tony's Timepiece demo went to such good use. Rather wished that you'd stayed in Mayfair though. Makes things bloody awkward you showing up.'

'I don't see why, Phil. Gives us a chance to catch up. Was it your idea to record Angie or hers?'

Phil dismissed the question with a roll of the eyes. 'Still thinking in straight lines.' he muttered. 'Such a redundant progression.'

Linda Sonne noticed I was awake and strolled over to join our conversation.

'Elis, I want you to know this isn't personal.'

'It bloody well is for me,' Geoff shouted.

'Yes, it is for Geoff, clearly,' Linda sighed. 'But right now, he is forgetting to focus on the circle rather than the straight line.'

'Silly old Geoff,' I said.

'He suffers from jealousy,' Linda continued. 'Jealousy, Elis, like all negative emotions, is a straight line. The circle doesn't allow for those negative emotions since there is no beginning or end...'

'Should I be taking notes?' I asked. 'Will you be asking questions later?'

Phil laughed nearby. 'Jonesy and his witticisms.'

'Talking of witticisms,' I asked. 'Why send me to Staines? Why Staines in particular?'

'You fool, Jonesy,' Geoff hooted. 'Lapping up that bullshit Linda fed you just so you could get your end away.'

Linda gave a pained smile as she knelt before me. I could now smell her, a strong intoxicating waft of earthy body sweat and honeysuckle.

'Geoff's parents live in Staines. He happened to know who their local MP was. Work with what you know was the first lesson at my drama school. My seduction was a means to an end. After we checked Billy's flat, we needed to make sure the tape wasn't hidden in yours. We had to be thorough. You remember how thorough I can be? Don't you, Elis?'

My mind was cast back to our lovemaking.

'I thought you'd at least ring me after our last meeting,' I mocked. 'I thought we had a special moment there.'

Linda leaned over and kissed me on the cheek.

'That was nothing but devotion to Apricus.'

'Like Phil killing Billy?' I asked.

'Shit! He really does know everything,' Geoff whined.

'He knows nothing,' Linda replied, now stroking my face just like she had once done in the afterglow of our lovemaking.

'I know the only reason Billy would have opened the door in the attic room,' I muttered, growing faint from the loss of blood, dazed by Linda Sonne's gentle touch.

I turned to Phil who was smiling, watching his wife – his astral guide – caress me.

'Billy opened the door because he saw a friendly face. You, Phil!'

Linda shook her head. 'We only have one friend, Jonesy. The circle.'

'The circle!' Phil responded.

I'd had enough of this craziness. I wriggled myself up to a sitting position.

'And because Billy forgot that, because he stole the tape from the studio, you killed him, Phil – stabbing him over and over and over. Did you know he was trying to sell the recording? Was that what made you so crazy. How long did you torture him till he told you where he'd hidden the tape?'

Geoff was getting agitated. 'Shut him up! Linda, shut him up!'

'Be calm, Geoff. Elis is just talking, talking, talking. Straight lines. Always straight lines. Isn't that right Phil?'

Phil nodded, though he seemed more than happy to resume talking, talking, talking.

'I was the one who guessed Billy was going to try and sell the tapes, Elis. I saved the day when I remembered where Billy used to hide out. I went back to Ryemuse. Rat-a-tat. Knocked on his door. Catch-up time. Let me in, Billy. Tell me where the tape is brother. Need some persuasion? Okay, if that's how you want it. It's surgery time. Precision. There's always a hard rain going to fall in these situations. He confesses, gives me the low down on Downview Hospital. What next? Our conversation has got me angry. Stealing the tape! That's really going against the circle. Not cool.'

'And sticking in a knife some fifty times?' I asked him. 'Is that cool?'

'It's like my beautiful astral guide Linda, says. It helps if you don't think in straight lines, Jonesy.'

My anger rose.

'Helps how, Phil? Is it how you stop the guilt, the horror over what you have done? Is that it? Did Angie turn against the circle? Did she forget all that 'we only have one friend, the circle' bollocks?'

Linda got to her feet slowly.

'I think that's enough. No more. Phil? Darling? Wouldn't you feel better lying down?'

'I might just do that. Nice to see you again, Jonesy.'

He got up from the chair and walked across the room to the door. It was pathetic, but I couldn't think of what else to say, other than: 'I once saved your life, you ungrateful bastard!'

Phil shrugged. 'I gave you a flat. Never even asked for it back. I believe that makes us even.'

'Fuck off, Phil!' I shouted as he left the room.

Once he had gone, Linda quickly turned to Geoff. 'Bring the car around. We'll drive him to the caves and do it there.'

'Good!' Geoff said, as he too left the room.

I was now alone with Linda and the ghost of Angie singing in the background.

'How long has Phil been back on the stuff?' I asked.

'A year or thereabouts,' Linda answered.

'You scored from Molly for his smack when you came to England.'

'A new convert, Molly was an addict, a troubled sun in the sky, obscured by clouds.'

'You lived in the King's Cross squat with her?'

'Our budget was tight. Phil and I were in a period of 'observation', not yet approved for our return to Apricus.'

'Molly must have been touched when you gave her Angie's gold dress after you wore it for me.'

'Circles, Elis. Think in circles. Remember our time together as a sweet joining of souls that will surely come again, just as it came before.'

Linda pulled her dress over her head. She was completely naked underneath.

I was played out. All I had left was jokes.

'Why Mrs Fratton!' I said, staring at her bareness. 'I'm not sure I can oblige in the circumstances, sorry.'

Linda laughed. It really was a delightful laugh.

'I don't want to get blood on my clean dress, that's all, silly,' she explained, reaching purposively into a canvass bag, then pulling out a pair of jeans and a t-shirt, which she quickly changed into.

Things were seriously spiralling. I needed to regain control.

'Before I left London, earlier today, I was telling the police all about what you have been up to.'

'Really?' she cooed, reaching into her bag again, this time producing a hand sickle.

'Yes, I was telling them why you wanted to record Angie. Apricus expelled Phil because of the drugs. You thought that you could get your way back in by recording Angie Bright-Silver, a new convert to promote your crazy religion...'

'You didn't talk to the police, Elis. We both know that. Or else they would already be here.'

She held the sickle high above her head, moving it in a slow, taunting circle as she approached.

'What did Angie do that was so wrong?' I demanded. 'She moved into the Apricus flat Billy managed, lit her incense, prayed to her circle and dot, and banged her chimes like a good little recruit.'

'Angie was indeed a beautiful sun in the sky, unobscured by the clouds.'

'So then why did you kill her?'

Linda looked at me, lowered the sickle and sighed. 'You killed her, Elis.'

'What…?'

'When you came to Ryemuse, Angie, Phil and I were hiding in the studio. Billy turned off the two-way camera in the control room but left on the intercom. I heard this wonderful Welsh voice, so deep, so resonant. The circle whispered to me that we were destined to be lovers. And so, I fell in love. But when Angie heard your voice, well, I could see it in her face: She didn't *fall in* love with you. She already was *in love* with you. Only now she was terrified. Not terrified you would tell Sporne. Terrified you would disapprove of what she was doing. Terrified she would lose you forever. We all tried to stop her. But she escaped. She ran after you. She ran *to* you. Then… sadly, as you know, it is a very steep flight of stairs, the lights were out…'

'She fell down the stairs?'

'Her neck was broken. She was alive. Just. Billy and Phil carried her upstairs. The circle spoke to us, telling us what we must do. Told us that an opportunity had arisen like a new day sun. No longer a forgotten pop star's tape, we could have the last recording of a dead legend as our gift to Apricus.'

'But she was still alive!'

'Geoff arrived. He also heard what the circle was telling us. We gathered around her broken body as, thanks to Geoff's administrations, Angie took the form of a sunset.'

'Fucking crazy bitch! He strangled her. Just say it.'

'...the form of a sunset...'

'He killed her! Murdered her! Billy didn't agree with all that shit, did he?' I shouted. 'Right at the end, he finally saw sense... he saw sense about what you did to Angie. He ran off with the tape. Then scared for his life, desperate for money he tried to sell it to Dave Cash, but Phil found him before he had a chance.'

I was crying impotent tears of rage and loss as Linda once more raised the sickle above her head and moved closer.

'Elis, once I felt the pain of tears, Phil and Angie too.'

She tensed, preparing to strike me down in the chest with the blade. 'Then we discovered Apricus. We discovered the circle...'

I stopped listening.

Though my eyesight was blurred by salt tears and seeping blood, I could see him coming, the baseball bat in his hands raised shoulder high. How long he had been listening, I was unsure.

Linda Sonne died exalting a religion that excused the murders of Angie and Billy. She died badly; the back of her skull driven through to the front of her head by the swinging baseball bat. I watched it happen and felt nothing but relief.

'What took you so long?' I finally asked Cliff.

'Shocking bloody traffic, Jonesy,' he replied.

INTERLUDE NO.9

January 1st, 1970: Mayfair

Less than five hours into the new decade I walked hand in hand with Angie Bright-Silver across Hammersmith Bridge. The party had finished and a group of us had set off to see the sun rise on the Thames. We found ourselves ahead of the crowd, just the two of us, alone together. Despite the season, Angie was barefoot, carrying both her high heels by the straps in her spare hand. As we crossed the bridge, the sun was rising, and our faces were golden. Everywhere was golden.

She placed her arm in mine and rested her head on my shoulder.

'Do you ever dream of being in a house you think you know well? But then a hidden room is discovered, a room that you never knew existed. And it totally changes your perception of the house forever. A doorway, a room: That's all it takes.'

We caught a taxi into the West End, hurtling down empty roads until we found ourselves outside the large townhouse.

'My hidden room,' she said with a smile.

The flat was on the second floor. She was my first visitor. I was still getting used to the dimensions, the lay out even. I hadn't unpacked any of my things. We made love amongst the boxes of books and records, suitcases and pots and pans. The carpet pressed into our flesh, chafed our skin as if in reproach, not that we noticed. Afterwards, spent, I held her in my arms. She seemed smaller, more fragile.

'Do you think you'll enjoy living in Mayfair?' she asked.

They were the last words I remember her saying to me. I must have fallen asleep. When I awoke, she was gone, and I was alone. The 1970s had begun, and it would be three years before I saw her again, dead in a recording studio.

Thirty-Five

Angie Bright-Silver was cremated in Golders Green Crematorium on a bright autumn day. The sun was shining, unobscured by clouds.

Teen Avenue was well represented with Mickie, Dick, Gordon Mills, Harry Baum and even Bertie Green showing up to offer their condolences. An impressive stable of pop stars from the sixties were also in attendance, from Lulu to Cilla, Ray Davies to Donovan, Peter Noone to Pete Townsend. I think Angie would have liked that so many people came.

Claire Gronwaulde sat next to me, her presence bolstering and consoling. I certainly needed it. Whether under Terry's guidance or not, the service was simple, and all the more moving for being so. The one unexpected moment was when Denis D'Ell took to the dais, the singer from the Honeycombs I had met at Joe Meeks studio, the singer nearly beaten up when Terry Sporne suspected him of having an affair with Angie. Denis and Angie really had been old friends back in Stepney, growing up two streets away. Denis might just have known Angie better than all of us. I thought he was there to say a few words. Instead, he sang unaccompanied Angie's last hit, 'Little Girl's Dream'.

'Holy men, princes, vagabonds and thieves,
Schemers and crooked men, promising you grief.
Love is a scheme.
Love is a theme,

Love is every little girl's dream.'

In the full to bursting room, Angie's pop song, as expressed through D'Ell's voice, rich with bluesy passion, became a profound statement on mortality. We all cried. Of course we did, Terry Sporne the loudest. I think he was allowed that. I found myself wondering how much he and Angie talked about her newfound religion. Whether she ever tried to explain the precepts and crazy theories behind that circle and dot cult. In the end, did it matter either way? No, not really. He was her manager. He was her partner. He loved her, and, just like me, he wanted to catch her murderers. Together, we achieved just that. Geoff was captured and driven back to a basement in Soho. As for Phil, the day before the service, Terry told me Viscount Fratton of Thakeham was already overdosed when Cliff found him, whether on purpose or by accident, no one would ever know.

Seabrook and Simkins went to bat for me, in the end. With Harry's help and encouragement, they accepted the whole story I gave them back in Mayfair. They chose to ignore my obvious lie about Linda being dead when I arrived at Clearwell, not to mention Geoff Birch being missing. They focused on Phil instead. Everything – the whole kit and caboodle – was dumped on him. Dead men make that sort of housekeeping logical. It meant they had their man, and it didn't even have to go to trial. I never asked Terry what happened to the tape. Just like I never asked him what his torturers did to Geoff. The manner of his demise was something I just had to live with, that is if I wanted to continue thinking in straight lines and not the circle. Straight lines had served me well so far. I saw no reason to change, not if I wanted to stay in touch with my humanity.

Phil had one last surprise for me.

The morning post on the day of the funeral had brought an official document from Farrer & Co – a deed for the flat in Curzon

Place, made out in my name, presumably triggered by Phil's death. It was official. I was the leaseholder. Mayfair was my home.

With Angie's service over, Claire stayed at my side as far as the Finchley Road and Golders Green tube station. She needed to get back to MAM, back to Mayfair. Tina Hoskins was being poached by Bell Records. Claire wanted to try and change Tina's mind.

'Honestly, Elis. With all her incredible talent, that kid's going to be a huge star and MAM don't seem to care a fig.'

'Bloody singers, eh?' I quipped glumly.

'Bloody singers,' Claire agreed, matching the gallows humour.

Neither of us smiled.

'Talking of bloody singers… have you spoken to Penny yet?' she asked.

I shook my head.

'I can't help feeling sorry for her,' she continued. 'It wasn't her fault she married a monster.'

'To stay with him was.'

Claire rested her head on my shoulder. Suddenly we felt like lovers again. It was a feeling I found myself enjoying. Nevertheless, I decided to share a thought that had gripped me all the way home from the Forest of Dean and then persisted, a thought I could not shake.

'You know, if they followed the original plan, Angie would never have died.'

'How so?' she asked.

'They were set to record in Wales when Angie got cold feet. Ryemuse was only booked as a fallback, once Billy, Phil and Linda had worked on Angie and persuaded her to go through with their plan.'

'And if they had gone to Wales, she might be still alive? Is that what you mean?'

'They would have never been at Ryemuse when I called in that night. Angie wouldn't have heard me talking to Billy. She would never have tried to run after me, would never have fallen down the stairs. I killed her by turning up in her life again…'

I stopped myself. It was too painful to go on because it was all true. I could sense Claire also felt the horror, the same terrible realisation. We walked on a few more steps before she came to a stop.

'No, Elis, I think you're wrong,' she said firmly.

'About what?'

'About where the responsibility lies. Angie was controlled by a domineering manager and partner for years, then manipulated by members of a cult. The one time, the only time, she ever sought freedom and broke away from that control is with you. The night she heard your voice coming through the studio intercom, for that single moment, you represented hope. And hope isn't a murderer. It never can be. That's what you were to Angie, Elisud Jones. Hope.'

'"An undiscovered room",' I nodded, explaining, 'it was something Angie once said.'

Claire turned to me and held my face with both her hands. 'You didn't kill Angie. A rickety staircase and a sociopathic bass player killed Angie. Don't you ever, ever, forget that.'

We walked on again, now in silence.

I could still feel the warm imprint of her hands burning on my face, her touch going beyond the skin, right through to the bone and sinew, the muscle and tendon. It was as if she were at a potter's wheel throwing clay, pushing me back into a more recognisable shape, a shape I could work with going forward. It was something she always did for me I realised only now, in that moment.

We reached the tube station.

'What will you do next?' she asked.

'Carry on doing what I do. The music business. Teen Avenue. Fixing the things people need fixing, when I can, when I'm able.'

'For a fee?'

'Of course, for the most part,' I said, gently sweeping a stray lock of hair behind her ear.

'Anything else?' she asked me.

'I'm still searching for that unsigned band. Only this time, when I do, I'll come to see you. Just so you can check I'm not hearing things that aren't there.'

'Please do, Elis.'

We parted with a kiss. Claire went into the station. I decided to find a pub; the famous Old Bull and Bush pub wasn't too far away. Without thinking, I sang the music hall song to myself:

'Do, do, come have a drink or two, down at the old Bull and Bush.'

A drink or two.

Absolutely. That should do it.

Then, as the afternoon slipped into early evening, I would take the same journey as Claire and head home to Mayfair, drifting through the elegant Georgian streets and squares lined by trees, their leaves now turning to autumn browns. And as the record company offices down Teen Avenue emptied, I would find some friends to go for a drink with, maybe try and hustle up some new work. Later, I would wander up to the Guinea Grill and have a steak with a bottle of wine. Who knows, I might even think about giving up smoking again. It would do me good to cut down on at least one of my vices.

A wind was coming in from the East. I fastened my coat and quickened my step. The strangest thought came to me, just popped into my head, and stayed there. It was this: I liked the seventies.

And for that, at least, I was grateful.

Printed in Great Britain
by Amazon

43084486R00169